GW00649860

'Madness in this book does not rest in a binary oppo.
playful experimentation and poetry of this text, the thrust is not so much toward break*down*, but break*through*. Gale confronts chaos, not as something to be conquered, but as a means to enhancing thought by removing it from the relentless repetitions of representation, classification and identification. In breaking loose from those old forms of humanist inquiry, the book opens out as a sparkling, embodied, sensory and unpredictable set of experiments, bringing to life the entanglements of language, of human and non-human bodies, and of desire.'

Bronwyn Davies, Emeritus Professor,
Western Sydney University, Australia

'Advocating madness as methodology is a tricky business: get it wrong, and you risk seeming either 'just' mad, or not really mad enough. Ken Gale gets it right. The book wears its erudition, its range, and its deep thoughtfulness lightly. It exemplifies exactly what it advocates – unruly resources for creative, ethical and experimental research encounters.'

Maggie MacLure, Manchester Metropolitan University, UK

'Madness as concept, madness as breakthrough, madness as movement, sensation, madness as life-giving, madness as in-formation, madness as the more-than. Madness as the force of a non-methodology that moves to the rhythm of a methodogenesis, a movement always processual, the movement of thought itself. This is the proposition: to compose, to write, to live in the midst of what refuses to know itself in advance. Not only toward new ways of writing, new forms of composition, but toward new forms of teaching, of learning, of living.'

Erin Manning, Research Chair, Relational Art and
Philosophy, Concordia University, Canada

'Treat yourself. Enter Gale's writing, his becoming, where assertion gives way to the possible. See how the nail rejects the hammer, the thread zigzags away from the seam, the mirror celebrates its shards. Gale's work is an assemblage of colourful fabrics and ribbons, always flowing, some wildly, some modestly, all caught in an always swirling wind. Embrace the pleasures of becoming with Gale, of moving with him and into your own terrain. His joyful methodological madness invites a performative immediacy of the moment, of movement. At the end, you may feel as I do: What pleasure surrendering to the space Gale opens!'

Ronald J. Pelias, University of Louisiana, USA

MADNESS AS METHODOLOGY

Madness as Methodology begins with the following quotation from Deleuze and Guattari, 'Madness need not be all breakdown. It may also be breakthrough.' This quotation firmly expresses the book's intention to provide readers with radical and innovative approaches to methodology and research in the arts, humanities and education practices. It conceptualises madness, not as a condition of an individual or particular being, but rather as a process that does things differently in terms of creativity and world making.

Through a posthuman theorising as practice, the book emphasises forms of becoming and differentiation that sees all bodies, human and nonhuman, as acting in constant, fluid, relational play. The book offers a means of breaking through and challenging the constraints and limitations of Positivist approaches to established research practice. Therefore, experimentation, concept making as event and a going off the rails are offered as necessary means of inquiry into worlds that are considered to be always not yet known.

Rather than using a linear chapter structure, the book is constructed around Deleuze and Guattari's use of an assemblage of plateaus, providing the reader with a freedom of movement via multiple entry and exit points to the text. These plateaus are processually interconnected providing a focal emphasis upon topics apposite to this madness as methodology. Therefore, as well as offering a challenge to the constraining rigours of conventional research practices, these plateaus engage with topics to do with posthuman thinking, relationality, affect theory, collaboration, subjectivity, friendship, performance and the use of writing as a method of inquiry.

Ken Gale works in the Institute of Education in the Faculty of Arts and Humanities at Plymouth University. His main philosophical and academic interests are to do with bringing the use of posthuman, process based forms of concept making as event to creative, experimental practices of pedagogy and research in education.

MADNESS AS METHODOLOGY

Bringing Concepts to Life
in Contemporary Theorising
and Inquiry

Ken Gale

To Katrina

I hope you enjoy this

Best wishes

Km 11/2/2019

Routledge
Taylor & Francis Group

LONDON AND NEW YORK

First published 2018
by Routledge
2 Park Square, Milton Park, Abingdon, Oxon OX14 4RN

and by Routledge
711 Third Avenue, New York, NY 10017

Routledge is an imprint of the Taylor & Francis Group, an informa business

© 2018 Ken Gale

The right of Ken Gale to be identified as author of this work has been asserted by him in accordance with sections 77 and 78 of the Copyright, Designs and Patents Act 1988.

All rights reserved. No part of this book may be reprinted or reproduced or utilised in any form or by any electronic, mechanical, or other means, now known or hereafter invented, including photocopying and recording, or in any information storage or retrieval system, without permission in writing from the publishers.

Trademark notice: Product or corporate names may be trademarks or registered trademarks, and are used only for identification and explanation without intent to infringe.

British Library Cataloguing in Publication Data
A catalogue record for this book is available from the British Library

Library of Congress Cataloging-in-Publication Data
Names: Gale, Ken, author.
Title: Madness as methodology : bringing concepts to life in contemporary theorizing and inquiry / Ken Gale.
Description: Abingdon, Oxon; New York, NY : Routledge, 2018. | Includes bibliographical references and index.
Identifiers: LCCN 2017047142 | ISBN 9781138066007 (hbk) | ISBN 9781138066021 (pbk) | ISBN 9781315159348 (ebk)
Subjects: LCSH: Methodology. | Ontology. | Deleuze, Gilles, 1925-1995. | Guattari, Fâelix, 1930-1992.
Classification: LCC BD241. M347 2018 | DDC 001.4—dc23
LC record available at https://lccn.loc.gov/2017047142

ISBN: 978-1-138-06600-7 (hbk)
ISBN: 978-1-138-06602-1 (pbk)
ISBN: 978-1-315-15934-8 (ebk)

Typeset in Bembo
by Keystroke, Neville Lodge, Tettenhall, Wolverhampton

MIX
Paper from
responsible sources
FSC
www.fsc.org   FSC™ C013985

Printed in the United Kingdom
by Henry Ling Limited

CONTENTS

(NOT A) FOREWORD

It's late August 2017. Ken and I have been exchanging emails and texts over recent days as the finishing line for the manuscript of this book has been coming into view. Amongst our other conversations, we have been toying with whether this is a 'foreword' or a 'preface'. I write to him, 'Oh, by the way, I'm going to start work on the preface on Friday', to which Ken responds, 'Thanks. I really appreciate it as I know how busy you are. But isn't it a foreword rather than a preface? Though what's the difference?' To which I respond, 'Ah yes, a foreword, not a preface, that's right', and leave it at that.

But Ken's question of whether I'm writing a foreword or a preface intrigues me. I search online and find publishers' various definitions. A foreword, my search tells me, is written by someone other than the author, with the purpose of giving the text their stamp of approval. A preface, on the other hand, is by the author themselves, standing outside their work (if that's ever onto-epistemologically possible), talking about why they wrote the book and/or how they found themselves writing it.

It would seem this is a foreword, therefore: I am not the author and I hereby give it my stamp of approval.

However, there's a problem with any notion of foreword (or preface) to this book, any 'fore-word' to *Madness as Methodology*. The work Ken does here disrupts both linearity and the privileging of discourse. Our encounter with Ken's book takes us into – immerses us within – a world (of theorising, of living, of bodies, of concepts) where notions of 'before' and 'after' become nonsense and where language needs to be understood as, at the very least, trembling with matter (p. 63).

A pause for breath. (Note: you also might find yourself needing breathers as you engage with Ken through this coursing, surging, enveloping book, which I mean as a compliment. To both you and *Madness*.) A pause, an aside. An indulgent aside, to say how different it is to be writing this. Ken and I have been writing together for a long time (a statement we keep writing at the top of our papers these days but it bears repeating here), since 2005. We once imagined a scenario where we would still be writing and presenting our work together in 2027 (Gale and Wyatt, 2009), well into our dotage, though 2027 does not seem so far off now. With luck (from our point of view, at least), that might still happen. However, here in this not-foreword, I am with Ken once more but I am beside him. I am not writing *with*, more writing *from*, from my encounter in this book with Ken, or better, with Ken-ing, becoming-Ken, and becoming-Ken alone. (Though, as Ken would point out, we're never alone, we're always 'co-labouring' with human, material, and post-human 'others'.)

Madness as Methodology is becoming-Ken in flow. It is vibrant Ken-force. Ken invites us to accompany him, bag containing our dog-eared copy of *A Thousand Plateaus* (and perhaps a Cornish ale) slung over our shoulder. He invites us to accompany him across the fields and hills from his house in southern Cornwall on a late summer's day, to hike along the cliffs with him – trying to keep pace – and follow him down the steep, winding path to the expanse of an empty beach. (Ken knows where the empty beaches are, even in high summer.) He wants us to run with him into the swells of the ocean and the maelstrom of the breaking surf as it takes us back and forth, lost but alive, surrendered, transported.

This event of a book is no place for a 'foreword'.

Instead, this is a happening, an encounter, in which Ken brings us into an unknown sense of what is possible, into a disruption of what we might expect, into, onto and beyond 'plateaus' (after Deleuze and Guattari) that do not follow one another but pick us up, turn us around and land us somewhere different through, as Ken might put it, 'a [text] constantly moving in animations of sensation' (p. 123). This book is flight, not travel (Deleuze and Parnet, 2002).

One further observation: it surprises me this is Ken's first sole-authored book. As someone who writes so prolifically and so fast, I know Ken has thousands of words in countless notebooks and elsewhere that have yet to find their way to readers, thousands of words – tactile, singing-and-dancing words – that could have found a place here. Maybe there's another book in him, maybe we'll be lucky. We're lucky to have this. I'm lucky to be here, with this. With Ken.

Jonathan Wyatt
September 2017, Edinburgh

References

Deleuze, G. and Parnet, C. (2002) *Dialogues II*. London: Athlone.
Gale, K. and Wyatt, J. (2009) *Between the two: A nomadic inquiry into collaborative writing and subjectivity*. Newcastle-upon-Tyne: Cambridge Scholars Publishing.

ACKNOWLEDGEMENTS

The thing about poetry, about all creativity, is that it is a compulsion; you never really feel you want to do it, you try to invent all sorts of jobs to prevent you from making a start, but it is a compulsion; you get a notion in your head that ticks and knocks away and it gives you no rest until it's been laid like a kind of ghost and then something slowly begins to appear. The great problem in writing poetry is to achieve resonances and hints and suggestions and reverberations and it's an endlessly difficult and endlessly fascinating task to get the thing to work somehow or other … the skin of a poem is never what it's really about.

Causley, 2017: 21–22

Charles Causley was born, brought up and lived his whole life in my hometown of Launceston in Cornwall. I have, what Cornish writer, poet and playwright Alan Kent (2010) refers to as, a 'hope of place' about this little Cornish town. For all of us who were born there it is 'Lanson' and pronouncing the name of the town in this way, using the Cornish dialect from which it originated, helps to keep it alive in ways that remain deeply potentiate and viscerally imbued in affect. Charles Causley's presence in my life was and continues to be wispy and ethereal; he was always there although I never really knew him. My father was the same age and they went to the same primary school together. I remember my father describing him as an unusually reserved and eccentric boy and something of an outsider. I attended another primary school in the town but I was struck by the knowing that many of my friends and peers were taught by him, talking fondly and often excitedly about his classes and his idiosyncratic approach to teaching. As Causley's pupils, they listened to him reading his poems, they wrote their own poems, some of which he published in books and magazines; in all, they seemed to have early experiences of living creatively in their school lives.

The quotation above that begins these acknowledgements was published in 2017 to commemorate the centenary of Causley's birth: the book from which it was taken was given to me by my good friend Colin Gregory (a former pupil and friend of Causley) on my seventieth birthday, on 9 August 2017. I sense a pleasant symmetry in this. My senses are alerted by this quotation. I sense a coming alive here that conflates the inner and the outer of the 'me' that is writing this book. It is a becoming that helps to exemplify the powerful forces that are in play in my own 'coming to writing' (Cixous, 1991).

I have written elsewhere about the humble beginnings of my life with my mum and dad in a tiny, two-up, two-down cottage with a cold, unwelcoming, outside toilet in Launceston in Cornwall in the early 1950s. Similar to Causley, I loved to read; books, comics, magazines, anything that I could lay my hands upon in the austerity of those early post-war years. By my early teens, as well as reading, I was always drawing, always writing. Now, as I look at the many boxes overflowing with sketchbooks, diaries and notebooks that fill numerous cupboards in my family home, I have a real sense of what Causley meant when he talked about the 'compulsion' to write. My parents were immensely influential in allowing me to do these things, never discouraging me, always encouraging and expressing enthusiasm about any aspect of my efforts that came to life in their lives. I am indebted to them for the space that they created in my life to find these writing ways. When I left Cornwall to go to live in London in the early 1960s, I used to exchange one, sometimes two, letters a week with my mum and dad; our busy, newsy correspondence not only kept me in touch with home but also continued to nurture in me the 'compulsion' to write. This 'compulsion' was not explicable in terms of, or premised upon, any particular logic or reason, intention or outcome: it was what I did.

All this and more tells me that it is my mum, Clarice Freda Gale, and my dad, Leonard Gale, first and foremost, for whom this book is written. I sense now that this 'compulsion' to write, this ticking and knocking that gives me no rest and that is now gradually being 'laid like a kind of ghost' as this writing, this book, slowly begins to appear, is deeply imbued with their presence and with the presencing that has emerged in that space making which they so lovingly and forcefully created in those early world-making days of this life. This writing is for them.

This book is also written for my children, Katy, Reuben and Phoebe, and my grandson Rohan. It is written with them and their presence in my life. I sense that they might never read this book but I know that they are always with me as I write it. In this confusing world of making sense of sense, I also feel them sitting down in some future world of theirs and turning these pages, taking in the worlds I have described here and coming alive in new ways with me as a continuing presence in the lives they go about making. As we are now, they sense me taking myself off in my car to go to work, travelling to international conferences and, more often, climbing the stairs, cup of tea in hand, to my little study room to write. They have a knowing what this is, what this is to me and what is in me, in them, when I go to write. My children give me love, joy and happiness. They are the love of my life and this is for them.

This writing wouldn't be here if I hadn't met Jonathan Wyatt. We have been buddies and writing partners for about twelve years. We met on the doctoral programme at the Centre for Narratives and Transformative Learning in the Graduate School at the University of Bristol in 2004 and a friendship and writing partnership that began and flourished under the tutelage of our erstwhile supervisor and now dearest friend, Jane Speedy. Only in fondness have we ever looked back. We discovered each other virtually at the outset of the programme. As Jane later said,

> And they had singled each other out quite quickly she remembered, the nomads, settling in together in her office. They had rooted each other out, those bright, sharp, edgy ones, in record time, she noticed ... and off they'd gone with the ball, full tilt. They were glorious.
>
> *Gale, Speedy and Wyatt, 2010: 26*

I am grateful to Jonathan for reading and commenting on earlier drafts of my manuscript and for writing the foreword to this book; in affect, whatever he has to say to and with my writing has been and continues to be a huge influence upon its continuing coming to life in the world. In many ways, the writing that Jonathan and I have engaged in during this period is, if nothing else, a testament to a deep, sincere and caring friendship and without the support and affection that Jonathan's friendship has given to me, whatever this book might be in its emergence, it would be much less without his presence in its making and in my life. Thank you, my friend.

I am indebted to Elizabeth Richmond for her reading of and feedback on many of the early drafts of the plateaus in this book. In both conversation and written response, her insights invariably enabled me to make new sense of my writing, encouraging me to engage in fresh re-compositions when the old accounts and exemplifications became tired or appeared to head in the wrong direction. I am also very grateful for the sustained diligent and hugely creative work that she carried out in the production of the book cover. In addition, and perhaps more than this, she was always there throughout the process of writing the book, encouraging, suggesting, prompting, motivating, querying and cajoling me whenever I began to flag, when my enthusiasm waned, when my interest veered too far off track and when the temptations of life became too alluring. Without her boundless energy, vibrant interest, ceaseless encouragement and love, this book, if written at all, would be substantively and qualitatively less than what it is now. Thank you.

This book has been a long time coming and in that history there have been many people and many instances that have contributed so much to its continued becoming. Jane Speedy, I can't stop mentioning her, she means so much and anybody who knows me knows why: dear Jane, thank you so much. The influence and encouragement of Alan Bleakley and Pat Sikes, so many years ago now, in helping me to bring this writing self into emergence was and remains very important to me and for that influence I am hugely grateful. For twelve consecutive years I have attended the International Congress of Qualitative Inquiry at the University of Illinois in the USA. My attendance there, the opportunity to present my work, both individually and collaboratively, and the ability to be able to listen to, appreciate and engage with a wonderful group of scholars who, in this time, have become more than colleagues, they are my friends. This book would not have appeared as it appears now without the friendship, personal support and intellectual generosity of Norman Denzin, Ron Pelias, Tami Spry, Elyse Pineau, Larry Russell, Bronwyn Davies, Susanne Gannon, Laurel Richardson, Maggie MacLure, Elizabeth St Pierre, Claudio Moreira, Marcelo Diversi, Alecia Jackson, Lisa Mazzei and the many more to whom I offer sincere apologies for not including in what will only ever be a partial list … I am hugely indebted to them and am so grateful that attending the congress has brought our lives together.

I have worked for twenty years in what is now the Institute of Education, in the Faculty of Arts and Education at the University of Plymouth in the UK. Many of the ideas, thoughts and practices that are presented in this book found nascent emergence in the many conversations I have had with my colleagues and students there over the years. I am sincerely grateful for the confidence, rigour and inventiveness that participation in those conversations, with those people, has given to me during this time.

Portions of this book, albeit in somewhat different form, have appeared elsewhere in the journals *Qualitative Inquiry*, *International Review of Qualitative Research*, *International Journal of Qualitative Studies in Education* and *Departures in Critical Qualitative Research*. I am grateful for the opportunity to publish them here.

Finally, my sincere thanks goes to Hannah Shakespeare, my editor at Routledge, for always being there to answer the many questions I sent her way and for the kindness, genuine interest and professional support that she has shared with me throughout the coming to life of this book.

INTRODUCTION? ON ARRIVAL FROM ELSEWHERE

> Madness need not be all breakdown. It may also be breakthrough.
>
> *Deleuze and Guattari, 2004: 143*

Madness as methodology: a method of inquiry? A book? Starting in the middle?

I have woken up this morning with this idea in bed beside me, with me, all around me. I have been circling this, unsure of what it is because I was not sure what it was or what it would be. This is how it begins, this is how it has begun, this is beginning, always beginning, always something, always with difference preceding repetition, difference preceding simulacra, difference as the creative force. This is the beginning of the book. Sense tells me it is starting. It will start with sense. In starting with sense I will posit this book's cartography as onto-episto-methodological. Sense takes me into the world, leads me to it and is its instrument of creation. In sensing, space becomes place, where 'becomes' is always processual, never an end point. I live this life with sense, in sense, for sense, to sense: it is how I create my world and in this constant process of creation my world creates me. Sense is palpability in touch, taste, smell, hearing, seeing and . . . and it is how I make sense of the world. It is also about the sense, the sense of sense, which perhaps is becoming lost and, occasionally, serendipitously comes alive in the instantaneous and always disappearing connection with the beautiful aesthetics of coalescing movement and moment. This is the movement in the moment, the moment of movement, as the ontology, senses and the experiences of the body becomes the epistemology, as the new epistemology as expression, in language, as discourse deterritorialises and becomes the new body. This is madness at play. This is where 'I' both lives and dies in infinite moments of creative energy. In this sensing/making sense is the diminution of the logic of rationality and reason through the growing magnitude of a logic of sense. This is the madness of the method of inquiry, it's *délirer*, it's going off the rails, it's coming to life. This is where rhythm comes to life, where the dance between sense and logic, between ontology and epistemology brings to life something new, energetic and life giving. Becoming-Ken: Ken-becoming. This is it. This is the starting point: in the middle of the vibrant matter of this life, in the melee of languages that try to make it, this is where it begins, this is where it already started, this is where it has never ended. This is this. Thisness. Haecceity. The incessant, perpetual and perpetuating dis/de/re/organisation of body becomes the place of always new origin, where the little plot of land is both figural and the land in which new life grows: space becomes place becomes space, always in the rhythmic play of smoothing and striating. The particulate, molecular multiplicity of organs becomes the always temporal transmutational in/tangibility of the body. What Guattari (1992) refers to as 'chaosmosis' is actually a way of confronting chaos, not as something that is to be overthrown or reduced in some way but as a means of enhancing thought in a struggle against the powerful discursive forces of representation, classification and modes of identification. This is how living is done and it is how sense is made, how sensing of the world becomes the world that always becomes something new. In this fragment of time, as these words appear on this screen, I sense this new writing being born; I sense becoming in making meaning that is making me making the world. This is working; this is my inquiry, this is what I will do, this is my madness as methodology.

In the introduction to her book *Cruel Optimism*, Lauren Berlant writes:

> A relation of cruel optimism exists when something you desire is actually an obstacle to your flourishing. It might involve food, or a kind of love; it might be a fantasy of the good life, or a political project. It might rest on something simpler, too, like a new habit that promises to induce in you an improved way of being. These kinds of optimistic relation are not inherently cruel. They become cruel only when the object that draws your attachment actively impedes the aim that brought you to it initially.
>
> *2011: 1*

This feels like an appropriate means of beginning to introduce this book. Berlant's words are enabling, they begin to help me to describe the emergence of this book or what I am now calling a 'book' as I start here, in the middle, having only written a few words. By writing these few words it feels like the beginning of a birthing process, beginning in a different way, a becoming that has always been there, a becoming, which perhaps because of 'cruel optimism', has never found a way with words, though very many words have always been there and are always being written.

I have heard people say, 'I have a book in me'. I take that to be saying that, perhaps in terms of affect, that person feels that they could, or they want to, or feel able to, write a book. Write a book. I think that will work for me. My desire to write a book has never been productive, perhaps it was Oedipal and all about lack: I don't know, I am writing here, now to find out.[1] And as I do this, as I tap these words into life perhaps there is a sense in which this book has already begun, perhaps I have already written many pages, perhaps there have been many false starts. Without doubt the idea has been in my head for many years so perhaps this is my modus vivendi. If something is nascent, it is still, nevertheless, alive. Already in its raw and emergent form it has becoming; it already has a beginning. This beginning is something that I need to talk to, it is a beginning that begins in the middle, it has already started and it has already ended, it is a beginning that is about heterogeneity and contingency, as the beginning of a book it is about now you see me, now you don't. I am writing parts of this 'introduction' when many other parts of the book have already been written so to talk of this as a beginning would be to offer a deceitful account of how this book originates and starts and continues to come to life. As a book its writing has been hugely influenced by writing in and with affect; many elements and atmospheres that are constitutive of the book could be signified as having certain posthuman[2] qualities and potentialities; all of the thinking and theorising and practising that it involves is greatly influenced by the writing of Deleuze and Deleuze and Guattari: I can say with confident honesty that this book would have had no beginning had it not been for the very many forays and encounters that I have experienced with these two writers over the last fifteen to twenty years. And so, with great conviction, I want to say that I understand and have a sense of the becoming of this book as 'assemblage'. In talking of a book as assemblage, Deleuze and Guattari offer in the introduction to *A Thousand Plateaus*:

> In a book, as in all things, there are lines of articulation or segmentarity, strata and territories; but also lines of flight, movements of deterritorialisation and destratification. Comparative rates of flow on these lines produce phenomena of relative slowness and viscosity, or, on the contrary, of acceleration and rupture.
>
> *1987: 3–4*

So this book is not conceived as having a life of linearity and I wouldn't want it to be used or lived with in that way. Just as this introduction is being written when well over half of the rest of the book has also already been written, I would hope that it might also be read in this way. In setting this up as a possible way of engaging with this book I have decided to borrow, or perhaps appropriate, Deleuze and Guattari's use of 'plateaus' rather than the more conventional and orthodox ordering form of 'chapters' as a means of providing multiple entry and exit points into and out of the book. I would like to think of the book as existing as a 'body-without-organs' and, therefore, I wish to keep my own organisational strategies and leanings to a minimum as I attempt to breathe life into the multiplicities and potentialities of its processually organic life. As I would also like to think of this book as, what Bennett might term, an 'agentic assemblage' (2010: 20), I would then also like to think of the reader of the book, through the use of these plateaus, as being encouraged to engage with its content not in a linear, developmental manner, page by page, chapter by chapter, but rather in indeterminate and free-spirited ways driven by experimental inquiries and impulsive curiosities, moving from one plateau to another as an insect might move from plant to plant in search of food and sustenance.

So, returning to those words of Berlant above, I want to take and acknowledge them and use them to animate and further provoke the writing of the words in these pages. It is as if the very object of my productive desire has been stopping me from flourishing, the Oedipal lack has held me back, inherent in the objectification of desire is its very demise and this is before a page has been written! So I think what shall I write? What will it be about? When will I have time to do it? Who will read it? So many questions! And of course these questions can be the becoming of the very inhibition of the writing itself. And now as these writings have found beginnings, as writing has its own becoming, as I begin to nurture a becoming in the writing, I sense the *object* of desire beginning to disappear, I sense an emergence of self in the writing, I hear Foucault asking 'If you knew when you began a book what you would say at the end, do you think you would have the courage to write it? (Foucault, in Martin, 1988: 9; see also Massumi, 2002: 18) and feel greatly encouraged by his words and the intentions they express. A sense of self is here, emergent. So, working with Berlant's words, I sense a diminution of the 'object' that hitherto has drawn my 'attachment', to the extent that, in affect, it no longer seems to be actively impeding the aim that brought me to it initially. Waking up with the idea of the book in bed beside me has wedded me to it. I sense it's becoming on a plane of immanence, with Deleuze and Guattari, I am aware of this in terms of 'concept, affect and percept'; it is as if, as I begin to conceptualise this book, it is, to use their words, 'a bloc of sensations . . . a compound of percepts and affects' (1994: 164). And so with affect there is a sensing of the fading of cruelty and a coming to light of warmth, generosity and the smiling face of a benign spirit.

Kathleen Stewart observes that:

> People are always saying to me, 'I could write a book.' What they mean is that they couldn't and they wouldn't want to. Wouldn't know where to start or how to start or how to stop. The phrase is a gesture toward a beginning dense with potential. They have stories, substories, tangles of association, accrued layers of impact and reaction. The passing gestural claim of 'I could write a book' points to the inchoate but very real sense of the sensibilities, socialities, and ways of attending to things that give events their significance. It gestures not toward the clarity of answers but toward the texture of knowing. What a life opens up to is still a problem and an open question: an object of curiosity.
>
> *2007: 129*

And as I come to this quotation I question Stewart's epistemological claim when she asserts 'What they mean is that they couldn't and they wouldn't want to.' I am guessing that this claim gains its force from the intonation that is contained in the word 'could' and the way that this intonation works within what I understand as the context of this passage. This epistemological claim seems to be deeply grounded in affect, in a sense of inability and within an absence of productive desire.

The productive desire that has animated much of the writing that is now part of the attempt to bring this book to life was prompted and inspired by my reading of Laurel Richardson's chapter, 'Writing: A method of inquiry' (2000). In writing about the genesis of the theory and practice of writing as a method of inquiry that she wrote about and originally published in 1994, she later said:

> I had been taught, as perhaps you were as well, not to write until I knew what I wanted to say, that is, until my points were organised and outlined. But I did not like writing that way. I felt constrained and bored. When I thought about those writing instructions, I realised that they cohered with mechanistic scientism and quantitative research.
>
> *Richardson and St Pierre, 2005: 960*

Recognising, in her words, that these 'writing instructions were themselves a sociohistorical invention of our 19th century foreparents' (ibid.: 960), I think of the excitement I felt at the time as I read her words about simply writing to inquire, invoking a kind of sitting down and doing it and a kind of seeing what happens when you do. Here was someone writing in a book containing an esteemed collection of chapters on qualitative research that was suggesting that it was worthwhile and, indeed, a creative practice to allow the writing that you do to inquire in and of itself. Reading this chapter released a little more of the madness that was constrained in me and now, as the writing of this book takes place, I sense an awareness of that reading, that event, that moment when things moved and shifted in a different direction. I feel a certain gratitude to Richardson for opening a door, for allowing a breeze to blow into that cloudy dark corner and of bringing a scent of the fresh air of possibility into the ways in which becoming in the world, my own creative world making was given fresh life. I have found that using writing as a method of inquiry has helped me in so many ways. It is now possible to think that using this writing process is liberating in terms of thought and concept forming; it is affectively stimulating in the way in which it helps confidence and self-esteem to grow and in the way in which it works to lift research and inquiry into creative, experimental and unpredictable ways of practice. So, for example, coming to Deleuze and Guattari's creative practice of concept making as event in their final collaborative book *What is Philosophy?* was also hugely influential and inspirational and was, in part, facilitated and enhanced by my interest in and use of writing as a method of inquiry in the kinds of research with which I was engaged at the time. Richardson's theory and practice is comfortably situated within post-Positivist, qualitative research and, from an epistemological point of view, is essentially sociologically and phenomenologically inclined. This places it in sharp relief in relation to the philosophies of the event and the realist ontologies of Deleuze and Guattari with which I was becoming familiar at the time. Nevertheless, both approaches animated in me a willingness to be both taken with and creative of processes of experimentation; the fluidity and the possibilities of transmutation and flux that both approaches enlivened in my approach to theorising, creative inquiry and research continue to have an influence as the writing of this book takes place.

I take a cue from Lecercle when, in his reading of Deleuze and Guattari, he argues that, 'antinomian thought (outside the main tradition, and beyond the control of the subject)' takes precedence in their work over that to be found in and characterised by the central rationalist tradition of philosophy emanating from Descartes and Kant, Aristotle and Hegel. Of this he says,

> its heroes are philosophers like Nietzsche or Kierkegaard, or poets like Artaud and Kleist; its form is not argumentative and logical, but aphoristic; its main characteristic is not *muthos* or *logos,* but *pathos* – personal involvement, the experience of suffering; not so much a foundation but a foundering. For them there is no Totality, and there is no Subject to grasp it, only a collection of fragments, particles, and flows of desire. And since there is no *logos,* there is no control over language.
>
> *Lecercle, 1985: 162–3*

In a similar vein, in her writing on shame, Probyn points to 'Deleuze's idea of the subjective disposition [which] allows us to understand something of the relationship between the writer, experience, expression, affect, and its effects' (2010: 81). In an important contribution, which also assists in the understanding of the workings of affect, she argues that,

> [s]hame cannot be conceived of as an external object that could be dispassionately described, nor is it a purely personal feeling. Shame is subjective in the strong sense of bringing into being an entity or an idea through the specific explosion of mind, body, place, and history.
>
> *Ibid.*

Writing, therefore, is not simply of the mind, writing is to do with this subjective disposition and the explosive coming together of, what Barad (2007) might describe as, the 'entanglements' of language with these 'fragments, particles, and flows of desire'. And so I sense that the writing to and of this book will shift me away from the *telling* and move me toward the *showing*. It will, therefore, encourage me to work less with what the writing might explain, interpret and critically engage with, in terms of what it might mean, and to work more with what this writing might do. Working with what this writing will do sensitises this writing in terms of what Deleuze refers to as the 'allotropic variations' (2004b: 45) of the body, the body of writing, as moving away from an emphasis upon its organs and the constraints of their organisation, its chapter and verse, its explanatory and representative elements, and more towards the vibrations of an intensive reality, its movements and sensations. Whilst this writing will pay attention to, what Manning refers to as, its 'ontogenesis' and, later, what I will refer to as, *its methodogenesis*, there is a constant need to be aware of the body of the book as working from and with thresholds and levels, flows and transmutations rather than being locked into the fixities of meaning and identity. As Manning says of her own writing:

> The tendency remains, through the writing, to give precedence to a stagnant humanist vocabulary that can be disciplined, controlled. It is difficult not to fall prey to this tendency. Politics of touch fights this impulse, continuing to challenge the ontological force of existing politics of identity . . . There is no stopping: ontogenesis requires invention. All radical engagements are inventions in some sense: unthought, untried, extraordinary. Let us improvise.
>
> *2007: 161*

So, working to introduce this book, as my starting stutters in the middle, I also have a strong sense, as I write these hesitant, early pages, of the way in which *what* I am writing is deeply entangled with *how* I write: the content/form binary is one that is deeply troubling and extremely unhelpful in coming to writing. There is something revealing and hugely important in Richardson's confession when she talks about 'yawning' her way through 'supposedly exemplary qualitative studies' and of leaving 'countless numbers' of these 'abandoned half read, half scanned' and how these affects gradually led her into her inquiries and experimentation with 'writing as a method of inquiry'. Elsewhere Massumi, in a somewhat self-deprecating manner, says, 'I might as well also admit that my prose has been compared to a black hole' (2002: 17). What is crucially telling about these two examples of how writing reads is their affective relationality in terms of what a body, in this case a body of writing, can do. For Spinoza this is a fundamentally important question: What can a body, any body, do? Multiple examples and considerations of this question, rather than what does something mean when it says, are of central importance to the writing of this book. The first example of this came to me a number of years ago when reading a paper by St Pierre (2004) entitled 'Deleuzian concepts for education: The subject undone'. I was engaged in trying to encourage a *doing* of what she talks about in the title of this paper. I was working with a group of students on a Master's in Education programme at a time when my interest in the philosophy of Deleuze was relatively new and when my enthusiasm for his work with the creation of concepts as events was growing at an extremely fast rate. I was eager to share this work with them and to encourage them in engaging in the kinds of concept making that his work with Guattari, particularly in their last collaborative work, *What is Philosophy?* was proposing. Whilst they found the work exciting they also found a great deal of the reading challenging. Consequently, and in this respect, I found the following quotation from Deleuze that St Pierre had included in her paper extremely helpful in the facilitation of their learning from the texts that we were using at the time:

> There are, you see, two ways of reading a book; you either see it as a box with something inside and start looking for what it signifies, and then if you're even more perverse or depraved you set off after signifiers. And you treat the

next book like a box contained in the first or containing it. And you annotate and interpret and question, and write a book about the book, and so on and on. Or there's the other way: you see the book as a little non-signifying machine, and the only question is 'Does it work, and how does it work?' How does it work for you? If it doesn't work, if nothing comes through, you try another book. This second way of reading's intensive: something comes through or it doesn't. There's nothing to explain, nothing to understand, nothing to interpret. It's like plugging in to an electric circuit. I know people who've read nothing who immediately saw what bodies without organs were, given their own 'habits,' their own way of being one. This second way of reading's quite different from the first, because it relates a book directly to what's Outside. A book is a little cog in much more complicated external machinery . . . This intensive way of reading, in contact with what's outside the book, as a flow meeting other flows, one machine among others, as a series of experiments for each reader in the midst of events that have nothing to do with books, as tearing the book into pieces, getting it to interact with other things, absolutely anything . . . is reading with love. That's exactly how you read the book.

Deleuze, 1995: 7–9

Encouraging the students to try to read in this second way was very revealing. They gradually found themselves breaking habits, connecting their readings with other readings, experimenting with the ideas they were encountering and creatively moving in many productive directions. In short, not only were they reading differently they were learning; learning differently. The form of reading that Deleuze proposes in the above passage is the way in which I hope this book will be read. I hope that this book will be read in a flow that connects with other flows. I hope that readers will plug their reading into other circuits and that, hopefully, this will help to make some sparks fly; I hope that these tentative experimental pluggings in will generate new ways of thinking and creative ways of doing.

With these hopes fresh in my body and animating my productive desire to write, I can only sense that if the madness that drives this book to some kind of completion is a motivating force, then it will be in relation to affect; it will be in relation to what it does in the writing in relation to what might be envisaged it might do in the future reading. In addressing what I have described here as the 'content/form binary', I am drawn to Manning's hyphenation 'in-formation' when she says 'When form becomes in-formation the body multiplies' (2010: 118). Thinking with what a body can do serves to trouble and make mute the generative force of this binary. I use it here simply to illustrate this redundancy and to highlight another aspect of what this madness might be in breaking away from traditional modalities and dualist constructions of practice. Manning's thinking on this is valuable, particularly when she talks of '(n)ot the body caught in the trap of hylomorphism where the individual is considered as created by "the meeting of *a* form and *a* matter"' (ibid.: 117–118). 'In-formation' is processual, it is about *individuation* and not about the *individualism* of the material body as somehow separate from its presencing in the world, in terms of its own world making. The body becoming of the person, of the idea, of the book is of this order and so, as Manning later says, 'The body's individuation is its force for becoming, not its end-point' (ibid.: 118).

Working with the shift away from what writing *means* to what writing *does* (and, indeed, to what reading *means* to what reading *does*) is a powerfully motivating force for the writing of this book and of offering conceptualisations of 'madness', whatever that might be taken to be, as an important energising force for its 'in-formation'. I sense this not in terms of somehow applying the concept of 'madness', whatever that might be, but rather that I will offer conceptualisations, concepts in process, concepts 'in-formation', if you will. In offering these conceptualisations (of madness) I am not trying to offer a repetition of the concept as it might be applied to a particular place, time or thing. Contextualisation of a concept suggests a kind of hylomorphism, a form of control in which the possible differentiations of the concept itself are limited by the representational relationality that might be applied to it in a particular context or setting. And so the non-beginning and non-ending of this book is about invention and experimentation in relation to the world-making possibilities of the concept of madness as methodology. In this I will take notice of Massumi's observation about how this might be done in relation to the 'in-formation' (Manning, 2007, 2013) of writing in the academy:

> The wager is that there are methods of writing from an institutional base in the humanities disciplines that can be considered experimental practices. What they would invent (or reinvent) would be concepts and connections between concepts. The first rule of thumb if you want to invent or reinvent concepts is simple: don't apply them.
>
> *Massumi, 2002: 17*

What Massumi has to say here might seem rather odd. If you have, say or write something that is exciting, that sounds good, that could be helpful in doing something in the world why not use it? You might argue that through engaging in the individuating, in-formative, processual becoming of conceptualisation you are experimenting and doing something new and worthwhile in the world, so, why not apply whatever it is you have created, make it do something, involve it in some form of world making that, in itself, creates something new? For me the key response to what Massumi is saying here is in relation to the usage I have intentionally mixed into my account in the preceding sentences. According to this view I understand that Massumi is referring here to 'concepts' and not 'conceptualisation': in my view this can be further explained by making my own conceptualisation that 'concepts' are more simply understood as nouns and 'conceptualisations' are more simply understood as verbs. In this sense 'concepts' become fixed, they exist in a representational domain of practice, they sit on shelves and are lifted down from time to time, dusted off and applied in different settings and contexts. Then, as Massumi argues, 'If you apply a concept or system of connection between concepts, it is the material you apply it to that undergoes change, much more markedly than do the concepts' (op. cit). In contrast 'conceptualisation' seems to be more about working with the concepts themselves, constantly bringing them to life, thinking about them and engaging in a doing with them that always involves something new, experimental, processual and transmutational. I think that Massumi's use of 'markedly' in the quotation above is significant in that it works to crush binary oppositions by pointing out that whilst it is the material that the concept is applied to that change, the concept also undergoes some kind of change. Equally, using Massumi's phrasing, it might therefore be possible to say that in the active process of 'conceptualisation' it is the conceptualisation that undergoes change, much more markedly than does that to which it is applied.

So the conceptualisation of madness as methodology that is part of the becoming of this book is about fragility and transversality, it is about moments and movements between practices of conceptualisation and what these might fold into other practices of world making and what unfoldings these foldings in might animate and bring to life. 'Conceptualisation' is the gleeful, anticipatory madness of 'what if?', it is the energising force that drives deviance, *délire* and digression; it is the creative dynamo that encourages incessant flows of flourishing, that brings new life to practices of world making that is full of surprises and that always offers new challenges. There is a sense in which Massumi's use of 'examples' and 'exemplification' resonates with this conceptualisation, as doing as event, that is being proposed here. Of this he says:

> The writing tries not only to accept the risk of sprouting deviant, but also to invite it. Take joy in your digressions. Because that is where the unexpected arises. That is the experimental aspect. If you know where you will end up when you begin, nothing has happened in the meantime. You have to be willing to surprise yourself writing things you didn't think you thought. Letting examples burgeon requires using inattention as a writing tool. You have to let yourself get so caught up in the flow of your writing that it ceases at moments to be recognisable to you as your own.
>
> *2002: 18*

In offering these stories of emergence, and in conceptualising *madness as methodology as event* in terms of movement, sensation, process and affect, this book is designed to open new digressions, new foldings and new processes of world making in the (post) Humanities. In this constant processualism in which madness is not seen as some *thing* to be categorised in difference within the solidities and fixities of a metaphysics of being, it is to be sensed within the fluidities and transmutational flux of becoming, individuation of posthuman movements and moments. In this sense, conceptualisation is forceful in offering exemplification. This provision of examples helps to expose and animate detail and divergence. It does not rely, primarily, upon the orthodoxies of the traditionally accepted academic practice of critique where one established body of represented thinking is set up against another and perspectives-driven critical discussions then ensue. Rather the use of examples is designed to trouble, tear and fracture, to cut through, perhaps using what Barad (2007) refers to as 'agential cuts' and, in so doing, leads to new possibilities and connections. Therefore, the emergence of madness as methodology in the writing of this book is designed to inattentively draw attention to diversity and difference and the possibilities that this offers, through the use of 'examples' and the ongoing use of practices of exemplification.

I recently found myself in the Round Room of Port Eliot House in St Germans, Cornwall looking at, or perhaps it is better to say, being a part of, the experience of *The Riddle Mural* (www.cornwalls.co.uk/photos/robert-lenkiewicz-riddle-mural-port-eliot-2308.htm) painted there by Robert Lenkiewicz over a period of thirty years in the latter part of the last century. I was attending the festival that is annually held in the grounds of the house and, despite living close by and attending the festival every year, this was the first time that I had found the opportunity to visit the Round Room and to look at the artist's fascinating and quite amazing work. The mural is over 40 feet in diameter, nearly 20 feet high and extends all the way around what is quite a remarkable room. Despite working on the mural off and on for thirty years, Lenkiewicz never actually completed it.

It is in two halves, with one half depicting death, destruction, insanity, unrequited love and the apocalyptic end of the world and the other providing images of love, affection, friendship, harmony and unity. Within the overall picture are concealed various references to his interest in witchcraft, the occult, metaphysics and medieval philosophy and many of the figures in the work offer resemblances to family and friends of the Eliot family and to people known to the artist. The presence of these hidden features in the work led Lenkiewicz to call this painting *The Riddle Mural*.

Whilst much discussion about the quality and value of the artist's work has continued since his death in 2002, there is no doubting that the scale, complexity and general immensity of *The Riddle Mural*, particularly when seen within the context of the artist's prodigious and prolific output, makes this an impressive piece of work by most standards. Drawn to searching for hidden meanings and attempting to 'solve' some of the riddles embedded in the complexity and chicanery of the mural, I found myself becoming immersed in the painting and in trying to imagine what it must have been like to have been involved in such a project. Lenkiewicz gained considerable notoriety in the Plymouth area where he lived for most of his adult life. His personal life attracted a great deal of attention due to his unconventional approach to familial relations and parenthood. He painted many large murals around the city and was involved in many projects, including faking his own death, all of which gave him a reputation which has lived on long after his death at the age of 61 in August 2002. All this has led me to ponder what it must mean to engage in such a massive and hugely time-consuming work. He was clearly a driven man with considerable energy, massive amounts of self-belief and a tremendous commitment to his engagement with the work.

My imaginings of Lenkiewicz in the presence of his mural in that sunny and spacious room on a Saturday morning led me back to my own inclinations and abilities to write a book and to Deleuze and Guattari's (2004) notion of 'desiring-production'. This powerful notion runs counter to the Freudian conception of desire, which is constructed as a representational signifier for a psychological sense of lack, something that is part of the individual and that, it is argued, exists as a human characteristic or trait. For Deleuze and Guattari, desire is a productive force and exists within the relational operation of multiple, interconnected 'desiring-machines' (2004) which are plugged into one another and which function as (machinic) assemblages and through which desire as an energetic and productive force flows.[3] Deleuze and Guattari imagine a multi-functional universe composed of such machines all connected to each other. So it is possible to make sense of the work of Lenkiewicz in this way. Each piece of work was part of an assemblage, connected, through transmutational tides, flows and currents, to other related and particular parts. Most his work took the form of what he referred to as 'projects' in which he would combine a whole series of thematically linked paintings with the publication of research notes, theoretical writings from his vast library of mediaeval philosophical books and observations and written narratives of many of his sitters. His 'projects' involved inquiries into vagrancy, mental instability and death and always set up inquiry into invisibility, ostracism, the positioning of minorities in society and the presence of the always not yet known. He often talked about these inquiries as 'surveys' or 'research' and, in attempting to diminish the status of his work as art, he insisted that it should not be seen simply as a series of individual paintings, rather that they should be looked at in their entirety and in relation to the other elements and features that formed the elemental particularity of his inquiry. In this respect he often described himself as a 'researcher', a representation which worked to further blur and trouble the various identifications, 'painter', 'lover', 'eccentric', 'researcher' and others that were used in the many futile attempts to categorise and classify him throughout his life. In this sense and within the context of his continual attempts to debunk the notion of his work as art, he often described his 'projects' as 'presenting information' (Mallett and Penwill, 1997) with all the individual elements contained in this 'presentation' being subordinated to and constituting the whole, and designed to elicit response and some form of action on the part of those who became engaged with them. In this sense his work and his whole approach to life seems to be intentionally provocative and I have come to have an understanding of it in terms of what Barad has referred to as an 'ethico-onto-epistem-ology', which involves

> an appreciation of the intertwining of ethics, knowing, and being – since each intra-action matters, since the possibilities for what the world may become call out in the pause that precedes each breath before a moment comes into being and the world is remade again, because the becoming of the world is a deeply ethical matter.
>
> *2007: 185*

And so the madness that I write with and about here, that attempts to make claims to offer a thinking and doing approach to working and becoming in the world, the very process of world making, is one in which selves are deeply imbricated in relationalities that are not bounded by the simply human and that the discursive construction of these selves into categories of representation that classify practices in particular ways needs to be challenged, questioned and ultimately broken down. As I read Barad in relation to the experience of *The Riddle Mural* on that sunny Saturday morning, I began to sense an immersion in that experience which was and continues to be a form of deeply ontological, epistemological and ethical mattering. In this sensing knowing is not a purely human practice and cannot be simply contained in, with and by such practices. In this sensing becoming is always intensively differentiated and those delineations of ontology, epistemology and ethics become increasingly fragile and much less full of meaning, value or practical use as they exist within these separations and categorisations. I turn again to Barad when she says that 'knowing is a matter of part of the world making itself intelligible to another part. Practices of knowing and being are not isolable; they are mutually implicated' (ibid.). When Bachelard talks of artists working to avoid allowing art being made into 'recipes', he argues that '(k)nowing must therefore be accompanied by an equal capacity to forget knowing. Non-knowing is not a form of ignorance but a difficult transcendence of knowledge' (1969: xxxii–xxxiii). I gain a sense in which he is saying here that the move away from *knowledge*, as a category of difference, to *knowing*, which involves being a part of the world and world making in all its differentiated becoming, is absolutely necessary and integral to the entanglements and elisions of ontology, epistemology and ethics that Barad is talking about in her work and that I am attempting to bring to life here. Bachelard cites a quotation from Jean Lescure describing the work of the painter Charles Lapique which says, '(a)n artist does not create the way he lives, he lives the way he creates' (ibid.). Whilst Bachelard's use of this binary construction seems to be more for literary effect than epistemological value, what it does offer is a thought-provoking statement of the ways in which a madness as methodology might be seen to form as creative practice and in relation to Deleuze and Guattari's engagement with concepts as events, an approach which I will return to again and again in the emergence of this book.

I am also aware that as I embark upon this project the need to engage with 'methodology' is hugely important. In proposing the concept of 'post qualitative inquiry', St Pierre (2011, 2015) and others have forcefully pointed out that the methodology and the methods of conventional humanist qualitative inquiry have become 'overdetermined by the publishing industry, university research courses, and journals and books that detail very carefully what it is and how to do it' (2015: 75). Therefore, my engagement with madness as methodology will involve me in working with both terms in their relationality; therefore, it might be a useful and provocative starting point to make in the introduction to this book that the methodology that I will propose here will be, in many respects, a non-methodology.[4] In proposing this in an apparently contradictory form, I wish to also show that it is the intention of this writing to work to show a madness as methodology, not so much in epistemological terms of naming and of offering a particular meaning, but rather to attempt to show what a madness of methodology might do. To return to an earlier theme in this introduction, the terms 'madness', 'methodology' and 'non-methodology' are offered as briefly existent representations in the constant processual play of conceptualisation. The world-making practice of conceptualisation will be engaged and folded in and returned to throughout the emergence of this book.

In September 2012 I attended the European Conference of Education Research. In that year the conference was hosted by the University of Cadiz and, spending nearly a week attending the conference and wandering through the narrow streets and *barrios* of the old town, I became captivated and entranced by the simple beauties of this ancient Andalusian city. That year Rosi Braidotti presented one of the main conference keynotes which addressed the question 'What is "Human" about the Humanities today?'[5] In this paper she described what she saw as a 'posthuman predicament' and proposed what she referred to as a 'posthuman affirmative ethics', in so doing making an argument for a pragmatic approach in readiness to engage with emergent forms of transformation and change.

> We already live in permanent states of transition, hybridisation and nomadic mobility, in emancipated, post-feminist, multi-ethnic societies with high degrees of technological mediation which, however, have not ensured justice for all, or resolved enduring patterns of inequality. These are neither simple nor linear events, but rather are multi-layered and internally contradictory social phenomena. They combine elements of ultra-modernity with splinters of neo-archaism: high-tech advances and neo-primitivism, which defy the logic of excluded middle. We therefore need great methodological creativity to cope with these challenges.
>
> *Braidotti, 2013: 1*

At this time I had already begun to tentatively formulate ideas for writing a book which would have as its focus an engagement with research methodology within the context of my own education practices in higher education in the UK, so Braidotti's call for greater 'methodological creativity' was both apposite and inspirational for me as I listened to her speaking in that crowded conference hall. Perhaps what was crucial for me in these listenings and frantic conference note-makings was the affective shift that her words inspired and prompted in helping to re-configure my ontological dispositions intra-relationally, in and beyond the world making with which I was engaging at the time. Her presentation offered a critique of the self-reflexivity of Cartesian rationalism, not simply within itself in its engagement with and perpetuation of narrow human individualism but also in the way that it had become manifest in, what she referred to as, a 'civilisational model' which she described, through reference to Hegel's philosophy of history, as producing a 'hegemonic cultural model'. Further, she argued, this model has in turn been responsible for creating a form of Eurocentrism that is 'more than just a contingent matter of attitude: it is a structural element of our cultural practice, which is also embedded in both theory and institutional and pedagogical practices' (2013: 2). These modalities of self-representation and the concomitant processes of subjectification which produce largely masculinist and Eurocentric selves, characterised as possessing consciousness, transcendent powers of reason and a form of ethical self-knowing, result from conditions of possibility that are deeply embedded and forcefully agentic in the discursive production of, what Braidotti describes as, 'the cultural logic of universal Humanism' (ibid.). My memory of sitting in that hot and packed conference hall, listening intently, enthusiastically making notes as quickly as possible and of being enthralled by the powerful rhetoric of Braidotti's argument stays with me and is here with me now. I remember leaving the excited vibrancy of that hot, packed conference hall and walking out into the warmth of the bright early autumn sunshine. I remember the refreshing feeling of Braidotti's words washing over me and, in the throes of this deep affective engagement, to begin to mobilise an ontology that was largely about, to paraphrase Foucault's words, a 'getting free of one self' (1992: 8), a self that as a researcher in higher education had also been at least partly culpable in allowing these discursive constructions to take place. Up until this point a good deal of my inclination to write in resistance to the largely Positivist inclinations and practices of the research culture of which I had grown to be a part had emerged out of my own genealogies and histories. As I have mapped elsewhere, here in this book, my research and writerly proclivities have always tended towards challenge, rhetoric and experimentation; my concerns to offer creative alternatives to the traditional orientations and practices of (post) Positivist research have always motivated and mobilised forms of pedagogy and inquiry that resist adherence to traditional authority and the constraints of bureaucratic strictures and controls. So listening to Braidotti's words, becoming alert to the power of the form and content of her argument and sensing the need for a looking out into worlds that hitherto were clearly being made around me, instigated a palpable ontological shift and one which empowers the methodological intent of this writing here and now. As Braidotti says: 'This new (posthuman) knowing subject is a complex assemblage of human and non-human, planetary and cosmic, given and manufactured, which requires major readjustments in our ways of thinking' (2013: 12–13).

With Braidotti's ideas circling the creation of these words, I continue to engage in the writing of this book, with due consideration of the multiplicity of process, the politics of productive desire and the influence of these humanist modes of 'paradigmatic self-representation' that are increasingly having an impact upon its coming together and upon what I hope it will achieve in the world doing and making that it conveys and, hopefully, begins to animate and activate in those who engage with it. This writing a book; this (be)coming together of *body-thing-called-book*, something named, something that, despite my best efforts, will function, at least in part, in worlds of discursive construction, identification and representation. As I work with the coming together of the writing of this book, I am aware of the multiplicity of human and nonhuman actants that play a part in this coming together. As Bennett pointed out as she was engaged in the writing of her book:

> the sentences of this book . . . emerged from the confederate agency of many
> striving macro and microactants: from 'my' memories, intentions, contentions,

> intestinal bacteria, eyeglasses, and blood sugar, as well as from the plastic computer keyboard, the bird song from the open window, or the air or the particulates in the room . . . what is at work here on the page is an animal-vegetable-mineral-sonority cluster with a particular degree and duration of power.
>
> *Bennett, 2010: 23*

I can now also draw into this assemblage, this *becoming-Ken-book*, further hetero-geneous and contingent elements and sense its changing constitution as, in this preceding passage, Braidotti's words also inflect its affective intensity and potential agentic force. In propagation, composition and ceaseless folding, as the emergent writing space that is this book takes place, these 'many striving macro and micro-actants' imbue this book with qualities, intensities and potentialities that are always processually and affectively shifting. As I write I am relieved when I read again the following well-known and frequently quoted passage from Foucault:

> I never think quite the same thing, because for me my books are experiences, in a sense that I would like to be as full as possible. An experience is something that one comes out of transformed. If I had to write a book to communicate what I was already thinking, I would never have the courage to begin. I only write a book because I don't know exactly what to think about this thing that I so much want to think about, so that the book transforms me and transforms what I think. Each book transforms what I was thinking when I finished the previous book. I am an experimenter, not a theorist.
>
> *Foucault, 2000: 239–240*

I have written books with others and it is only now that I am tentatively beginning to embark upon the writing of this book in a very different kind of assemblage. I have included this quotation here because it carries with it so many thoughts and assertions that I want to say about the writing of this book. How Foucault says this, how I read this, how I appropriate this for my purposes and how the reader has just read it are all beautifully and aesthetically indeterminate and are constitutive of my sense making. His sense making is imbricated within a desire to produce something from the multiplicities of which I feel a part and at the same time partial to creating. Foucault talks to me in this passage of the politics of madness in its battle with what I want to refer to as the irrationality of reason. In this writing it feels to me that he is working in the play of a Deleuzian 'logic of sense', working with a sensing that, in the working of his writing, conveys his acute honesty and a conviction to write, just to write. Writing in these ways works to trouble some of the myths and organisational discourses that surround the conventionalities and orthodoxies of book writing and production and, in so doing, works with what the writing and the reading of a book can do. So the politics of madness that I am working with and to which I am beginning to give presence here will require a methodological approach that pays due attention to the concerns of St Pierre referred to earlier in this plateau. In paying respect to her concerns this book will not offer an approach to methodology that 'detail(s) very carefully what it is and how to do it'. I have already, somewhat obliquely perhaps, suggested that my methodology will be a 'non-methodology' and I know that I will need to work with what the use of such a potentially unusual signifier might be. Therefore the subsequent reading with other plateaus in this book will offer encounters with process, affect and posthuman relationality. As already suggested, the book will offer and approach the works with the dynamisms of multiple elisions and entanglements of ontological, epistemological and methodological considerations in carrying out research and inquiry. In this approach, detailing 'very carefully what it is and how to do it' will be anathema to the presencing and worlding that the (non)methodological approach described in this book sets out to do. In this I can therefore begin by saying that this approach will actively work with what Barad refers to as 'ethico-onto-epistemology' (2007: 185). Further it will build upon Manning's working with Simondon's concept of 'onto-genesis' (2007: 106). By using practices of and being alert to processes of 'individuation' and 'in-formation' (Manning, 2007, 2013), I will formulate what I will tentatively refer to at this stage as a *methodogenesis*. If in these elisions and entanglements ontogenesis can be seen to work with the always becoming of bodies in movement, in contrast to ontology, which tends to work with bodies as established categories of being, then *methodogenesis* might attempt to offer how this work might be done rather than describing and identifying very carefully what it is and how it should be done. Such an approach might be seen to, using Manning's words, involve an approach in which '(a)ll radical engagements are inventions in some sense: unthought, untried, extraordinary' (2007: 161). In offering this creative conceptualisation of *methodogenesis* I am, therefore, concerned to free research and inquiry from its containment within practices that are based upon Kantian forms of reason and which are designed to discover facts and lead to the establish-ment of knowledge. *Methodogenesis* works against those methods that use practices of organisation, reason and judgement to capture and work to define knowledge.

Of such an approach it is also possible to draw upon the thinking of Deleuze when he says, 'you see the book as a little non-signifying machine, and the only question is "Does it work, and how does it work?" How does it work for you?' (1995: 8). As a machinic assemblage, the book can be plugged into other machines and we can see what work it does. This shifts the emphasis of the methodological approach described in the book away from originative conceptions and designs, in terms of what it might prescribe and mean, towards an emphasis upon action and to what it might be able to do. In the entanglements of the material and the discursive, the important ontological question might therefore be to do with how a body functions in affect. Therefore, in relation to this book as a whole, a transversal approach of this kind is designed to cut across representational and hylomorphic hierarchies of meaning and fixed categories of interpretation and critique. In so doing, challenges will be offered to, what Deleuze refers to as, the 'arborescent' nature of the Cartesian rationalist approach, in which branches and leaves reach up for light and roots dig deep to become established and foundational, intent on producing the anthropocentric individualism of the Enlightenment model.

And so as I tentatively 'introduce' this book, as I write from its middle, unsure of its starting and ending points, already deeply immersed in its process, knowing that I have always been writing it and that I will never stop, reading another passage from Deleuze and Guattari, I find myself in excellent company when they write of

> [s]trange Anglo-American literature: from Thomas Hardy, from D. H. Lawrence to Malcolm Lowry, from Henry Miller to Allen Ginsberg and Jack Kerouac, men who know how to leave, to scramble the codes, to cause flows to circulate, to traverse the body without organs. They overcome a limit, they shatter a wall, the capitalist barrier. And of course they fail to complete the process, they never cease failing to do so.
>
> *2004: 144*

It is about conceptualisation, about becoming as spatialising; it is about creating space in these kinds of ways that gives comfort; a form of comfort that is imbricated with ambition. This is the becoming of the space in which I will write and it is this writing that will be the becoming of this book, or not.

Notes

1 Desire and specifically, in this example, productive desire, is, in a Deleuzian sense, not to be understood as attributable to or rooted in a subject, therefore, it is not, in a Lacanian sense, to do with lack. Rather it is to be understood in terms of what it does; in intentional and unintentional ways, it produces effects of a certain or uncertain nature.

2 Throughout the book I shall be using the term 'posthuman' in this elided form rather than the, possibly more familiar, hyphenated form of 'post-human'. To this purpose I suggest that 'posthuman' refers to the more than and not simply human and that 'post-human' refers to after or following human.

3 As Deleuze and Guattari moved in their writing of *Anti-Oedipus* to *A Thousand Plateaus*, they made a transition from the apparent subjectivism of 'desiring machines', preferred in the former, towards the use of the more impersonal concept of assemblage, sometimes translated as *agencement* or arrangement which is preferred in the latter.

4 At this point in the emergence of this book, I spent a great deal of time considering whether or not to replace the term 'madness as methodology' with 'madness as (non) methodology'. For the sake of consistency of conceptualisation and presentation, I have decided against this course of action. However, I would entreat the reader to be alert to my concerns about the use of the term 'methodology' and to pay attention to the rhetoric of this work that wishes to present the concept and practice of methodology as always being in play; continually fluid, processual and working in world making and encounter rather than within the containment of a fixity of meaning

5 Since published as 'Posthuman humanities' in *European Educational Research Journal* (2013).

SOME STORIES OF EMERGENCE: ROUTINES, SURPRISES AND EPIPHANIES

When he came to writing it began to save his life. He began to find a self that he could not just identify but sense. His writings became palpable in emergent materiality; no longer simply representations acting like coat hooks in the hall. His vibrant self began to hum in his sense of others. He began to write to and with his gender, his class, his insecurities and his strengths. His writing increasingly became suffused with the energies of the wind, the incessant flows and transmutations of the tides. His deserts became more populous as birds, fish, animals and, yes, people began to grow their presence in his words. Like meeting new lovers, making love on these shores was an awakening. And with this becoming in the saving of his life grew a sense of community, a knowing of others, a reading and a writing, a talking and a listening with beautiful others.

And with this becoming, like the worm in Blake's rose, grew an infection, a resistance, a new sensing that all was not right with this new world he was now helping to grow and not simply live in. He began to sense the ephemeral representational quality of identity. He was aware of his body bleeding over the page and the blood being mopped in ways that was not saving his soul. And, with this becoming he began to question the 'I' that he was making for himself and that others were busy making for him and that he was busy making for others. The emergence of this troubled sense of self grappled increasingly with the use of signifiers, those 'I's', 'you's', 'we's' and 'them's' that worked to ossify selves in the shelves and drawers of classification and categories of difference. Therefore, and with this becoming, he wrote and spoke to trouble the preposterous and pugnacious 'I' that populates the world with nouns and beings and identifications of fixity. He took himself back to the beach, he walked barefoot in the sand, swam naked in the cold crashing of the waves. His glistening wet body dried in the cooling breeze of the westerly wind, he picked up wet shells like glistening treasure, collected seaweed for his garden, sensed oyster catchers tolerating his madness and was attentive to the slow dipping arc of the sun moving toward its home beyond the horizon. His new knowing was of a loss of 'he' and 'his' in the growing sense of this vibrant yet ordinary relationality. A sensing of gentle immanence in the grittiness of sand between toes, the stiff skin of a salt dried body, the first star in the freshly darkening sky, herring gulls preparing to roost in the precarity of their homes on the cliff, a lightening of the breeze from the west, the incoming tide and the emergent desire to draw pictures in the sand.[1]

The preceding passage can be seen to portray nervousness, apprehension, uncertainty and many other affective flavours, hues and possibilities. Now, some two years since I initially drafted that piece of writing, I sit with its words and I gain a powerful sense of intensities and of the potentialities that exist within the concerns and procrastinations it might be seen to express. The very context in which it was first revealed in the form of a presentation paper for the inaugural session of an Autoethnography Special Interest Group at a conference in which the majority of delegates would probably describe themselves as autoethnographers was itself problematic. At this time I had already begun to write and to attempt to engage with what I was beginning to understand as the humanist and pheno-menological tendencies inherent in the naming, the principles and the practices of autoethnography. With Jonathan Wyatt, I had presented at conferences and written papers (Wyatt and Gale, 2013a, 2013b) that engaged with and problematised the precession and domination of the 'auto' in research practices of this name. In offering a practice conceptualisation which we named 'assemblage/ethnography' (ibid.) we began and continue to write to, with and against the very practices with which we had begun our early incursions into qualitative inquiry a number of years previously.[2] And, as the previous introductory plateau begins to address questions and problems to do with the naming of 'madness' and 'methodology' both in the title and in describing the experimental nature of this project, in this plateau I will also begin to describe and engage with the problem of authorial presence in the writing and presentation of this and indeed any book of this kind. A substantial part of this becoming-book and the journey it takes over the com-ing pages and plateaus will at least in part involve an engagement with and a destabilisation of what St Pierre (2011: 75) has referred to as 'conventional humanist inquiry'.

These stories of emergence will, in part, offer narratives of a historical nature and in so doing will bring those narratives into the presents that are both the writing and the reading of this book as events. In presenting these (past) events and encouraging a drawing from them, I wish to open spaces to further inquiry, I wish to offer a mistrusting of concepts and inducement to further conceptualisation and, in so doing, to nurture the creation of new events that will contribute to new sense making and continue to promote the possibilities and practices that the preceding writing begins to speak to and talk with.

It is always to start in the middle. In naming this plateau *Some stories of emergence*, I am not necessarily intending to offer starting points or places where this book and these ideas of methodology as madness somehow began to emerge and form as part of some kind of linear process which had a beginning, in the past tense, is being presented here and now in some kind of present and will have an ending in some kind of future. In these conceptualisations I am influenced by Manning's reading of Simondon when she says, '(w)hen form becomes in-formation the body multiplies' (2010: 118). I conceptualise the body of this book in this way: it is a body that is always in and of emergence, it is never fully conceived, it is '(m)odulated by information, the body resonates with affect's propulsive potential which moves across the becoming-body's intensive surface', it is liberated 'from the presupposition of a form, demonstrating how a body is always alive across lives. The body's individuation is its force for becoming not its end-point' (ibid.). I see these stories of emergence as part of highly plural and multiple processes of actualisation that will never be complete and as always belonging to the virtual. I see these stories as offering a sense of this book-becoming, this person-writing-book as event and as a force of intensification in the possibilities offered for a madness as methodology.

In taking what he refers to as a 'topological turn', Massumi, as a means of engaging with the 'virtual', animates a philosophy of the event in which trans-formation, variation and change take precedence. On first reading this paper, some while ago, a particular passage, which I will quote here in full, provided a stimulus which I will now use as a context for considering some of these stories of emergence.

> We do not see or experience perspectival forms from the outside: they occur to our experience and in it, as arrest events that befall it. We ourselves, as spatially located forms in interaction with other forms, as embodied subjects in reciprocity with objects, we ourselves must be co-occurrences with depth and boundary, co-emergences of concretion and stoppage, companion arrests' fall-out of the befallen. 'We' ourselves are stoppage events in the flow of experience.
>
> *1998: 21*

Movement with starlings

Starlings, thousands and thousands of starlings, flying together in the darkening light of the evening sky over the Somerset Levels. Even on wobbly and grainy video footage this is such a sight. It is easy to slip into cliché and call the sight incredible. Its very credibility is what makes these images so powerful: this is something that happened, is happening and will happen again, and again and again, until the diminishing population of starlings becomes so small that its visibility ceases in its new becoming. The Royal Society for the Protection of Birds website (www.rspb.org.uk) describes these amazing circlings, soarings and swoopings of thousands and thousands of birds as murmurations. On the site the question is asked 'What's going on?' and the keen ornithologists on the site tell us that:

> It's basically a mass aerial stunt – thousands of birds all swooping and diving in unison. It's completely breathtaking to witness.
>
> We think that starlings do it for many reasons. Grouping together offers safety in numbers – predators such as peregrine falcons find it hard to target one bird in the middle of a hypnotising flock of thousands.
>
> They also gather to keep warm at night and to exchange information, such as good feeding areas.
>
> They gather over their roosting site, and perform their wheeling stunts before they roost for the night.

Many, many years of teaching, learning and the representations that are squeezed from the discursive construction of reality with which this is imbued tells me that such reflexivity 'aims to reflect upon, and systematically take account of, the investigator's role as an instrument in the constitution of evidence' (Barad, 2007: 86). The need to tell, identify, represent and somehow mirror reality is paramount within the ontological predispositions and hence the epistemological accounts and methodological practices of generations of scientists and scholars whose realities are grounded both within and by these discursive constructions of reality. Using perhaps a Foucauldian genealogical inquiry into the conditions of possibility that might be attributed to this, Barad cites Keller and Grontkowski in suggesting that the use of these optical tropes of representation and hence reproduction of our worlds is based upon an 'intertwining of vision and knowledge in Western thought [arguing] that "the tradition of grounding our epistemological premises on visual analogies dates back to the Greeks"' (ibid.).

I know that I prefer to sit in awe, to let the sight wash over me and allow the breeze created by a thousand furiously flapping wings and millions and millions of tiny feathers to disturb the insolence of rational explanation. I want to sense, perhaps with Barad, the beauty of these awesome intra-active material entanglements and to experience a knowing that simply makes this real, and allows me to ask with incredulity: How can the body, *any body*, be generalisable?

> How can the body be generalisable?
>
> The body works, without measure, in encounter.
>
> Each new movement of body brings to life moments of new life.
>
> These glow with the iridescence of birth, fresh into the world, naked leaves in emergence in the dewy freshness of dimsy woodland glow, bloody babies squealing in excited celebration of coming to life in the wild thrusting of their new post-foetal lives.
>
> These are becomings.
>
> They are the always more than of the event.

This event/ful/ness is the energetic potency of the vibrational force of the new, the new that can only live in its relationality to the ever presence of the not yet known.

So, this new, is the living vibrational force of the always new.

It is the death of the stases of identity, certainty and stability, its bell is tolling the demise of the representational.

It rings goodnight to the coercive, individualising frailties of reflection, interpretation and the critical; bodies transitioning, becomings in knowing of bodies in movement and relationality.

It never dwells in the facile fabrications of this or that, me or you and the idea that one and the other are the means by which meaning is made of the world.

It is not necessary to make meaning of the world only to see what it does, to sense what worlds it makes only to live in with and through the movements of its world makings.

In the madness of my methodology I increasingly find that working with this kind of knowing grows in me, in the insidiously gradual annihilation of temerity and doubt, a new logic of sense. My moving in and out of Deleuze's (2004a) *The Logic of Sense* since I bought and first began to read it back in September 2004 has infected me in ways that allows my madness to grow in welcome ways: like an unwanted virus that adjusts my living to its lowest ebb through the dark months of winter, this book grows into me in ways that gradually and insidiously allow me to celebrate the madness that is allowing me to tap out these words and to tentatively will this book into its fragile stuttering existence. In my frequent returns to this book and in my living with its introductions and continual seductions of Deleuze's philosophy of the event and of becoming has also helped me to live to explore the paradoxes of meaning and meaninglessness and to nurture the confidence to work with the practices of common sense and nonsense, your sense and my sense and to encourage others, students, colleagues and friends alike, to do the same. Increasingly, I find that these non-totalizing modes of sensing in multiplicity and ceaseless transmutation animates an immanence of becoming that troubles the metaphysics of being and shows me that it 'always more than one' (Manning, 2013).

In the early pages of *The Logic of Sense*, Deleuze engages the work of Lewis Carroll and in giving an account of Alice's loss of identity during her travels in Wonderland has provided me with a growing sense of what a practical philosophy of event can both be and do for me in my becoming:

The loss of the proper name is the adventure which is repeated throughout all of Alice's adventures. For the proper or singular name is guaranteed by the permanence of *savoir*. The latter is embodied in general names designating pauses and rests, in substantives and adjectives, with which the proper name maintains a constant connection. Thus the personal self requires God and the world in general. But when substantives and adjectives begin to dissolve, when the names of pause and rest are carried away by the verbs of pure becoming and slide into the language of events, all identity disappears from the self, the world, and God . . . In it words may go awry, being obliquely swept away by the verbs . . . personal uncertainty is not a doubt foreign to what is happening, but rather an objective structure of the event itself, insofar as it moves in two directions at once, and insofar as it fragments the subject following this double direction. Paradox is initially that which destroys good sense as the only direction, but it is also that which destroys common sense as the assignation of fixed identities.

Deleuze, 2004a: 5

I have always felt reeled in and cast up on the shores of identification. I have understood the logic of Foucault's discourse theory; I can sense the way in which the innocence of a discussion about a person, an event or a philosophy of meaning can turn into fixed representations about the world. The chilling shift and the emerging disciplinary effect of the potentially benign subject *of* the conversation becoming transformed as subject *to* the conversation always creates affective incisions. The materiality of affect entangled here with the discursively constructed and seemingly helpless docility of the body has always been disabling for me as I engage with the struggles of my life. And so Spinoza's consideration of the power to affect and be affected seems deeply imbricated with and animated by naming and the permanence of *savoir*. And so Barad, in her critique of the practices of reflection and reflexivity points out that 'representationalism – the belief that words, concepts, ideas, and the like accurately reflect or mirror the things to which they refer – makes a finely polished surface of this whole affair' (2007: 86). And so I am left with and excited by the possibilities of this logic of sense, this philosophy of event, this practice of doing, over naming. Whilst I live with the sense that speech acts, I allow this sense to live in the eventfulness and eventualities of these moments, encouraging the materiality of the self to live against the identifications that act to name and represent it in particular ways. I will murmur and stutter in my emergent language as the reeling dance of the murmuration of starlings seething, wheeling and soaring around and above my head fills me with brief ecstasies of wonder and the intensities of joy.

Sensing with Patti Smith

Reading Patti Smith's deeply moving and visually poetic book *M Train*, I found myself being taken on an odyssey of grimy cafes, sensually alluring coffee bars and anonymous hotel rooms. Absorbed by the delicate intimacies of her writing, I found myself drifting from simple stark awareness of mundane material realities, the pungent, aromatic smell of coffee, the stark coldness of a hotel room, the gift of a book from her mother, to becoming immersed in a hazy, shifting, dreamscape of affect, where hope, curiosity, despair and fascination all somehow fuse together through the multiplicities and intensities of her diffractive lensing. The following account is at once a highly realist descriptive passage and at the same time is suffused by the warming aesthetics of a dream.

> I wound up reading The Master Builder until late afternoon before the fireplace in the hotel library. It was a bit warm and I was nodding off when a man in a tweed overcoat tapped my shoulder, asking if I might be the journalist he was supposed to be meeting.

>   – No sorry
>   – Reading Ibsen?
>   – Yes, The Master Builder
>   – Hmmm, lovely play but fraught with symbolism.
>   – I hadn't noticed, I said

> He stood before the fire for a moment then shook his head and left. Personally, I'm not much for symbolism. I never get it. Why can't things be just as they are? I never thought to psychoanalyse Seymour Glass or sought to break down 'Desolation Row'. I just wanted to get lost, become one with somewhere else, slip a wreath on a steeple top solely because I wished it.

> *Smith, 2015: 58–59*

From an email to Jonathan (Wyatt), 10.09 Monday 1st June 2015

I started my book yesterday. It came to life as I was waking up. It was in my head, a title, a surge of ideas which I immediately sketched into my iPad and which I have built upon this morning. I have a strong feeling about this that I can bring something to life. What is this tide that is up surging on to my shores, flooding them with new life?

Diary writing, Thursday 4th June 2015

There is a poetics in our madness that opens fissures in the indistinct relentlessness of relational spaces. It is a poetics of affect and it is sensitised in the aesthetics and sensualities of becomings in space. Working with the affective offers alerts to haecceity and the vibrancy of moments of 'This is this'. It is the point where everything stops, perhaps only for an instant, and then in that brief instantaneous stopping that defies language and all discursive construction, becoming is the surging tide of beautiful temporary knowing that is recognised in gestural simplicity, a smile, a nod and a gentle moving on in the world.

In this diary writing, as now, events happen and carry their force, despite our attempts to describe them, classify them and organise them within what we call bodies. They can only live, really come alive, in the beautiful brevity and potentialities of intensities. These are fleeting, they float like translucent skeins in the delicacy of a fresh morning breeze that often eludes life in origination and form. It is their very resistance to forming and shaping that gives them their existence. Their intrinsic qualities of elusiveness are their life force and if they are brought to life within the limits of a name, they are already dead. As Berlant says:

> The aesthetic and sexual scenario induces a mode of impersonality that is fully felt and dispersed in relationality and in the world. The seismic shift takes place in yielding to the proximity of an intimacy undefined by talking, made by a gesture of approach that holds open a space between two people just standing there, linked newly.
>
> *2011: 32*

There is great suspense here in what she refers to as 'suspended space'. Perhaps this is because we are so unused to living in worlds where talking and writing are bereft of the ability to capture such movements in moment. Perhaps it is because the incessant discursive constructions of our realities, the very stuff of representation that codifies and that identifies and defines 'me', 'it' and 'them' in such vivid and persistent ways has trapped us within what Deleuze and Guattari (1987: 268), in drawing from the work of Simondon, call 'hylomorphism'. These externally originating systems of order, unity and classification can often be seen to constrain and mould our becomings in determining ways, making them more to do with measurable developments and shifts that gain their life from the ease with which they are constructed and allowed to live. The interfering diffractions that Haraway and Barad encourage us to work with in our engagements with the world, in living our 'entanglements' between materialities and the languages that attempt to construct them, offers a powerful resistance to the practice of reflection as 'a pervasive trope for knowing' (Barad, 2007: 72). Reflection is often conceptualised and practised as a means of engaging with these determining normative and prescriptive forces working to consolidate and enforce them, reinforcing the confessional modalities of self-forming. So, reflection as a practice style can be seen to valorise sameness and difference between, *qua* other, where the mirrored image becomes the reassuring reality of the artifice of the phenomenological self. However, diffractive practice, as Barad describes it, illuminates the cracks in the mirror by always placing difference prior to constructions of the self in the world, by recognising and articulating difference as the basis of knowings and our conceptualisations of the world. Barad offers a major ontological claim that becomes the substantive rhetorical force of her book when she says 'that there is a deep sense in which we can understand diffractive patterns – as patterns which make a difference – to be the fundamental constituents that make up the world' (ibid.).

Diary writing, Friday 5th June 2015

Staying with the spaces between/within and working with intensity and living for haecceity, 'moments of being' (Woolf), assemblage, desiring machines,[3] and the molecular over the molar, the minor literacy over the major and differentiation over categories of difference and . . . living in the presence of space/time as always relational. I sense my self, a self perhaps, engaging in writing that is trying to move more and more to the rhythm of a Deleuzian 'logic of sense' in time with space/time of 'processual sensualism' (Thrift, 2006) and therefore working with the vague, the intangible, those indistinct morphologies to be found in Goethe's thought, bathing in perfume, scent, pheromones, moods, tones, vibrations, inclinations, intonations, tendencies, inferences, implications . . .

I remember reading Annie Proulx's gripping and atmospheric novel *The Shipping News*, and being moved by how the central character, Quoyle, is represented at a human level as a hapless, shambling and desolately alone individual and yet, somewhat paradoxically, in a posthuman sense, he has a oneness with the materiality of the stark, grey, frozen world around him and of which he is, almost inevitably, a part.

> Nothing was clear to lonesome Quoyle. His thoughts churned like the amorphous thing that ancient sailors, drifting into artic half-light, called the Sea Lung; a heaving sludge of ice under fog where air blurred into water, where liquid was slid, where solids dissolved, where the sky froze and light and dark muddled.
>
> *Proulx, 1995: 5*

As I read the words of my diary entry again, well over a year since I first wrote them, I can now sense ways in which the indeterminate cloudiness to what my writing appeared to be alluding was to do with my readiness to lose and find affective ontological ways of self-forming in the mercurial, elusive and shifting elemental spaces of an always becoming-self. In drawing from Whitehead's process philosophy, Manning offers a clear and concise sense in which it is possible to think of bodies in relation to the kinds of fields of experience that I talk about in the diary entry above: 'There is never a body as such: what we know are edgings and contourings, forces and intensities: a body is its movement' (2014: 163). As I begin to work with the madness of, what is still an early stage of writing this book, what I will refer to as its methodology, what I shall later develop as its 'non-methodology', I am drawn to Deleuze when he says: 'We can seek the unity of rhythm only at the point where rhythm itself plunges into chaos, into the night, at the point where the differences of level are perpetually and violently mixed' (Deleuze, 2004b: 44). I will offer these Stories of Emergence as bodies as movement, as levels, perhaps, always becoming, always 'perpetually and violently mixed'. The Deleuzian figure of the Fold (1993) exists in rhythmic movement, never stopping: the ceaseless exogamies and endogamies of unfolding, folding in, unfolding, folding in . . . can be used to begin to address Manning's question, '(h)ow does movement produce a body?' (ibid.: 162).

Becoming-student, student becomings

He studied Philosophy as an undergraduate in the late 1960s, early 1970s, in an old and somewhat august red-brick university in the UK. He had read what he thought was Philosophy prior to attending university. Camus, Sartre, Dostoyevsky and many others had whetted an appetite for argument, discussion and critical engagement. Studying for a degree in philosophy seemed the way to go. His father had gently and somewhat knowingly pointed him to an article in a Sunday paper prior to leaving home to start the first year of his degree that over 40 per cent of philosophy graduates were currently unemployed: that did not seem to deter him in the least. With the optimism of those heady opportunistic times coursing through his body, he thought little about the need for an equation between undergraduate study and future employment.

Despite this optimism and initially indulging in all the social pursuits of university life with great enthusiasm, a few weeks into his undergraduate studies led him to begin to question the study of philosophy that he had embarked upon. At the outset, study comprised a two-year course entitled A History of Modern Philosophy, a study exclusively centred around the philosophical works of Locke, Berkeley and Hume, a two-year course entitled Formal Logic, a two-year course entitled Ethics and a two-year course entitled Introduction to Philosophy, a course almost entirely based upon the recently published book written by a leading professor in the department emphatically and confidently entitled *Truth*. Although these were early days, the rigour and discipline of Analytic Philosophy was clearly not something that he had bargained for or could buy into. Wittgenstein's *Tractatus Logico-Philosophicus* was a huge influence upon undergraduate Philosophy courses of study in the UK at this time. Published in English in 1922, this hugely complex and unusual book made a fundamental impact upon philosophical thought and upon the ways in which the theory and research in the social sciences and the humanities were practised. The growth of Logical Positivism through the work of the Vienna Circle was a direct consequence of the group's reading of *Tractatus* and, in the UK in 1936, the publication of AJ Ayer's *Language Truth and Logic* led to huge transformations in philosophical thought and the way in which the subject was practised and taught in universities. This was the 'philosophy' that he studied as an undergraduate from 1969 to 1972.

Central to the philosophical practices involved in engaging in this programme of study found him grappling with Ayer's account of and arguments for the Principle of Verification. Deeply rooted in Positivistic scientific inquiry, this states that the meaning of a proposition is its method of verification, which means, in short, that if there are no means of verifying a proposition then it can have no meaning. In this book, for example, Ayer refers to ethical concepts as 'pseudo-concepts', claiming that the presence of ethical symbols in the proposition adds nothing to the factual content or truth value of the proposition. For Ayer the 'pseudo-concepts' of ethics are to be seen as 'emotional utterances', there to express feeling but unable to contribute anything to the meaning of the proposition because of the inability to provide a method which enables what was said to be verified. According to this view, there are no criteria for determining the validity of the judgements of ethics. Ayer's arguments were highly controversial and seen by many as being heretical due to the means by which the Principle of Verification could also be applied to propositions of a religious nature.

In the *Tractatus* itself it was clear that Wittgenstein began to question the role of the logical practices of analytic philosophy in relation to problems such as these, problems that he considered to be 'outside' the world: 'There are indeed things that cannot be put into words. They make themselves manifest. They are what is mystical' (Wittgenstein, 1922: 6.522). In the final pages of the book, Wittgenstein veers towards what might be seen as religious considerations and in many respects what he writes there could be regarded as antithetical to the kinds of strict Logical Positivist stance and positioning of the *Tractatus*. In these pages he talks about these 'mystical' and transcendental aspects of life such as ethics, aesthetics and the existence of God that cannot be discussed meaningfully. The misgivings that he began to express here also suggest that trying to explain language is impossible for exactly these reasons.

These were difficult questions and the concerns and doubts present in Wittgenstein's work were also reflected the intense struggles involved with studying philosophy at this time. Whilst as an undergraduate the philosophy that he was studying was of a particular space and time, it was, nevertheless, causing him pain. So, he continued with his struggles with the early Wittgenstein, the propositions of the *Tractatus* and the ensuing arguments of the Logical Positivists. Reading that a logical language can only reflect the world and that therefore any attempt to discuss the mystical, the affective and the metaphysical immediately loses all sense and cannot in fact be meaningfully engaged with caused him great trouble and concern.

And then, at this time, in the madness of this struggle, a quite serendipitous and, what turned out to be, highly significant, life-changing event took place which had a profound effect upon the way in which he went about his study of philosophy. The following extract offers a sense of how this came about:

> I remember stumbling across the following quotation from Wittgenstein's *Philosophical Investigations* (2001) as a young philosophy undergraduate struggling with the arid complexities and mathematical intricacies of Logical Positivism.
>
> > Describe the aroma of coffee. —Why can't it be done? Do we lack the words? And for what are words lacking? —But how do we get the idea that such a description must after all be possible? Have you ever felt the lack of such a description? Have you tried to describe the aroma and not succeeded? (sec. 610, p. 134)
>
> . . .
>
> I found myself reading, not reading, flipping from one stanza to the next, staying with one if it stuck itself to me or sliding off into another as adherence turned into lubrication. This was ideal for the state of my mind; finding myself in a becoming, glancing from one place to another, not focusing and then only momentarily as flashes from last night's excesses literally sprinkled new vistas into my vision, fuelling my desire to read more, to jump a page and then to stop, recount, retrace, recall and read again, read again. What? What was that?
>
> 'But how do we get the idea that such a description must after all be possible?'

What?

In a stanza on the seemingly innocuous musings on the aroma of coffee, the simple rhetoric of this question startled me, sitting there, quietly, almost inconspicuous among all these other questions.

'But how do we get the idea that such a description must after all be possible?'

I had never thought to ask such a question. Now nearly forty years after that apocalyptic moment, it is the kind of question I ask all the time; with Foucault, it is always to problematize, to inquire into conditions of possibility, to employ archaeologies and genealogies, to work, and to always challenge provenances, justifications, and truth claims.

And in one sense my story ends here.

And in so doing, I continue in the middle of this new beginning. My remaining time as an undergraduate was joyful; philosophy became and continues in its becoming to be my creative practice of preference. I have often thought of the serendipity of that revelatory moment, of that coming across that little piece of rhetoric, partly hidden within a small stanza in Wittgenstein's ground breaking book. I think about questions, particularly about questions of this kind and I am with Deleuze when he says,

> It's the same when I am asked a general question. The aim is not to answer questions, it's to get out, to get out of it. Many people think that it is only by going back over the question that it's possible to get out of it . . . It's very trying. They won't stop returning to the question in order to get out of it. But getting out never happens like that. Movement always happens behind the thinker's back, or in the moment when he blinks. Getting out is already achieved, or else it will never be.

Deleuze, 2002: 1
Gale, 2014: 1001–1002

Challenging identification

As I felt at the time of writing this passage, I want to go where my sense of the writing in this passage leads. The questioning approach that Wittgenstein uses thinly veils a powerful politics in which the logic of identity, which makes the subject possible in particular ways, has to be problematised and challenged. I feel that Wittgenstein wants us to see this and to do something about it. It is as if he senses that the processes which produce individualised selves are the contingent result of processes of subjectification and, as Deleuze would have it, that difference is prior to and actually constructs the subject.

> Something in the world forces us to think. This something is an object not of recognition but of a fundamental encounter. What is encountered may be Socrates, a temple or a demon. It may be grasped in a range of affective tones:

wonder, love, hatred, suffering. In whichever tone, its primary characteristic
is that it can only be sensed.

Deleuze, 2004a: 176

I have sensed that my sensing of this at this time was somehow animate; almost as if
an individualising self was being told something. I have carried this little stanza from
The Philosophical Investigations for a long time: in my sensings I have come to see this as
an epiphany, that somehow within my naivety and a politics of affect this worked as an
encounter that was meaningful in terms of my emergence – a sensing of an individualising
self in its becoming. As I return to these events and look at them again, my sense of
these sensings shifts from those that offer individualising realisations of being and move
towards a challenge to the humanism and subjectivism that is inherent within them.
My sensings now take what I have to refer to as this 'I' into a world that is immanent
in its becoming. These sensings lead to a presencing of processes of individuation that
actively troubles the politics of identity and representation that works to establish the
foundational stability of Being and the individual that have held precedence at least
since the time of Plato. A Deleuzian 'logic of sense' works to eradicate a binary
distinction between being and becoming by arguing that becoming is all there is; there
is no being to be discovered or given meaning, becoming is immanent and in this sense
becoming is everything in its becoming. In this, Deleuzian thought offers profound
challenge to the simply and exclusively human, it demands a thinking without the
constraining containments of models, codes, identities and representations and gives
the task to philosophy and to writing to undo the metaphysics of being by creating
concepts that are always new. Colebrook neatly describes these Deleuzian powers of
becoming in terms of the task of philosophy, science and art when she says:

> Philosophy allows us to think the forces of becoming by producing concepts
> of the differential or dynamic power of life; science allows us to organise
> matter by creating functions that allow us to extend our perception beyond
> what is actually given; literature allows us to become by creating affects that
> transform what we take experience to be.
>
> *Colebrook, 2002: 126*

What follows in the continuing emergence of this book, as new concepts are formed
and that live in connectedness and challenge to those that might have remained from
the energies of an earlier tide of thought, could perhaps be described as exemplifications
of encounters, as the doings of these writings will hopefully bring to life on these
pages some sense of the rhythmic play of ideas that give life to its always becoming.

Notes

1 The opening passage of this plateau emerged within and has been adapted from a piece of
   introductory writing presented at the inaugural session of the Autoethnography Special
   Interest Group at the International Congress of Qualitative Inquiry on Wednesday 20 May
   2015 and later published as Gale 2017.

2 The concept of 'assemblage/ethnography' is discussed in more detail in other plateaus in the book.
3 As Joughin, one of Deleuze's translators explains, desiring machines are 'the free functioning of any configuration of linked components, considered as an oriented process or a processing of other configurations with which it intersects or shares components – as desiring production' (Deleuze, 1995: 84)

BRINGING MADNESS TO LIFE

The temptation to write chronologically, to trace the life course as a journey that follows a line over a given period of time is discursively substantive and alluringly present. The phenomenologically oriented and dialectically infused accounts of the humanist project are discursively constructed around the bookends of birth and death and, within the limits of such parametric fabrication, in which life is seen as some kind of arduous journey between these beginning and end points, a sense of self emerges that isolates life as individual and insulated from intensive relationality in molecular space and time.

As the writing of this book begins to take on a shape, since I have begun to say in actuality and with affect, 'I am writing a book', as I sense the emergence of and a living within a cartography that is fluid, tidal, rhythmic and transversal, I have also found myself saying something like 'I have been teaching for forty years'. I have found the emergence of this kind of statement as acting as some kind of animating prefix to what is relevant to the action which I am about to embark upon within a particular context and, once uttered, it becomes performative, it does, it places and it makes content and context. And so the statement acts in this way here. It acts for me in a number of ways that seems obvious at the moment. I see teaching deeply bound up in research. In many respects I see the methodology of madness as being as much to do with pedagogy as it is to do with inquiry. I hear people in education talk about 'research informed teaching' or 'pedagogic research' as if it is something new and I ask myself and those who talk about it, how can we not talk about teaching and learning without talking about research and investigation, experimentation and inquiry? And so, when I say something like, 'I have been teaching for forty years', I want to infuse whatever I say and do with a presence that cannot separate itself from forms of doing that have been part of a creative evolution that has been taking place for a large portion of my life.

With this in mind, with this as extant in affect, I want to say something about *chronos* and *aeon* and, in so doing, to attempt to trouble the fabrication of a life spreading out like a channelled rivulet over a specific period of time and within a particular location. I prefer to think of what Deleuze and Guattari say about the rhizomatic nature of language, that 'it evolves by subterranean stems and flows, along river valleys or train tracks; it spreads like a patch of oil' (1987: 7) and liken this to the capillary nature of life in which leakages and absorbencies are the everyday particularities of existence. Bodies bleed and grow and in so doing their very fabrication is part of incessant processes of exogamy and endogamy where, with each unfolding, something new folds in: incisions and scarring do not exist in binary form, they are processual.

> Matter thus offers an infinitely porous, spongy, or cavernous texture without emptiness, caverns endlessly contained in other caverns: no matter how small, each body contains a world pierced with irregular passages, surrounded and penetrated by an increasingly vaporous fluid, the totality of the universe resembling a pond of matter in which there exist different flows and waves.
>
> *Deleuze, 2003: 5*

These continual, multiple and intensive processes of folding have to be seen 'after finitude' (Meillassoux: 2008). They have no beginning and end points, and if they are given them, then these can only exist as convenience and as a means of capture, classification and coding into a discursively created frame of reference. So I want the statement 'I have been teaching for forty years' to be seen in this light and not to be taken as a means by which the narrative of this book should be framed. This is where the play between ontologies, epistemologies and the doings of madness as methodology catch fire and sparks the rhythmic dance of the inquiry and opens up the space where landscapes and territories emerge.

> In the madness of these foldings and unfoldings, as writing energises the becoming other of this relational space, I sense the emergence of a machinic ontology where subjectivity is always of the moment, where the momentum of the writing is the force that moves a 'getting free of one self' (Foucault, 1992, p. 8), where the latencies of emergence become manifest in nodal points in the flows of possibilities of each new rhizomatic encounter.
>
> *Gale, 2014: 999*

The 'getting free of one self' is what comes alive in the becomings of the 'fold' and that is brought to life in the emphasised separation of 'one' and 'self' in this quotation and so, in what follows, therefore, the emphasis upon *aeon* is intentional; the awareness of *chronos* is full of palpability and is intended to adjust the focus towards and upon the intensive nature of time and space rather than its obvious and often more observable quantifiable forms and in terms of its visible extensive qualities. Writing has always been a dynamic, energetic force in the emergence of these spatio-temporal immersions and creations and it continues to be so in the movements and moments of this becoming-book.

The use of Deleuze and Guattari's (1987) neologism 'becoming' is central to the evocation of this emergence. In their work 'becoming' runs counter to the fixity of the Cartesian 'I' that exists as an essentialised category of being and which dominates humanist and post-Kantian forms of phenomenological thought. 'Becoming' is processual in space and time and, as the coalescence of concept, affect and percept exists as events, selves are always forming, re-forming, de-forming in the constant play of event/uality. In other plateaus in this book, Deleuze and Guattari's concept of the 'conceptual persona' (1994: 61–85) is also used to trouble the anthropocentric and exclusively human-centric proclivities to be found in the conventional orthodoxies and usages of the Cartesian 'I' in relation to the ways in which conceptualisations and practices of collaboration and friendship are enacted. Therefore, and in relation to this, it is possible to suggest that 'becoming' is about the continual potentiality and processual emergence of 'conceptual persona' and that 'thought's aptitude for finding itself and spreading across a plane' (Deleuze and Guattari, 1994: 64) passes through bodies in many ways and, in event/uality, produces and accentuates 'becoming'. This can be animated further, through Deleuze and Guattari's use of the medieval philosopher Duns Scotus' term 'haecceity' (1987: 262). In their usage, the term can be simply described as 'thisness', as a portion or block of space/time, as a non-personal individuation and not as a Cartesian modality of individualisation. Duns Scotus' use of the term is meant to describe a form of personal development and change, where individualisation is concomitant with actualisation and, where, through certain practices, the person will become some *thing*, *qua* category of difference, individualised and, hence, fixed as a person. For Deleuze and Guattari, however, 'haecceity' designates a unique assemblage of moments and movements that come together as a set of relationalities and then processually, in contingent and heterogeneous ways, disperse, diversify and emerge in-formation.

> There is a mode of individuation very different from that of a person, subject, thing or substance. We reserve the name *haecceity* for it. A season, a winter, a summer, an hour, a date have a perfect individuality lacking nothing, even though this individuality is different from that of a thing or a subject. They are haecceities in that they consist entirely of relations of movement and rest between molecules or particles, capacities to affect and be affected.
>
> *1987: 261*

'Haecceity' provides a means of coming to know the writing of this book. And so whilst the emphasis upon the transversality of the moment that continues across the hierarchical solidity of the fixed linearity of chronological time is one which this madness as methodology lives to nurture and to grow, its usage is not designed to set up binaries between formed objects and objects in flow or between fixed periods of time and the inspirational glimpse that dis/appears in the wink of an eye. So I have a sense of one self writing this book, that self that has 'been teaching for over forty years', that self that loves the writing and cries with pain as the emergence of each word and phrase is part of a process of difficult birth. This sense is in play with that sense of living in the moment, of *aeon*, that almost imperceptible, just perceptible time of the event that time as event and, as Deleuze and Guattari put it, 'the floating line that knows only speeds and continually divides that which transpires into an already-there that is at the same time not-yet-here, a simultaneous too-late and too-early, a something that is both going to happen and has just happened' (1987: 262). So in this early attempt to bring this madness as methodology to life I need to talk more about the sense, the sense in which in continuing to introduce this book I will bring into play a Deleuzian 'logic of sense'.

In *The Logic of Sense*, Deleuze (2004a) works to trouble the coupling of sense and its modernist location within a logic of reason and rationality and from its traditional conceptualisation within humanist and phenomenological denotations of perception. In this sense it is understood as somehow belonging to the body and as such as working to provide 'logical' and 'rational' explanations of the world. Emerging from such a view of sense is the modernist notion of 'common sense' which works discursively to construct a 'sensible' perception or understanding of the world. In philosophy, for example, the influence of Logical Positivism in the early part of the twentieth century was based upon a Principle of Verification (Ayer, 1936) which asserted that the meaning of a proposition about the world was dependent upon the methodological possibility (or not) of verification. In other words, if it was not possible to posit a method that enabled proof of the existence of something, then the proposition used to assert such a possibility was itself meaningless. In *The Logic of Sense*, Deleuze works, first of all, to demonstrate that the logic and use of sense to be found in Modern and essentially Positivist philosophy is part of a logic of reason (e.g. common sense) and, second, that this elision, whilst not entirely false, is, in certain ways, flawed. The following note from Joughin, the translator of *Negotiations*, is helpful in providing an explanation of how Deleuze's 'logic of sense' does not simply highlight and provide a binary separation between reason and irrationality. Rather he argues that it works to incorporate it within a logic that is not simply fixed in one particular form of thought and language of expression.

> Etymologically, *délirer* is to leave the furrow, go 'off the rails,' and wander in imagination and thought: meanings, images, and so on float in a dream logic rather than calmly following one another along the familiar lines or tracks of cold reason. But for Deleuze and Guattari solid 'reason' and free floating délire are simply converse articulations of a single transformational 'logic of sense' that is no more anchored in a single signifier . . . than in any supposedly fixed system of reference.
>
> *Joughin in Deleuze, 1995: 186*

The binary logic of Cartesian Dualism that employs rationalism and empiricism as the basic means of meaning making and, in so doing, creates the philosophical and humanist 'problem' of the separation of mind and matter comes under sustained fire in its use of sense in Deleuze's book. In this I am taking a lead from Deleuze, I am attempting to employ a logic of sense that moves away from and challenges Western thought and modern philosophy's logic and use of sense. Therefore, the madness as methodology that I will attempt to bring to life in this book will work to conceptualise and situate the logic of sense within a philosophy of immanence, as Deleuze has done in his book. In this respect Deleuze makes it clear that the domain of sense is inherently fragile in that it can easily topple over into the domain of non-sense. In other words, 'nonsense' can be seen as the ontological basis of sense. The term is not used in its conventional form to denote something that is somehow and of itself, as a category of being, nonsensical, rather it emerges from elements that do not, in these conventional terms, necessarily have a sense. Deleuze offers an ontological sense of sense which is imbricated within pure difference, intensity, virtuality and immanence. As MacLure says of this *Logic of Sense*, 'Deleuze identifies a "mad element" in language: something that exceeds propositional meaning – a Dionysian spirit in language. He called it *sense*' (2017: 53). In this book, through the sustained use of Deleuzian conceptualisations of becoming, chaos, desire, force, the 'body-without-organs', et al., I will attempt to offer a madness as methodology that is wholly infused with such a logic of sense.

Deleuze's engagement with and challenge to the pre-eminence of voice and language in *The Logic of Sense* demonstrates the ways in which, not only in philosophical terms but also in everyday usage, modernist and phenomenological forms of sense making are used to fix identity, knowledge and meaning within a logic of meaning and representation. He talks there of voice 'which speaks and comes from on high', likening this as a kind of discovery, something that is similar in Freud and his stressing of 'the acoustic origin of the superego'. He says:

> For the child, the first approach to language consists in grasping it as the model of that which pre-exists, as referring to the entire domain of what is already there, and as the familial voice which conveys tradition, it affects the child as a bearer of a name and demands his insertion even before the child begins to understand. In a certain way, this voice has at its disposal all the dimensions of organised language.
>
> *2004a: 221*

Crucially, and as Deleuze goes on to emphasise, the voice presents these 'dimensions',

> [w]ithout yet being able to grasp the organising principle according to which the voice itself would be a language. And so we are left outside sense, far from it, this time in a *pre-sense* (*pre-sens*) of heights: the voice does not yet have at its disposal the univocity which would make it a language, and,

having unity only in virtue of its eminence, rests entangled in the equivocity of its denotations, the analogy of significations, and the ambivalence of its manifestations.

Ibid.

For Deleuze these entanglements in the equivocity of denotation are to do with those transcendent practices that posit beings as categories of difference, intelligible bodies with 'voices' that 'know', 'interpret' and 'represent'. In this respect the transcendent proclivities of Western rationalist thought, anthropocentrism and the separation of mind and matter are based upon equivocations of this kind and provide a basis for a binary logic that sets one kind of being above another and an ethics that provides a moral justification for doing so. In this madness as methodology I wish to offer a Deleuzian logic of sense that sets univocity against equivocity, that offers immanence over transcendence and that sees the multiplicities of becoming and individuation as the pre-eminent condition of one common existence.

The seriousness with which I want to explicate and argue for this madness as methodology is also infused with Deleuze and Guattari's elision of concept, affect and percept (1994: 163). I cannot think of these elemental ontological features of self forming and world making independently of processes of what Whitehead (1929) has referred to as 'individuation'; they exist and work for me as assemblage, they are always in play and they play out the energising forces of worldly sense making. As this ontological sense making continues to unfold and in so doing imbricates and folds in with the becoming of this book, I am with Manning when she works with sensing bodies within what she talks of as a 'politics of touch'. For her:

Sensing bodies in movement are ontogenetic. They are ontogenetic because they are always in genesis, in a state of potential becoming. An ontology of the body presupposes a concrete category of Being. Yet, bodies in excess of their Being: they become.

2007: xxi

Ontogenesis articulates with and animates processual individuation, making vibrant the pulsing energies of Deleuze and Guattari's 'body-without-organs' and always offering challenge to those reactionary forces of representation that somehow serve to enact identification and to miraculously write bodies before they are created. Therefore these processes of 'individuation' are to do with and cannot be separated from a univocal plane of becoming and are used by Deleuze to counter the equivocalism of the traditions and practices of Cartesian individualism. Deleuze and Guattari's engagement with concept, affect and percept offers an animation of creative practices of univocity that works to free life from the organising principles of the transcendent position of the individual observer and the organising systems of representation and identification. When Deleuze talks of '*a* life' (2001), he talks of bodies that are more to do with the heterogeneity and contingency of assemblage than the fixed structures and given forms of identity and representation. In this sense it is not about bodies *having* particular ideas, *experiencing* certain emotions or *seeing* the world in given ways, rather it is about bodies in becoming always subject to the interplaying forces of concept, affect and percept and living 'a life of pure immanence, neutral, beyond good and evil, for it was only the subject that incarnated it in the midst of things that made it good or bad' (Deleuze, 2001: 29). In the intensity, diversity and potential of multiplicity, the logic that attempts to identify subject and object, to create an 'either' and an 'or' and to substantiate the world in reason and a metaphysics of being, becomes an artifice and an attempt to capture and hold reality within the confining forces of representation.

As I continue with this process, I know that some things will emerge in my design and equally I know and I am excited by the sensing that other things will surprise me; words will appear that will pull me up short, make me feel good and make me wonder should I do this, should I carry on? So I know for sure that I will make claims, again deeply influenced by the work of Deleuze, posthumanism, affect theory and the new materialisms, for a new empiricism; one that lives in its resistance to that Positivist empiricism that works to simply contain and catalogue the world. I could not write a methodology book without doing this. Deeply ingrained in my knowing is a valuing of an approach which is closely aligned with my commitment to challenging those Positivist philosophies and procedures that have dominated inquiry and investigation in the world of education that I have absorbed myself in for these past forty years. So in the discussions that I have been trying to set up in this plateau and that I hope will further help in bringing my madness as methodology to life, I have a number of motives in mind. I want to trouble through strategies of conceptualisation and territorialisation the very conceptual force of methodology itself. As I have already suggested, methodology, as it is conceived and practised in conventional humanist qualitative inquiry, is an over-determining and highly prescriptive force, limiting the active experimental qualities of research practices through the use of discourses that have established these conditions of possibility in research methods textbooks, journal articles and research methods courses in higher education institutions. Madness as methodology might well offer an engagement with non-methodology as methodology, a possibility that I shall take up again and pursue later in this book. Linked to this, I also want to trouble the foundations of the very notion of data and the binary artifice of data collection and analysis that emanates from it. From an ontological point of view, by engaging in such an approach I want to bring to life new empirical, materialist and inquiry-based practices that challenge those metaphysics of being that serve to consolidate and not trouble the conscious reflexivities and individualism of Cartesian approaches to the self and subjectivity. I want to set up approaches that clearly demonstrate that what might emerge from making inquiries cannot 'capture' moments and movements and then proceed to an engagement in processes of coding, interpretation and classification that work to solidify them in statements of fact, philosophies of truth and arguments that lead to the implementation of practices that purport to be based upon them.

And so deeply ingrained in affect are senses of trust and mistrust or is it *dis*trust? I live in wonderment with the possibilities that mis/dis/trust brings. I am with Stengers when she talks of affirmation, when she argues

> that to be interested by something has the character of an event, since it gives to that something a power it does not generally possess: the power to cause us to think, feel and wonder, the power to have us wondering how practically to relate to it, how to pose relevant questions about it.
>
> *2011: 374*

In 'Working at the wonder' (Gale and Wyatt, 2016), in living with the astonishment of event, I revel in the possibilities of scepticism. As a young philosophy undergraduate, Descartes' malign spirit of scepticism began to seduce me with its enticements to doubt and the possibilities that could come from always asking questions, always problematising, ever involving me in the sensual delights of discussion infused with laughter and lubricated by the devilish whims of playing on and with the edges of narcosis that further fuelled the way my life began to grow and spin in multiple directions. Later, reading Nietzsche, I found myself becoming enthralled by the writing of a great philosopher who was saying things that I had been living and wanting to live and live and never been able to find the words, the accomplices, the writers who were always willing to take me to new and exciting spaces where difference was always emergent. And so as I studied I found myself reading passages like the following:

> [We] must no longer accept concepts as a gift, nor merely purify, and polish them, but first make and create them, present them and make them convincing. Hitherto one has generally trusted one's concepts as if they were a wonderful dowry from some sort of wonderland.
>
> *Nietzsche, 1968: 409*

Reading this wonderful writing; writing that was saying things that were running like drugs in my veins, in ways that were totally counter to all the words and theories of all those masters and professors that I was being told to study and grow to respect. This was writing that was taking the nascent energies of my rebellious youth and saying, why not try this? Why not do that? And so in becoming older and perhaps wiser, I started to learn again, to relearn, to start anew, from elsewhere, studying and becoming immersed and delightfully lost in research in my doctoral studies. It was Deleuze who helped me to surf this beautiful rising Nietzschean wave a little higher, a little further and a little more adventurously. There was a finding of a self that began to come to life as I studied with Jane Speedy on the doctoral programme in the Centre for Narratives and Transformative Learning at the University of Bristol, when I later met Jonathan Wyatt there, when I started to write – no, when I started to believe in writing. The surfing the wave metaphor has been imbricated with a materialist ontological realism through all this time. I test it frequently, I worry that it slips off the tongue, that it inevitably sparks from my tapping fingers like the habitual force of the cliché and as I test it I know that it is OK. Swimming and surfing in the sea around my home allows me to believe in the materiality of this usage here: when the swimming out to the swell becomes the recognition of the lifting power of the wave and the wild tumbling ride that follows I sense a bodily force that also comes alive when I am writing:

> That swell having lifted you both up to its peak, that mountaintop point where for an instant you share that wide eyed exhilarating all round vision, then tips you, as its crest begins its startling downward gravitational lash and that wild, swimming, tumbling, surfing ride takes you both, down and through the crest, immersed in the great, gargantuan body of the wave and finally into the seething, spinning relief of the shore break: smiles, laughter and the funny, exciting but welcoming shock of sand under your feet.
>
> *Gale and Pineau, 2011: 319*

And in the swim of these new writing forces, the self that I was finding was not alone, 'The desert expanded, but in so doing became more populous' (Deleuze and Parnet, 2002: 17). I was swimming, surfing and writing with others, the materiality of these spaces became vibrant in their incessant and ever increasing palpability:

> When words wash you and invigorate your body, when you find yourself surfacing again, struggling for breath, heaving the frantic swimming weight of your body up onto the rising power of a new surging swell and you look across that iridescent glassy surface and another face, in that same astonishing rush, grins with you and shares a mad laughing smile as you both tip and surf slide down the next ever accelerating edge, then you know you are not alone.
>
> *Gale and Pineau, 2011: 319*

Movements in beautiful moments: the great transversal shift occurring with the emergence of these logics of sensation. And with these flows and transmutations something else seemed to be happening in my life. As a teacher I found myself working more and more with my students in very different ways. I found myself becoming aligned with and working to animate and activate the mistrust of concepts that Nietzsche talked about both in relation to my understanding of power in a general sense and in a more specific sense in terms of the relations I was trying to bring to life with my students. I have always worked in what has been referred to as 'student-centred' ways, I have always found the constructivist practices of facilitation far more beneficial in the promotion of learning than the didactic methods used by many of my contemporaries and, in so doing, I had never fully articulated my pedagogical practices with the relational dynamics of power. So with the words of Nietzsche in mind, rather than accepting concepts as gifts, or merely purifying and polishing them, increasingly, I began to encourage my students to make and create them as a means of animating and activating vitality in relational pedagogical space. The discovery of Deleuze and Guattari saying the following, that in philosophy 'concepts are not waiting for us ready-made, like heavenly bodies. There is no heaven for concepts. They must be invented, fabricated, or rather, created, and would be nothing without the creator's signature' (1994: 5), further underlined for me the value and huge potential in engaging the Nietzschean mistrust of concepts to the teaching and learning spaces that I was beginning to open up in my pedagogical practice. Such an approach was encouraging me to look with fresh eyes at the politics of concept forming both in the classroom and in my relationships more generally. I began to see more and more that power resides and lives a healthy life in the ordinary, in the habitual and the customary and in the perpetuation of a general willingness to accept discursive constructions of reality. As a Marxist since my undergraduate days, I had nurtured a sense of power that was based upon a binary construction that was made understandable through the practices and actions of coercion, repression and inequality and whilst I have never dispensed with this notion I began, at this time in my life, following these readings of Nietzsche, Foucault, Deleuze and Guattari, to see that power also needs to be understood in other ways. By working with a mistrust of concepts, by challenging the theory practice binary construction through a realisation that practice is not simply an extension or consequence of theory I began to work with myself and others with theorisation and conceptualisation as practice. As Deleuze said in a conversation with Foucault:

> Yes, that's what a theory is, exactly like a tool box. It has nothing to do with the signifier . . . A theory has to be used, it has to work. And not just for itself. If there is no one to use it, starting with the theorist himself who, as soon as he uses it ceases to be a theorist, then a theory is worthless, or its time has not yet arrived. You don't go back to a theory, you make new ones, you have others to make.
>
> *2004b: 208*

Deleuzian theorising as practice, in engaging active processes of theorisation, conceptualisation and contextualisation, involves making shifts away from textual fields of representation and movement towards ontologies of realism and materiality. Deleuze suggests that we are in 'situations which we no longer know how to react to, in spaces which we no longer know how to describe' (Deleuze, 1989: xi)

CONCEPTUALISING MADNESS AS PROCESS?

I wouldn't want what I may have said or written to be seen as laying any claims to totality. I don't try to universalise what I say, conversely what I don't say isn't meant to be thereby disqualified as being of no importance. My work takes place between unfinished abutments and anticipatory strings of dots. I like to open out a space of research, try it out, then if it doesn't work try again somewhere else. On many points . . . I am still working and don't know if I am going to get anywhere. What I say ought to be taken as 'propositions', 'game openings' where those who may be interested are invited to join in; they are not meant as dogmatic assertions that have to be taken or left en bloc.

Foucault, 1991: 73

In this and the following plateau I want to spend some time focusing upon my take on madness and to offer a consideration of what influences me in helping to make my view of what it might be and how, in my view, it becomes a methodology, a methodology that is inevitably imbricated with my own always emergent and relational onto-epistemological dispositions. I am not unhappy to use the term 'methodology'. In the opening plateau I made reference to the questions raised by St Pierre (1997, 2011, 2015) in relation to the methodological approaches employed in conventional humanist inquiry. I also agree that in addressing these questions there is a fundamental need to uncover, to problematise and to trouble the conditions of possibility, mainly of a Kantian origin and way of thinking, that have made these discursive constructions of research reality possible in many fields of qualitative inquiry at the present time. In these answerings, as this inquiry unfolds, I wish to suggest and tentatively formulate what might be referred to as a *non*-methodological methodology, a *non*-methodology perhaps, what I have already referred to as a *methodogenesis*, in which research doings are always becoming and in which conceptualisation and inventive research process is given precedence over the fixities of set methodological representation and signification. In the politics of research practice I offer this as a means of deterritorialising the methodology grip that has tightened itself around most forms of qualitative research in recent years. At the moment I will offer a sensing in relation to my own movements: in taking an ontogenetic approach that does not fix the body in any pre-determined sense I am happy to work experimentally with madness as methodology in terms of encounter and event. In this sensing of a *non*-methodology as methodology and in proposing this *methodogenesis*, I can offer an ontologically informed account of the feeling and thinking that might be associated with affective doing – my machinic pluggings in, my rhythmic riffing off, my philosophy of action. I think of this *methodogenesis* in similar ways to what Massumi describes as being 'imbued with an immediate understanding of what is under way, what might be coming – and what we are becoming. This is enactive understanding: it is one with the action. It is what I call thinking-feeling' (2015: 94). I sense that his description has some resonance with the openness implied by what Koro-Ljungberg calls 'fluid methodological spaces' (2016: 79) and begins to address the need for what Braidotti referred to as 'methodological creativity' (2013: 1) to cope with current challenges in the Anthropocene. In making these expressions, I also want to make the argument that methodologies matter.

And I think that this 'conceptualisation of madness as a process' will need to break free from those orthodoxies and foundational modalities that identify and ontologically and epistemologically ground madness as a category of being that can somehow be objectified, classified and ascribed to the humanist construction of the Individual and the individualised subject. Therefore the emphasis that this book places upon process is not intended to posit a preferential meaning but rather to engage with what this process based philosophy of practice might do. In thinking with Spinoza about what *any* body might be able to do and with Deleuze in terms of the potentialities of bodies-without-organs, I wish to draw upon and emphasise the processual movements and dynamics that animate bodies in their relationality and to exemplify this in these discussions here.

Recently a colleague from another university talked with me about a student of his who was experiencing 'extreme neuroses' and he was concerned that this might turn into something that he described as 'psychogenic psychoses'. He clearly saw these conditions as substantive and substantially inherent within and *of* that young person in his genuine concern about his well-being and his life. I found myself challenged by the fixities inherent within my colleague's use of these determinations and classification of the student's severe maladies and was only able to express my concerns to my colleague in terms of the processual and relational aspects of the agentic assemblage in which I saw our discussion and engagement to be immersed.

In perhaps bringing to the fore another *Story of Emergence*, this experience revived my own recollection of being similarly 'fixed', along with thousands of other contemporaries, as young children in the UK in the late 1950s and 1960s, by the 11+, a test that provided the basis of selection of children in their journey from primary to secondary schooling. The 11+ was based on the notion of an intelligence quotient (IQ) that could be measured by a test. Originally developed by psychologist Cyril Burt, the IQ tests were used to 'measure' intelligence and were based upon the theory that IQ is hereditary. This theory was based upon the assumption that intelligence is a fixed thing and which is susceptible to various methods of measurement and grading. The system created successes and failures. The former were selected to attend secondary grammar schools and were destined for careers involving likely attendance at university and subsequent lives in the professions. The latter were 'selected' to attend secondary modern schools and were destined for working lives in trades and occupations. At the time the 'failures' could be characterised as mainly being from the working class, usually girls and members of ethnic minority groups:[1] this system of selection at the age of 11 served to perpetuate and sustain the inherent inequalities and socially divisive nature of society at that time. I failed the 11+. I enjoyed my experience of four years of secondary schooling. At my school the curriculum was built around crafts and the acquisition of practical skills: I remember whole half days of woodwork, rural science, art, sport, drama and small portions of Maths, English, History and Religious Knowledge thrown in to leaven the curricular mix. At the time I didn't find being identified and fixed as possessing a lower level of intelligence was in the least inhibiting. I remember being baffled, amazed and quite proud about my dad's ability to accurately predict the 11+ results of all my class: it was many years later that I worked out that he simply did that on the basis of knowing the occupations of all my classmates' fathers at that time. So, I didn't feel particularly disadvantaged by a system based upon Burt's claim, itself based upon forty years of research, which supposedly proved that a child's intelligence was fixed by genetic inheritance with social and cultural circumstances playing only a small role. I was happy!

Looking back at these experiences, over fifty years later, I suspect that the challenge that I now offer to the kinds of substantive fixities and classifications that are offered by the psychologising tendencies of certain academic disciplines and practices has at least some origination in my realisation of the injustices that the 11+ test and the system of selection into secondary education connected to it inflicted upon many thousands of children.

Increasingly I have grown to work with Whitehead's assertion that in our thinking and doing we need to emphasise process over substance. As a young undergraduate studying philosophy in the late 1960s, I found that the metaphysical approach to philosophy offered by Whitehead and others was anathema to the Logical Positive content and tenor of the Philosophy curriculum predominant at this time and to those who constructed it and taught it. Coming to Whitehead's (1929) book *Process and Reality* and the philosophy of organism that it offers, helped me at a much later stage in my life in challenging the metaphysical problems to do with dualism, materialism and idealism that I had encountered as an undergraduate. This introduction to Whitehead's process philosophy that refuses mind/body dualism and that offers what he called an 'organic realism' (ibid.) has been hugely influential in helping me to work to bring this book to life. The rejection of the Cartesian Dualisms of mind/body, rationalism/empiricism, subjectivity/objectivity and so on and an engagement with the idea that perception is not simply a representation of the external world but rather it is part of the world has been hugely energising. Whitehead's notion of 'prehension' (ibid.) replaces the traditional view that perception offers a representational relation to and with the external world with what can be described as a part-to-whole relationality. This part-to-wholeness is processual; it is about individuation and becoming in which what was hitherto referred to as a perception of reality is actually part of that reality and not a representation of it.

What Whitehead referred to as 'actual occasions' (ibid.) and 'occasions of experience' (ibid.) can be used to animate our understanding of a Deleuzian concept forming as event: these 'occasions' are event/ful and activate becoming in the world and world making, in Manning's terms 'worlding' (2007). I found these considerations animating my thought as my colleague talked with me of the problems that his young student was facing. I wondered about the effectiveness of this giving of precedence to the search for explanation, meaning and the seeming need to fix these objects of inquiry within an objectification of madness over an engagement with the process, relationality and activation of what these bodies could do. In these considerations I wondered about the usefulness of the kind of binary thinking that proffers bi-polarities of meaning in terms of categorisations of sane/insane, rational/irrational, neurotic/psychotic and so on. I realised that I had carried these uncertainties and hesitations with me for a long time. I had read the work of R. D. Laing and David Cooper in the 1960s and had already developed an acute sensing from their work that madness is better understood less as a condition or as some thing that is possessed by some person and more as a form of emergence in relationality, where the supposed categorical difference between 'normal' and 'abnormal' is a representational artifice rather than a substantive reality. As Barnes and Berke point out, 'More often than not, a person diagnosed as "mentally ill" is the emotional scapegoat for the turmoil in his or her family of associates, and may, in fact, be the "sanest" member of this group' (1982: 84). Therefore, the madness as methodology that this book is attempting to bring to life can only offer challenge to the foundational and substantive establishment of nouning and naming and to provide a practice of processual doing that works to trouble and undo their dominance and colonising tendencies. Deleuze and Guattari's treatment of desire is helpful here because by bringing production into the conceptualisation of desire they help to shift the emphasis and concern away from what desire means and towards what it does. The shift that this animates from a logic of reason towards a logic of sense also helps me to bring to the fore the conceptualisation of madness that I want to work with here.

The notion of *délirer,* referred to elsewhere in these pages, is helpful in beginning to bring this concept of madness to life. I have quoted Joughin as saying, in more detail, that '*délirer* is to leave the furrow, go "off the rails," and wander in imagination and thought: meanings, images, and so on float in a dream logic rather than calmly following one another along the familiar lines or tracks of cold reason' (Joughin in Deleuze, 1995: 186). I take this to mean that it is not simply the individual that is freed from the constraints of formal logic and reason to follow creative paths of inquiry but, rather, that it is the interrelated human and nonhuman processes of collective individuation and transversality that are given freedom by such transgressive and transformative movements and deviations:

> Between the contingent moment or the chance caress and the hand given according to convention, a day goes by; a multitude of disequilibria mark the waiting with slight deviations. She loses her head, he feels his heart beating; her voice is strained, his trembles; he is beside himself with emotion. Like a river leaving its bed, the story seeks new points of stability, is churned up only to settle into a new stability. A new whole is reorganised as if from vibrations, sounds of words and heart, movements and wind: a storm is brewing, the warm breeze chases the clouds in the sky; the two women, like clouds, go for a walk: a ramble.
>
> *Serres, 2008: 298*

The synaesthesia that *délirer* opens up and that the above quotation can be used to evoke are a central feature of the madness of methodology that is being created here. The creative 'going off the rails' that the 'dream logic' of *délirer* puts into action involves an aestheticising that heightens engagement with and making of the world, in contrast to the narrow, limiting and ultimately dulling an/anestheticising that conventional logics of reason and rationality are used to promulgate. The interrelated sensing of synaesthesia involves a becoming that is both of and beyond the body: it is a seeing that is the sound of church bells; it is a tasting that is the tingling of the touch of a hand on bare skin.

Within the emergence of a realist and processual ontological logic that offers challenge to the ascendancy of identification, representation and interpretation, the traditional divisions that are based upon Cartesian Dualism, those that supposedly exist between organic and inorganic, sentient and non-sentient and so on are troubled, destabilised and diminished. Jane Bennett's (2010) espousal of 'vibrant matter' is a direct descendant of Whitehead's thinking in its argument that all bodies, to varying degrees, display potentiality, intensity and possibilities of sentience. The fluidity and flux inherent within Whitehead's 'organic realist' philosophy posits that we are not simply in the world and that the world is in us. His monist challenge to the ascendancy of Cartesian Dualist thought brings into focus animating notions of the Will to be found in the philosophy of Schopenhauer, Nietzsche and others and begins to cultivate genealogies that lead to those philosophies of Deleuze and Guattari that play a central driving force for the idea of madness as methodology that is being offered in this book.

In her book *The Outrun* Amy, Liptrot (2016) writes about her wild and carefree life as a child on Orkney, her later hedonistic life in London, which led her into alcoholism and ultimately to her eventual return to a life back on the island: a new and different life, a life of sober reflection on her past and an immersion in the remoteness and the testing natural environment of the island. On her many walks across the island she searches for a fault line, a crack in the earth's crust resulting from the displacement of one side with respect to the other. In geological terms fault lines are usually to be found in fault planes indicating the surface of a fault. In cartographic terms a fault trace is used to plot fault lines and to generally indicate the presence of a fault in the earth's surface. Whilst she is unable to discover any trace of the line in her walking, she begins to apprehend her tracings in terms of herself, her struggles with alcohol addiction and the travails associated with it. She seems to sense fault lines in herself and she increasingly draws them together in a plane of existence that is always becoming in its transmutational fluidities. Musings on her inner torments flow into and become articulated with her immersive gazings into the infinite vistas stretching out in the cosmos, as she stretches her head back and stares up into the beauty and wonder of the sky above her.

Increasingly in her writing she grows to exist not simply as a category of difference that is somehow classifiable in referential and binary forms casting her as sane/ insane, alcoholic/reformed alcoholic and so on, it is rather that she is always in flow in terms of her material actuality and the discourses and ideations that might be used to pin her down in particular ways. Difference precedes and forms her becoming and it is these transmutational fluidities that are the essence of these continuing movements in and through her life. Each new 'immediation' is agentic in these flows and is an event in the ceaseless worlding that she actualises with each fusing encounter between the interior and the exterior of selves moving on, in and through the flow of these 'fault lines'. In the intensities and potentialities of these flows and growing transmutations, she takes the attempted fixities of representational and identifying forms, such as 'addiction', 'addict' and 'alcoholic', away with her and in the moments of her constant movement, walking, looking, touching, she engages her body in doing (something with them):

> In grandiose moments, high on fresh air and freedom on the hill, I study my personal geography. My body is a continent. Forces are at work in the night. A bruxist, I grind my teeth in my sleep, like tectonic plates. When I blink the sun flickers, my breath pushes the sun across the sky and the waves roll into the shore in time with my beating heart. Lightning strikes every time I sneeze, and when I orgasm there's an earthquake. The islands' headlands rise above the sea, like my limbs in the bathtub, my freckles are famous landmarks and my tears rivers. My lovers are tectonic plates and stone cathedrals.
>
> *Liptrot, 2016: 219*

As she walks along the wild windswept cliff top or picks her way along the shoreline, the crashing waves a few metres from her slightly wavering body, she is always on the edge. In the seething relationality of her ever-moving body, the tumbling, stumbling, perhaps only steadily stepping into new realities is the becoming of self always in flux, always in encounter and ever present in the movement from the one to the many. As Manning says when talking of the work of Simondon, 'he liberates [the body] from the pre-supposition of a form, demonstrating how a body is always alive across lives. The body's individuation is its force for becoming, not its end-point' (2010: 118).

And, therefore, in these terms, it is possible to think with 'madness' not as a condition, a malady that can be ascribed to an individual that has been constructed through activities of arborescent rationalism, not as a category of difference that can be seen to exist in this or that form but rather as a force that, in multiplicity, seethes in and through all forms of relationality. In offering further challenge to the kinds of metaphysics of being alluded to here, we can think with Spinoza in terms of the constant rhythmic play of the capacity of bodies to affect and be affected and can then think and act with the immersion and absorption of bodies always in encounter. The constant event/ful/ness of the encounter is about the play between *affectio* and *affectus* existing on a plane where bodies are not described as doing some thing to an other and the other responding in certain ways, as is often the case when interaction is used as an avoidance of the complexities of intra-action, it is about, as Guattari has pointed out,

> rather than moving in the direction of reductionist modifications which simplify the complex, 'schizoanalysis' will work towards its complexification, its processual enrichment, towards the consistency of its virtual lines of bifurcation and differentiation, in short towards its ontological heterogeneity.
> *1992: 61*

And so the 'event/ful/ness of the encounter' is a complex, all-consuming relationality of space and time. In these relationalities, organic and inorganic bodies, in their 'entanglement' (Barad: 2007) with one another and with the discourses that construct them in particular ways, are affectively what Massumi describes as 'differential attunement' (2015: 94), they are rhythmically absorbed in processes of becoming.

With Deleuze and Guattari's engagement with and critique of Freudian psychoanalysis acting as a potent context and energising force for the processual considerations initiated by the kinds of thinking to be found in Whitehead's 'organic realism', I wish to offer a consideration and activation of madness as methodology in relation to the concepts of 'desiring production' and a 'body-without-organs' to be found in *Anti-Oedipus* and *A Thousand Plateaus*, both subtitled *Capitalism and Schizophrenia*. These conceptualisations can be brought into focus through the use of the following quotation from *Anti-Oedipus* in which Deleuze and Guattari, in citing Engels, also provide some ontologically oriented lines of reference to my earlier discussion related to the productive desire involved in wanting to write a book:

> [I]t has been a long time since Engels demonstrated . . . how an author is great because he cannot prevent himself from tracing flows and causing them to

circulate, flows that split asunder the catholic and despotic signifier of his work, and that necessarily nourish a revolutionary machine on the horizon. That is what style is, or rather the absence of style – asyntactic, agrammatical: the moment when language is no longer defined by what it says, even less by what makes it a signifying thing, but by what causes it to move, to flow, and to explode – desire. For literature is like schizophrenia: a process not a goal, a production not an expression.

Deleuze and Guattari, 2004: 145

In working with process over substance I also notice becoming, what Deleuze brings to life in terms of being in sensation 'pure immanence . . . A LIFE, and nothing else' (2001: 27). In this I sense a going beyond the simply human where the process is not just about this life or that life, or about this person interacting with that person. In this I prefer to think about what Thrift refers to as 'processual sensualism', where a life is about bodies, human and nonhuman, that are in play, engaging in the rhythms of movement and momentary realisation, where this making real involves constant foldings and unfoldings that are interminably about life making. In this vein Manning talks of 'a force for life that extends beyond this human life to the life of organic-inorganic ecologies or speciation' (Manning in Massumi: 2015: 140) where these processes of 'speciation' release practices from the reductivist closures of classification and categorisations of difference that impale species into binary cages of this or that and which allow for understandings in terms of relationalities of becoming and constant intra-action. As Manning offers elsewhere:

> Individuation does not bring a life into an individual. The individual expresses a life as the force of its continuing individuation. The individual is but an aspect of being's becoming. A body as individual is relational more than substantial, in relation, always, with the discontinuous force of becoming, with life in all its forms.
> The body never fully actualises.
>
> *2010: 121*

Body-without-organs

Deleuze and Guattari borrowed the concept of the 'body-without-organs' from Dadaist poet and dramatist Antonin Artaud and used it in their initial collaborative work to energise and animate their conceptualisation and use of the productive nature of desire and, in so doing, worked to free it from its individualising and psycho-analytic location and association with lack. By dis-locating desire from these psychologising proclivities and human-centric connections, Deleuze and Guattari brought the conceptualisation of desire to life, initially within what they term 'machinic production' and later in the form of assemblages or *agencement*. They worked to free it from the purely personal, subjective and psychological and, in so doing, offered a conceptualisation that embraced and activated its connection to production in multiple social, economic and political spheres of activity. Therefore, their work on capitalism and schizophrenia involved a linking of this productive conception of desire with the 'body-without-organs' in what Dosse describes as 'a universalising programme, a limitless process, a constantly reiterated ability to transgress limits, to carry out a release' (2010: 199). In this respect Deleuze and Guattari used the 'body-without-organs' as a plane of immanence which not only offered this radical re-conceptualisation of desire within machinic production but also used it to give force and energy to engagement with all bodies: human bodies as well as nonhuman bodies, bodies of thought, bodies of words, bodies of sense and so many more. Of this approach Dosse points out:

> With Anti-Oedipus, this entirely immanentist conception of the body without organs became the source of the life-giving energy for words and things. It was a critical, clinical, anti-institutional weapon and a new tool for defining a political philosophy.
>
> *ibid.: 198*

Finding this concept and putting it to work, not just in research practices but also in relation to all bodies and particularly those of an institutional nature, has been hugely energising for me. I now think in this way of my body, the body of my writing, bodies of thought, affective bodies and so on; 'bodies-without-organs' territorialises my doing in the world. So in thinking and working with the concept of the 'body-without-organs' it might be of value to return again briefly to Spinoza and to the oft-repeated criticisms of Cartesian Dualism that are to be found in this book by stating that it is not about what a body is, or indeed might be, it is more about what a body can do. And so my sense of the articulations that I want to propagate from this are powerfully agentic in helping to also formulate, not so much what madness as methodology is, but, in parallel fashion, a more careful focus upon what it can do. With Whitehead and central to this thinking is also to think of bodies more in terms of process and less in terms of substance and, in a similar vein, therefore, to think of relationality not in traditional terms of representation-to-object but rather in terms of part-to-whole. In this I am reminded of a small section of conversation between Donna Haraway and Thyrza Nichols Goodeve:

> TNG: There's this quote I saved from the 1985 'A Manifesto for Cyborgs' where you say, 'Why should our bodies end at the skin or include at best other beings encapsulated by skin.'
>
> DH: And other organisms as well as built objects. There are all kinds of nonhumans with whom we are woven together.
>
> *Haraway, 2000: 86–87*

In these respects it also becomes more and more necessary to think of bodies as activities, as always in flux and as part of processes of transmutation, where little is fixed and movement is ontologically ever present and in movement in the becoming of selves. In this, becoming of madness as methodology questions to do with subjectivity abound. The very word 'madness' lives within orthodoxies and semiotics that represents bodies as objects placed within categorisations and classifications of difference. This difference is of a binary form whose very discursive construction sets up a malevolent presence in the sensing of selves within processual differentiation. Bodies and their representational signification in different forms of situated identification become subjected to the regimentations of fixity inherent in these systemising hylomorphisms of power and control. Bodies are understood and their subsequent subjectification and colonisations practised through the societally normalising and legitimising procedures of these categorisation, procedures which regulate and inform us what a body is or is not.

In this plateau I wish to offer a sense in which Deleuze and Guattari's engagement with Artaud's 'body-without-organs' can be used and as a means of conceptualising madness in processual terms. As already stated, this thinking takes a lead from Whitehead's placing of process over substance and which, therefore, is designed to encourage a thinking with 'madness' not within a metaphysics of being and not as an object of inquiry within a fixed category of difference but in terms of flows, transmutation and always in differentiation. In this sense madness is not conceptualised as other, as not sane, as not rational, as clinically defined but rather in terms of allotropy, where differentiations in intensity and potential are creative of immanence, of difference in itself, where bodies exist and act affectively within the constant flux of movement and moment, elusive to reductions in terms of content and form.

I first read about the 'body-without-organs' on a sunny day in June 2006, sitting on the sand at Porthmeor beach at St Ives in Cornwall. It was Father's Day. I suppose that, following numerous highly weighted clues from me, my family had bought me a copy of Deleuze's (2004b) book on Francis Bacon. We had all spent the morning visiting the Tate Gallery and, with my children's interest in the exhibits there stretched to the limits, we then moved to the beach where the delights of sun, sea and sand were more to their liking. My Father's Day indulgence was also enhanced by our choice of beach for the day. Porthmeor Beach is one of the many beautiful beaches in Cornwall whose dazzling white sand sparkles in the sunlight with the play of the bright summer sun on its shining granite crystals. The beach is backed at its western extremity by Man's Head and the imposing presence of the Tate and at the eastern end, closer to the town, by The Island and, at first sight, the somewhat ramshackle row of buildings both fringing and overlooking the beach, known as Porthmeor Studios. The Studios, originally a random collection of store houses and sail lofts used for generations by members of the local fishing community, have become, over the years, the home and workplace of a thriving and increasingly well-known 'colony' of artists, potters, sculptors and painters. Of these studios, well-known British abstract expressionist painter Patrick Heron, who lived and worked in them at various times, once said:

> Where else in the country are there 13 studios, with a total floor space of over 8,200 square feet, placed at the same time at the centre of a painting

community and (most dramatically) on the very edge of the ocean, where in consequence, the light is of a brilliance that is unique in England?

Heron, quoted in Tufnell, 2006: 11

At this time I had become fascinated by the work of Francis Bacon and had begun to include references to this in my own writing (Gale, 2014) and from reading an earlier biography I knew that Bacon had spent some time working in studio number 3 at Porthmeor in the winter of 1959. During his short stay in St Ives, Bacon's presence caused quite a stir. Various biographers of Bacon seem unable to fully explain his reasons for going there, particularly as his work bore little affinity with the abstract expressionist movement that was central to the artist community in St Ives at that time. So I had become fascinated, not only by Bacon's work and increasingly with Deleuze's writing about it but also by the vivid stories of his brash and aggressive clashes with the abstract painters and sculptors living there at that time. Therefore, my Father's Day plan, after visiting the Tate, was to take my children to Porthmeor beach to find a spot on the sand close to the studios and, in between swims in the sea, making sand sculptures and feasting on pasties, to begin to read what Deleuze had to say about the work of Bacon. This early reading was and continues to be inspirational. Reading Deleuze on Bacon after already having been absorbed by the work of this great artist shifted me bodily. Sitting there, in the sunshine, on Porthmeor Beach, below the iconic presence of the Studios with my children, and beginning to read this book set in process for me what MacLure (2013a) describes as an intensity that 'glows'. The intensity of this glowing continues and is sustained in the varying hues and shadows, lights and darknesses of its continuing presence. In this I find myself always becoming in my conceptualisation of madness as methodology as process and affect. On that sunny afternoon in June, reading this book in the way that Deleuze recommends a book should be read, I randomly opened *Francis Bacon: The Logic of Sensation* at page 44 at the beginning of Chapter 7, the plateau entitled *Hysteria*, and began a reading that lives on in its processual intensity, that always has the potential to shift me seismically in my thinking and that will pull me up short if my mental acuities start to dull and the resolution to always inquire begins to lose its shine.

On this page Deleuze introduces Antonin Artaud and the body-without-organs:

> Beyond the organism, but also at the limit of the lived body, there lies what Artaud discovered and named: the body without organs: 'The body is the body/it stands alone/it has no need of organs/the body is never an organism/organisms are the enemy of the body.'
>
> *Deleuze, 2004b: 44*

I loved the imagery in this and the writings that followed on the subsequent pages. I found the ideas that they evoked exciting and inspirational. I filled my diaries and journals with jottings. My sense of discovery, of uncovering something new or of recovering something that I had, perhaps, lost in the more recent years of my life began to be heightened and as I read on the glow became luxuriant, brighter. I began to find a self-bathing in the warmth of this glow, something was comforting in the wash of this imagery, in swimming in the waves of affect that these readings were beginning to bring to life. At first I struggled in my concept forming: how could I begin to imagine and formulate an idea of a body that had no organs? At this time still, at least partially, anchored in humanist and phenomenologically oriented conceptions of the self and subjectivity, how could I make sense of such a thing, having lived for all these years with *this* body, *this* pulsing, heart thumping, sweating, head aching, living and breathing thing? As if he is aware of the kind of confusion that Artaud's words in the above quotation could generate, in the following sentence, Deleuze offers a really helpful and crucially significant take on Artaud when he explains: 'The body without organs is opposed less to organs than to that organisation of organs we call an organism. It is an intense and intensive body' (ibid.: 44). Bonta and Protevi have suggested that 'body-without-organs' (BwO) is 'a misnomer, the BwO is responsible for much confusion; it would have been better to call it by the more accurate but less elegant term: "a non-organismic body" (2004: 62). Sitting there enjoying the sensual pleasures of that beautiful Cornish, sun-sparkling beach with the roar of the Atlantic surf rushing in my ears, with my children happily playing close by, the puzzlement and surprise of reading that phrase for the first time and then the massive evocation that my first conceptualisation of it inspired has stayed with me and I wouldn't be without it!

I am aware as I write these words here on these pages that I am identifying a 'me', an 'I' and various 'we's', 'others' and 'them's' to try to give sense through expression of what I was and am living then and now as a lived and living body. The a priori logic of Cartesian arborescent reasoning has allowed the 'I' signifier to dominate senses of self and the representational discursive construction of subjective reality. Attachment to this practice troubles me and I shall be using this book to try to unravel the entanglements between these materialities and the discourses that construct and represent them in particular ways. Deleuze offers hope through guidance in the first lines of this very important passage of writing when he says:

> This ground, this rhythmic unity of the senses, can be discovered only by going beyond the organism. The phenomenological hypothesis is perhaps insufficient because it merely invokes the lived body. But the lived body is still a paltry thing in comparison with a profound and almost unliveable Power (*Puissance*).
>
> *2004b: 44*

And, for the madness as methodology that I was beginning to conceptualise and become excited about at that time, 'We can seek the unity of rhythm only at the point where rhythm itself plunges into chaos, into the night, at the point where the differences of level are perpetually and violently mixed' (2004b: 44). I began to think about the organisation of the body; the organisation of *my* body, the organisation of any body. I was already fascinated by Bacon's work, by the ways in which, through the practices and processes of painting a canvas, bodies would emerge, forms would change, a bird would become an umbrella. As I have said elsewhere:

> In the work of Francis Bacon, the very action of the painting brings to life the amorphous indeterminacy of every moment of becoming alive and becoming death, in the building up and the scrubbing away as the paint expresses and lives hesitantly in fragile mortality on the canvas, images come alive and sparkle in their vivacity, to be washed away in the forceful rinsing of insistent subtleties and powerful tides of instant imagery.
>
> *Gale, 2014: 1000*

As my thinking led me more and more in the direction and awareness of these allotropic variations and of the intensities afforded by the potential of the body to exist processually in different forms, it became and continues to become difficult to resist the allure of working with the 'body-without-organs' in everything I do. In *Hysteria*, this hugely important chapter, Deleuze adds powerful impact to some of the practical suggestions that he and Guattari made about the 'body-without-organs' in *A Thousand Plateaus* when they put forward the important question, 'How do you make yourself a Body without Organs?' (Deleuze and Guattari, 1987: 149–150). It seems as if what they ask here is of central importance when we ask Spinoza's question that informs, both by its rhetoric and by its practical intent, much of what this book has to say about madness as methodology: what can a body do? The capacity of a body to affect and be affected in many senses is informed by our understanding of and engagement with power. Power is often understood as being external to the body in the way in which forms of determinism might have upon free will or, in this plateau, how the organisation of the body has a controlling influence upon the organs of the body. An understanding of power in terms of *Puissance* suggests the fluid potentiality and force of intensity, a kind of amorphous and indefinable energy that works in ways that are not simply explicated in coarse hylomorphic modalities of division, hierarchy and control. In this respect Deleuze encourages a thinking of power, not in terms of the controlling hylomorphic organisation of organs, but rather in terms of intensities, thresholds and levels that can shimmer and shift in and through space and time. These are not simply recognised and represented through identification but rather as intensive reality where the moments of allotropic movement from one state to another is the becoming through which power (*Puissance*) is differentiated, sensed, encountered and enacted. It is within the territorialising rhythms of this affective play that the capacity of bodies can be understood. As Deleuze and Guattari say of the 'body-without-organs':

> At any rate, you have one (or several). It's not so much that it pre-exists or comes ready-made, although in certain respects it is pre-existent. At any rate, you make one, you can't desire without making one. And it awaits you; it is

an inevitable exercise or experimentation, already accomplished the moment you undertake it, unaccomplished as long as you don't. This is not reassuring as you can botch it. Or it can be terrifying and lead you to your death . . . It is not at all a notion or a concept but a practice, a set of practices. You never reach the Body without Organs, you can't reach it, you are for ever attaining it, it is a limit.

Deleuze and Guattari, 1987: 149–150

There is a crucial ontological shift in thinking and feeling to be found in what they have to say here. When they pose the question 'How do you make yourself a Body without Organs?', they avoid offering any kind of conceptualisation of how it might be *made*, how it might be *formed*, rather they assert that it is 'a practice, a set of practices' and crucially it is sets of practices that are always being made. In terms of methodologies of inquiry this is helpful in troubling and helping to break down those binary constructions that in research practices are used to separate theory from practice. By never reaching the 'body-without-organs', by never being able to reach it, in active and experimental ways you are for ever attaining it. As Bonta and Protevi say:

A BwO retains its organs, but they are released from the habitual patterns they assume in its organism form; in so far as the organism is a stratum (a centralised, hierarchical and strongly patterned body), a BwO is a destratified (decentralised, dehabituated) body.

Bonta and Protevi, 2004: 62

Using the Deleuzian practice of always creating concepts as events has led me elsewhere to suggest and argue for a 'theorising *as* practice' research methodology and pedagogic practice which can be used to activate 'the processes and practices of using forms of writing to disrupt a metaphysics of being . . . in the promotion of the flows and transmutations of becoming-researcher' (Gale, 2016b: 248). Such an approach is not only active in the animation and activation of concepts but also pays attention to Deleuze and Guattari's practice of 'plugging in', which involves not only creating concepts but also bringing them to life by plugging them in elsewhere, 'when one writes, the only question is which other machine the literary machine can be plugged into, must be plugged into in order to work' (1987: 4). These processual pluggings in are part of the active practice of challenging the entrapments of metaphysics of being and of releasing bodies from the habitual patterns that they have hitherto assumed in their prior organisational form. Here we can conceive of the 'body-without-organs' as experimental, always transmutating, always reanimating the relationalities that are ever present in the play between the power to affect and be affected. For Deleuze and Guattari the striation of space can be associated with the hylomorphic practices of the organism; for them striation organises and, in their words it 'imprisons life' (2004: 45). What they conceive of as smooth space, however, 'is filled by events and haecceities, far more than by formed and perceived things. It is a space of affects, more than one of properties. It is haptic rather than optical perception . . . a Body without Organs instead of an organism and organisation' (1987: 479). And, as Manning argues generally, the 'force of process philosophy lies in its ability to create a field for experience that does not begin and end with the human subject. There is no subject "of" experience, no consciousness outside of the event in its unfolding.' (2014: 164). Active processes of 'smoothing' could be seen to alter striations in space and time and, in so doing, also territorialises those organisational striations in always different ways. In the work of Bacon, referred to above, 'smooth space' is created by the scrubbing and brushing of the canvas, working to neutralise preceding forms that have organised the canvas in particular ways.

In the plateau 'Year Zero: Faciality' of *A Thousand Plateaus*, Deleuze and Guattari offer a conceptualisation and complex theorising of 'faciality' in terms of the play between subjectivation and significance which they call 'the *white wall/black hole* system' (1987: 167). This can be understood as a correlative system of holes and surfaces in which '[t]he face is a surface: facial traits, lines, wrinkles; long face, square face, triangular face; the face is a map, even when it is applied to and wraps a volume, even when it surrounds and borders cavities that are now no more than holes' (ibid.: 170). In the constitution of 'faciality' the 'white wall' is like a projection screen on which signs and images are reflected and 'the black hole' is that dark, unknown space in which the potentialities of intensity and affect have their play. Deleuze refers to the 'movement-image' (2005) as the becoming of the spatial and temporal possibilities of this correlative system of signification and subjectivation and which in film he sees as being exemplified in the cinematic use of the close-up. Deleuze and Deleuze and Guattari's theorising of 'faciality' clearly serves a micro-political purpose. It does this by drawing attention to and challenging conceptualisations of the face that might attempt to fix it as a site of psychological investigation and analysis or that work to present it as an idealised and preferred form of beauty and human attribution. So seeing '(h)ow tempting it is to let yourself get caught, to lull yourself into it, to latch onto a face' (Deleuze and Guattari, 1987: 187), they argue for a getting free from the limitations and fixities of facialisation and, in this, place great value on literature and art that enables a getting out and a getting away, 'to cross an horizon . . . go across, get out, break through, make a bee-line , don't get stuck on a point' (ibid.: 186). As discussed elsewhere, Deleuze's treatment of the work of Francis Bacon in *The Logic of Sensation* offers a powerful exemplification of work that refuses the fixing and identification of self in the representational establishment of the face. The molecular fluidity of Bacon's 'scrubbing and brushing of the canvas' referred to above, his morphing of faces into bodies, of heads into walls, of birds into umbrellas, serves to animate a politics of the face through a refusal to accept the tendencies and pressures that would choose to form, fix and establish it in particular ways.

Therefore, the madness as methodology that is being proposed in this book is one in which the 'body' of methodology that has been organised by conventional humanist qualitative inquiry hitherto will be actively dis-organised in the ever-flowing multiplicity and constant becoming of an inventive and experimental *methodogenesis*: non-methodology as methodological approach. In this, process as movement always precedes the actualisation of bodies. Therefore the capacity of bodies to affect and be affected is processual, it is relational and, in event, it is about bodies always in becoming: 'From noun to verb, what movement does is make apparent that nothing is quite what it seems' (Manning, 2014: 165).

In this plateau I wish to animate madness as methodology by bringing its conceptualisation to life through an engagement with it that is energised in processual terms. Through the *methodogenetic* use of argument, exemplification and personal account, I offer challenge to some of the accepted views of madness as substance that can usually be understood in materially different ways through the offering of different kinds of madness as categories of being. I want to offer one more account here which is designed to continue with this approach and to raise some questions which the rhetoric of this presentation has yet to engage. It is another narrative account. It is a remembering. It exists in the frailty and insubstantiality of recall. It is a narrative fragment that connects with other fragments that are offered here and that are also likely to appear here in the future.

I encountered chance at an important transitional stage in my life in an encounter that moved my thinking and doing in the world in ways that I find continues to reverberate in and through me now, as I write these words. In July 1972 I graduated with my degree in Philosophy, I spent the summer in Cornwall, working in hotels, swimming and sunning myself on the beach and generally having a good time, hanging out with friends and family. In September I went to live in London and began a Post Graduate Certificate of Education (PGCE) programme at Garnett College, which was at the time the only dedicated lecturer-training college, as distinct from teacher-training college, in the UK. The curriculum there was based around the History, Sociology, Psychology and Philosophy of Education and, after the rigours of studying a highly Logical Positivist-inclined Philosophy degree as an undergraduate, the Garnett College course was a delight. The introduction to the teaching practice component of the course was difficult and a rude awakening for those of us who were new to teaching but doing this one-year full-time course sprung me into a career which I have been engaged in for over forty years.

The encounter with chance was serendipitous. It was not part of the official PGCE curriculum; the historical, sociological, psychological and philosophical elements of the programme were enjoyable and relatively mainstream in terms of content and delivery. What was exciting about the programme was that we were not discouraged from bringing our own ideas to bear upon our participation and we were actively encouraged to think about how we could make these work in terms of the teaching and learning practices with which we were beginning to work. A great deal of our approach to study was politically inflected; institutional education was less disciplined by central government policy in those days so a great deal of thinking to do with education was still contested, different practices continued to be introduced into curriculum and classroom practices. The discussions that we engaged in on the course were vibrant and full of life. Many of us had read Postman and Weingartner's (1971) *Teaching as a Subversive Activity* and, following the disturbances we had been involved in at our universities in the late 1960s, were keen to use their methods and approaches to challenge the hegemonies and discursive practices of institutionalised mainstream education. However, our idealism was also imbued with a degree of pragmatism; on the course we had all been encouraged to read Leila Berg's (1968) account of the closure of Risinghill, a co-educational comprehensive school in Islington, North London in 1965. Berg's book offers, as its back cover details, 'a passionate indictment of educational bureaucracy . . . a story in which the word "love" occurs again and again . . . as a key word in a basic conflict about the state education of children'. Michael Duane, the inspirational and eventually sacked headmaster of Risinghill, was a visiting lecturer at Garnett College during my time there and his impassioned descriptions in his lectures of what happened there had a great influence upon me as I took those early initial steps into a career in education. And so this tentative entry into a new world remained full of excitement and tempered by a degree of caution.

Also at this time, chance, the occurrence of an event or events in the absence of any obvious intention or cause, brought me into contact with another important book which continues to be relevant to the madness as methodology which I am attempting to bring to life here. Today it is easy to describe the spread of material on the internet and digitalised space as viral. The publication and subsequent spread of Luke Rhinehart's (1972) book *The Dice Man* could also easily be described, within the relative slowness of those times, in exactly the same way. Published in 1972, and then reprinted twice in 1972 and 1973, and then again in 1974, 1975, 1976, 1977 (twice) and numerous times after that, it is evident that the book was widely read. I owned three, perhaps four copies of the book and, at various times, would have to replace my own copy as the copies that I had originally lent out would then be passed on to others keen to read. The book describes the life of an initially bored psychiatrist who takes to absolving himself from the responsibility of decision making and gives this over to the throw of the dice. Left in the hands of the dice, Rhinehart's life takes many highly unpredictable twists and turns, described in the book in a lively, graphic and often amusing style.

My understanding of the notion of chance at the time related to its clear inconsistency with theories of causality and with any forms of determinism and was explicable as the occurrence of an event having no apparent or obvious intention or motivational cause. Consequently, I found Rhinehart's book and the seeming indeterminacy of chance very seductive; its apparent challenge to the scientistic rigours of Logical Positivism, to which I felt I had been subjected as an undergraduate, fuelled me with interest, excitement and optimism.

My memory does not enable me to fully describe the motivation for what followed my reading of this book. All I know is that I introduced some of the ideas and passages from the book, my version of Rhinehart's dice theory, to some of my classes whilst engaged in my teaching practice on the PGCE programme. The effects were never of the magnitude achieved by the practices Rhinehart described in his book but, nevertheless, the pedagogical and experiential outcomes were always notable. I suppose that I must have exercised some control over the choice and weighting of the options that my students chose and whilst, on occasions, some classes finished their sessions early, or watched an entertaining video, others involved them in writing an essay or reading a difficult passage from a book. My greatest achievement (!) took place during a teaching session observed by my PGCE tutor where a group of engineering students, at the whim of the dice, wrote, acted and filmed a play during their General Studies lessons with me: the feedback I received from my tutor was glowing!

Chance and the use of dice theory and practice encouraged me to revisit the binary construction of free will and determinism, an essential ingredient of political philosophy courses and a great influence of the application of the agency and structure distinction so prevalent in social theory at the time. Whilst my thinking only began to fully develop much later in life, this working with dice decision making provided me with an early introduction into the possibilities of indeterminism, to a belief that no event is certain and the entire outcome of anything is probabilistic. Further, and in a linked sense, the emergent belief in the possibility that all bodies, not just human bodies are, in varying degrees, agentic. In short, Rhinehart's attempt to diminish the control of the ego through the throw of the dice led me to think more and more about those forces and potentialities at work in, in posthuman terms, the coming to life of encounter and event. Deleuze has talked about the 'dice throw' and of how the coming together of many forces can bring about 'a singular composition, an idiosyncrasy . . . marking the unique chance that *these* entities had been retained and willed, that *this* combination had been thrown and not another' (1997: 120). The power that the italicised emphasis gives to this quotation is immense, telling us that this coming together is powerful, unique and not some thing other.

This engagement with chance also offers a creative engagement with some of the problems associated with Zeno's paradoxes if they are simply looked at through the lens of a logic of reason. In the race between Achilles and the Tortoise, Achilles, who is obviously the quickest, can never overtake the slower runner, since, as the pursuer of the ponderous tortoise, he must always first reach a point that is between himself and the next destination point whence the pursued started, so that the slower must always hold a lead and the faster can never catch up. According to rationality, reason and the rules of common sense, this is absurd. However, if a processual ontology of fluidity, multiplicity and movement is proffered in which the 'race' is not simply seen and coded within the binary logics of linearity and chronological time, but instead, in terms of differentiation, distribution and potential, there is always the possibility of becoming and the in between, in which the opportunities for chance, gestural interference and the play of diffractive suggestion and emergence is always present. If we accept the possibility that Zeno's problems could be coded differently, their so-called paradoxical qualities can then be seen in a positive light rather than in the somewhat pejorative terms of the *reductio ad absurdum* of a rationalist logic of so-called common sense.[2] As a consequence, a madness of methodology is one that operates within an engagement with flows and transmutations which are not exclusively human. These work to displace a Cartesian notion of individualism, consciousness and approaches which address and locate agency within a purely humancentric mode of reasoning. So, in looking at the opportunities afforded by chance and in seeing movements as being coded in ways other than those which are simply initiated by human bodies, interferences and diffractive possibilities always have the potential to act and to influence other actions in ways that are not simply foreseen by human agency.

Play in the dance of chance is one example of where movement in the momentous works to trouble the pre-eminence of the fastidious and often narrow search for meaning in research and inquiry. Post-Positivist forms of inquiry appear to have allowed its practices to reside in forms of research that accept pre-determined worlds of identification and difference and that perpetuate this through attempting to minimise doubt, complexity and uncertainty in the representation of their outcomes. The application of strategies of coding, the concerns with potential bias in the use of findings and the construction of generalist themes that provide controlled and rationalist conclusions are all examples of the ways in which desired propositional meanings are 'discovered' and established. So the question to be asked at this stage of my inquiry is one that has also been put forward by MacLure when she asks, 'In trying to free thought from the hierarchies of representation, and restore ontologies of difference are we trying to get a little of that murky, impure Dionysian blood into the "clear and distinct" veins of Apollonian representation?' (2017: 49). I wish to sense the spirit of this question unexpectedly appearing and mischievously lurking in the nooks and crannies of my inquiries here. I want this presencing to disturb me, to trouble my work if I slip back into the orthodoxies and discursively constructed languages of worlds that I am trying my best to disturb and take to task. I am aware, with St Pierre, that 'conventional humanist qualitative methodology described in textbooks and handbooks and university research courses is, indeed, an invention, a fiction' and that 'we made it up' (St Pierre, 2017: 38). Therefore, these fabrications have to be seen for what they are and, in proposing what might be deemed a non-methodology, I am aware that I might also be held to ransom for what I am in the process of proposing here as I engage in the writing of this book, as, in some respects, the non-methodology that I am proposing can be seen, of course, as a methodology. However, I wish to argue that the processual nature of my notion of *methodogenesis* resists such critical observations by the abilities of such an approach to always keep inquiry in play, never allowing it to reside in the comfortable stability of a named and substantive body of practice, supported by a rationalised representation of its distinctiveness as a separate category of difference.

Notes

1 Most of the data available from this period to do with educational (under)achievement focused largely upon relative achievements according to social class grouping and was often drawn from an exclusively male cohort (e.g. Halsey, Heath and Ridge, 1980). Although gender inequalities were evidently present, it was only in later years that studies were carried out that demonstrated this.

2 Within the formal logic of Positivism, the term *reductio ad absurdum* is used to describe a reduction to absurdity. It is a form of argument which attempts to disprove a statement by demonstrating that it leads to an impossible or 'absurd' conclusion', to a positon that common sense would determine as unreasonable, illogical or impossible.

CONCEPTUALISING MADNESS AS AFFECT?

My Found Poem

My found poem exists like life on the beach.

The sun shines brightly, the breeze comes out of the west, a cloud drifts over and the day turns chill.

I turn from the sea, my wet, salt stained body replenished by the vitality of immersion in water and jousting in the waves.

I amble across the sand, my body slowly dries, my eyes dip, scan and pick up things shining here, an unusual shape nestling there, curiosities and surprises teasing my walk into further distances.

I search for serpentine and discover worn black elvan.[1]

I marvel at the deep quartz veins incising through the killas[2] all over the beach.

The ironed, eroded and decomposing shell of a Coke can catches my eye; it is like a piece of parchment drifting unnoticed on the windswept pavement outside a church.

I pick it up and change its life; it is now marking a page in my book.

Sticks like bleached bones in the wreckage of a desert cemetery are scattered all around, with no body to connect them together and make them represent; they exist like living ghosts to me, always becoming new forms.

Today they shine in parched expressions of aridity, tomorrow they might soak up the juices of a rain shower or become sodden from the soaking of a brazen Spring tide; each new form is new life, is world making.

I know the carcass of the dead dolphin still silently rests where it was stranded weeks ago by a giant tide near a cave at the top of the beach.

I look at it from a distance.

I couldn't go near it because it filled me with sadness, the still remaining beauty living on in its dying life shining in my eyes like a spear.

I can't go near it now, its dead body stinks; I witness its foul decomposing becoming other from a trembling distance.

I turn to watch oyster catchers nervously conversing on the tideline, delicately feeding on the morsels that the gently lapping waters carelessly shares.

I love their fragile beauty, their now you see me, now you don't way of living.

I try to be casual, quiet and unassuming as I allow the limbs of my light stepping body to gradually drift toward them.

I want to be with them, to share this beautiful space, to let them know how much I love being here with them but, all of a sudden, they can tolerate me no more; as one they lift, fly and are gone, skimming over the water in a busy, piping, dipping and flowing bustle.

Alone again in my wandering. I feel the now warm sun on my neck and am reminded that life is good.

I wonder about the pace of the incoming tide and bend to marvel at the smooth delicate pinkness of a dead discarded peeler crab's shell, making the word carcass sound good again.

Mussels audibly sigh as the tide washes over them, turning their bleached sun burnt shells into dark, sleek, shiny effervescence.

Sea anemone breasts lose their shiny brown pendulous seductiveness and grow seething nests of tentacles that delicately sway in the gentle wash that slowly surrounds them, their venomous surprises hidden in the beautiful endless wafting of their water-borne flows.

It is the moon, now silent and barely visible in the clear azure sky, which makes these plays.

In her third quarter she becomes restless, growing with feline animation and voluptuous strength and lives in the endless energising of the vibrant particularities of this world pulsing in, with and around me.

I have gendered the moon in my writing here.

It makes me self-conscious, aware of stumbling with this common and over used trope in facile, idle self-expression, always searching in the flawed findings of words, movements, and flows of these gentle moments of waking.

Wiggle Beach, Whitsand Bay, Cornwall, 9 June 2016

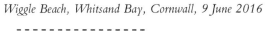

I think that my comfort in living with this book becoming, becoming-book, comes in large part from my growing encounters with what is generally described as the posthuman. Obviously living with Deleuze for all these years has prepared me for this but it is the more recent readings that I have engaged in with Spinoza, Bergson, Haraway, Stengers, Grosz, Stewart, Bennett and others that has accentuated my leaning in this general direction. In my *Found Poem* I want bodies, human and nonhuman, in exemplification, to simply come to life in their relationality and, in so doing, through divergence and diversity, to encourage new life, new ways of looking and the openness of relationality to spread.

Early this morning I wrote using the imagery of magnetism to energise the way I was feeling in terms of looking forward to enjoying the sun, sea and sand, of walking on the beach and swimming in the waves. This imagery has stayed with me and now manifests itself in thoughts that turn themselves into these words. I think about how magnetism and certain other forces, such as gravity, are 'understood', moulded and readily accepted within the scientific discourses that generate our relationality to them. We have all experienced those 'experiments' in school laboratories where teachers demonstrated these forces with iron filings on pieces of paper and objects sliding down inclined planes. These experiences have so deeply embedded themselves in our senses of the world that we readily use them in metaphor and cliché to identify and represent without any sense of confusion or perturbation. We harness the materiality of these forces to animate the discourses that construct and constrain us and then, in turn, these animations energise our actions and behaviours and in so doing instrumentalise our relational engagements in time and space.

This frisson between language and matter is vividly described and brought to life by Barad (2007) in her use of terms such as 'intra-action' and 'entanglement'. The intensities that are the life force of these 'entanglements' are the very stuff of these inquiries; 'after finitude' (Meillassoux, 2008) their complexity is integral to the becoming of this madness as methodology. How can I live in any other way? It is as if the visibility of magnetism and gravity give them meaning and that that is enough; because we can see them then we can live with and accept their power: this is how the scientific discourse seems to work. So when looking at becoming in the simply *interactive*, therefore, it is possible to gain understanding of this through direct visible exchange; a question might be followed by an answer, an alluring smile might be followed by another smile, a tentative touch, perhaps a kiss. When looking at becoming in the *intra-active*, however, this gaining of understanding would be dependent upon less direct or obviously visible forms of exchange. Here nuance, inflection, mood and intonation, the very presence of forces, would provide a much less distinct measure of the exchange. The articulation of the intra-active transmutation would be noticed, perhaps, through the shimmering vibration of a slight tremor, the inflected mannering of a phrase. So where the *inter-active*, as a space where prior difference is brought into contact, is perhaps understood through the structural logic of language and reason, the *intra-active* is more likely to be understood through a logic of sense as space in which difference is produced.

I have a sense of other forces at play here, what Manning describes as 'beyond me and mine' (2014: 165) and they are the ones that cannot be seen and that, nevertheless, play a huge part in the lives we live and that I want to bring to life in the writings in this book. In June 2011 I bought Deleuze's book on Spinoza (1988). I loved the edition that I bought because it is published by City Lights Books, Lawrence Ferlinghetti's publishing house that had such an energising influence upon Beat literature and which published the likes of Ginsberg, Kerouac and others in the 1950s and 1960s when other publishers were very reticent about doing so. In the early 1960s, as a young aspiring beatnik and a new and avid reader of continental philosophy and contemporary American literature, I loved carrying around those little black editions of Ginsberg's *Howl* and *Reality Sandwiches* and Kerouac's *Book of Dreams* in the pockets of my donkey jacket and my faded blue jeans. So now, owning a copy of Deleuze's *Spinoza: Practical Philosophy* from the same publisher carries with it a deep and powerful resonance. At the time of my first enthusiastic reading of this important and influential book, the following quotation enveloped me:

> [T]hese image affections or ideas form a certain state (*constitutio*) of the affected body and mind, which implies more or less perfection than the preceding state. Therefore, from one state to another, from one image or idea to another, there are transitions, passages that are experienced, durations through which we pass to a greater or lesser perfection. Furthermore, these states, these affections, images or ideas are not separable from the duration that attaches them to the preceding state and makes them tend towards the next state. These continual durations or variations of perfection are called 'affects,' or feelings (*affectus*).
>
> *Deleuze, 1988: 48–49*

I had not formed ideas of affect in this way. I had not fully thought about affect working in terms of action and power and in terms of a relationality that could somehow be both with and beyond the human. The powerful influence of affect upon these increases and decreases of action brought into sharp focus the oft-quoted phrase from Spinoza that talks of 'the power to affect and be affected'. In this powerful relationality, *affectus* is the force which embodies the power to affect and *affectio* is the impact, it is the power to be affected. The duration of this relationality varies; it might be fleeting, almost like a glancing blow that is felt and then quietly dissipates and is perhaps forgotten, or it might be more enduring, perhaps by making a lasting impression, residing with a presence for a much longer period, perhaps leaving a residue. And of course this is not a binary construction that can be used to divide affect into two parts because in *affectio*, where perhaps there is some emotional impact upon the body, there will also exist *affectus*, where the impact upon the body is the becoming of a new energising force, which generates further impacts and affective disturbance. Not long after I had read this I was having a conversation with my eldest daughter, Katy, we were talking of my recent divorce from the person who was then her stepmother and she reminded me of how I was at the time and how sadness was a deeply constitutive force in my becoming. She went on to describe how this was not only having an impact upon me but also, in terms of the energy that I was giving out, the forces that were pulsing from me were having a profound affect on her and my other two children. So here the power to affect and to be affected was not limited to a single, isolated one-dimensional relationality but was, in this rhythmic play, imbricated within and generative of a whole new series of forces and impacts. *Affectus* and *affectio* were constitutive of a certain state (*constitutio*) of our affected bodies and minds, which, in this case, at this time, suggests less perfection than in our preceding relational state. There is a sense in which this is what Massumi (2002: 17) might refer to as an 'example', an event perhaps that exemplifies movement and a dynamic in the ever-shifting energies of relationality. This is something that happened seven, maybe eight, years ago now; those relational dynamics continue to play a tune but the refrain is now different as the intricacies of our affective turns become more complex, carrying certain residual elements with them and leaving others behind, dependent upon the fragility of memory for their existence.

My many encounters with Deleuze have been enlivened by the way in which his writing encourages me to question the boundedness of the body. I think of discovering Donna Haraway questioning the Enlightenment-driven, scientific discourses that tell us that our bodies end with our skin and now, through Spinoza, I am drawn to the idea that our bodies are part of the constant relational play between the multiple forces and impacts of the 'entanglements' of language and materiality. In the moment of every movement change takes place: as I think of my example above, it becomes increasingly clear to me that within the intensity of the whirling affective twists and turns of a marriage break-up feelings were in flow, not in separation, not in an isolable individual state, but always in relation to the movements and moments of all those involved. Affectively they can only be understood in this way. And now as I read Haraway again I am enthralled and share her excitement when in talking of the highly distributed and diversely populated nature of 'the mundane space I call my body' she says:

> I am vastly outnumbered by my tiny companions; better put, I become an adult human being in company with these tiny messmates. To be one is always to become with many . . . I love that when 'I' die, all these benign and dangerous symbionts will take over and use whatever is left of 'my' body, if only for a while, since 'we' are necessary to one another in real time.
>
> *2008: 4*

In writing in this way Haraway brings into focus the notion of figurative realities in which the distributed agentic forces of all these tiny 'companions' and 'messmates' in play with one another coalesce and come together in the brevity of movements in space and moments in time. So in our 'figuring out' of the world, in our processes of explanation and world making, we must cease to grapple with the elusiveness of fixity, we must recognise the futility of trying to capture any movement or moment, knowing that this can only be done through the superficial and politically imbricated mannerisms and fabrications of representation and identification. And so for Haraway, 'figures are not representations or didactic illustrations, but rather material – semiotic nodes or knots in which diverse bodies and meanings coshape one another' (2008: 4).

In these ways I am drawn by the realist nature of this ontology. I am struck with awe as my growing sensing of these forces and energies enlivens my praxis in the world and I am seduced in my thinking of subjectivity as 'figure', whose embodied self needs to be understood in terms of the way in which these biological and discursive forces come together: I cannot conceptualise 'me' in any other way. In this respect I sense 'my' self, this 'figure' as an event, as something that is both preceded by difference and produces difference, something that never repeats, something that is eventual in its always becoming and something that is eventful in its continually differentiating engagement and involvement in active world making. This is always processual, always in play, never constant and always surprising. As Manning (2007: 106) suggests, it makes sense to talk more of the constantly processual notion of 'ontogenesis' in preference to the more seemingly fixed concept of ontology. In these sensings the flows, transmutations and durational forces at play in the constituting of figures as events and the frisson between the power to affect and be affected can be further illuminated by Barad's (2007) use of 'intra-action' in preference to the more familiar form of 'interaction'. Also, in this respect, her use of the notion of 'entanglements' to describe the intense relational forces and impacts at play between language and materiality in the constant re/cognition and re-construction between words and things resonates powerfully with the energies at play in the emergence of Haraway's 'figures'.

And so, as I write here, talking of madness as methodology, I am drawn by these observations and to remembering what Deleuze writes about in relation to the work of Spinoza. In talking of the unconscious nature and potential of thought and the unknown of the body he says, '(t)he fact is that consciousness is by nature the locus of an illusion' (1988: 19). I revel in the paradoxical nuances and inflections that this assertion provides me with as I carry out these considerations of madness. In this brief quotation, Deleuze is claiming that the conscious, sentient and rational world that we have come to know through the thinking of Kant, Descartes, Hegel and the whole of Enlightenment philosophy and science, the world of first causes, the one which helps to provide us with explanation and meaning and which works to make us sane, is one that is actually premised upon an illusion. It is through and with the conceptualisation and application of a 'logic of sense' that enables him to be able to make claims for the existence of laws of composition and decomposition that, as conscious beings, he argues, eludes us through our adherence to these traditional logics of reason and meaning that serve to discursively construct our thinking and doing in particular ways.

Deleuze's 'logic of sense' helps to animate a shift away from (not an abandonment of) the world of ideas and the separation of mind and body that emanate from the a priori thinking of Cartesian logics of reason. In drawing upon the work of the Stoics, Deleuze argues that 'there are bodies with their tensions, physical qualities, actions and passions, and the corresponding "states of affairs"' (2004a: 7). We can understand these 'states of affairs' as events which are created by the constant mixture of (human and nonhuman) bodies and as no longer representing the disembodied ideas of reason, identity and categorisations of difference that are constrained within traditional notions of common sense, identification and reason. Instead, a 'logic of sense' is concerned with difference in itself and with the event/full processes of differentiation and becoming that are inherent within it. By engaging in concerns with the imbrications and instantiations that are part of the relational eventfulness of the play language and substance, the application of a Deleuzian 'logic of sense' shifts our attention towards Spinoza's question that asks 'What can a body, *any* body, do?' This movement helps to shift our attention away from *effect* towards the world of *affect*. Hitherto we might react joyfully or with sadness to how another body appears to us or to the effect of such a body upon us or how a particular idea impacts upon our thinking but because of consciousness we only notice these as effects. In this what we fail to sense are the encounters between bodies, between ideas that, through processes of composition and decomposition, change those bodies and change those ideas:

> And this is what is prodigious in the body and the mind alike, these sets of living parts that enter into composition with and decompose one another according to complex laws. The order of causes is therefore an order of composition and decomposition of relations, which infinitely affects all of nature.
>
> *2004a: 7*

It is as if we have grown to live by these appearances whilst allowing the world of reality to slip by us without noticing it. With the presence and animated chatter of Haraway's 'tiny companions and messmates' all around me, I am taken by the view offered by Hurley in his introduction to Deleuze's book on Spinoza when he says,

> the elements of the different individuals we compose may be nonhuman within us. What we are capable of may partake of the wolf, the river, the stone in the river. One wonders, finally, whether Man is anything more than a territory, a set of boundaries, a limit on existence.
>
> *Ibid.: iii*

It is the durations and inclinations and disinclinations to and from perfection that are at the heart of Spinoza's oft-quoted dictum about the power to affect and be affected that energise this beautifully insane take on engaging with the world. I love the sense in which I can consider myself and my place in the world not as some fixed entity that is the product of some lazily incurred, discursively inflected process of naming, some noun, some fixed category of being susceptible of classification and predictive possibility and that instead I can sense myself becoming-wolf, becoming-river and becoming-stone and animating the multiple possibilities after finitude. And so I am with Kathleen Stewart when she describes her book *Ordinary Affects* as 'an experiment, not a judgment', when she talks of her work in the book as provoking 'attention to the forces that come into view as habit or shock, resonance or impact' and when she talks of 'something' that 'throws itself together in a moment as an event and a sensation; something both animated and inhabitable' (2007: 1). The thinking behind what it is I am doing and that what I want to do resides here.

Its residence is not comfortable and luxurious, its inhabitants, its 'tiny companions and messmates', do not sit still for long, they are fuelled by curiosity, the excitement of experimentation and the sense that one blink too many might mean that something is missed. And so this residence is one of animation, it is where the activation of mind and body takes off, where lines of flight are agentic in multiple becomings and in the unbridled fascination of the always not yet known. These human and nonhuman residents have alerted and encouraged me to be present with Jane Bennett's ascription of 'thing power', of the power of the nonhuman as well as the human to affect and be affected and thus to acknowledge and practise notions of 'distributed agency' and the idea that assemblages are agentic (2010: 21).

This brings me back in touch with transmutations that come about due to the play of forces and energies and in so doing encourages me to be curious about the possibilities of invisibility, opacity and corners of shadowy presence. This is to feel and talk about the wind, to smile with its animation of children in playgrounds and the ever-present vibrancy of relationality that is always there to be tapped into when wonder plays its part. Stengers says,

> that to be interested by something has the character of an event, since it gives to that something a power it does not generally possess: the power to cause us to think, feel and wonder, the power to have us wondering how practically to relate to it, how to pose relevant questions about it.
>
> *2011: 374*

The philosophy of Spinoza offers us the opportunity to engage with potentialities. When we consider the *capacity* of bodies, all bodies, to affect and be affected, we are bringing into play notions of possibility, we are sensing what a body can or might be able to do. This is not a phenomenologically inflected consideration that enacts a humanist sensibility such as a feeling or an emotion, it is not about consciousness or having an experience, rather it is a movement in a moment, a moment in a movement, it is unstructured and unformed, and, in affect, it is about intensity, difference and the potential to bring about change. In this respect Shouse asserts that affect 'is the body's way of preparing itself for action in a given circumstance by adding a quantitative dimension of intensity to the quality of an experience' (2005: 1). This affective sense in which we can think about 'preparing for action' is about potential and resonates powerfully with Deleuze and Guattari's treatment of the virtual and the actual. In this the virtual and the actual do not exist in binary form, it is not about an actual or 'real' world being 'represented' in the virtual and brought into life by the transcendent authority of man, rather, as Colebrook points out, life is

> just this actual-virtual imaging: each flow of life becomes other in response to what it is not. The anticipation goes beyond what is actual, but also produces a new actual. The image is neither actual nor virtual but the interval that brings actuality out of the virtual.
>
> *2002: 87–88*

As the rhizomatic emergence of this book multiplies in its becoming, there is a sense of a powerful madness coming to life in the possibilities and potentialities for the practices and methodologies that can be seen to emanate from it. I am full of what Stengers refers to as the power of wonder and sense, an animating madness in living with the tangible invisibilities of these forces that are both folding into me and which I fold into. I am seduced by and addicted to the energising affectiveness of these forces. When Manning says '[t]his kind of wonder-ful movement-event is rarely ascertained as such – as it is too quickly subsumed into the nextness of movement-moving' (2014: 166), I sense the animation of Davies and Gannon's powerful elision 'mo(ve)-ment' (2006: x) where, in the processual vitality of space and time, something is always being done, something is happening, haecceities occur and the vibrant intensity of becoming is the always potential for new life.

My sense of Deleuze and Guattari's treatment of the virtual and the actual brings into focus, through implication, the experimental possibilities of the new, the always not yet known and the emergent and creative dynamics of potential. What Colebrook describes as 'the interval that brings actuality out of the virtual' is about the possibilities of change and a sense in which we can continue to make sense of Deleuze and Guattari's philosophy of the event. Practising concept forming within the context of such a philosophy works as a challenge to the containing and restricting practices of transcendence. The creative practice of concept forming inheres potential and the possibility that in any given context or situation the experimental forming of concepts as events will enable an always going beyond existing circumstances and actualities. This is where my enduring interest lies, where the fire is sparked and where the seeds of madness as methodology are sown. These are times and spaces where world making is about awe and wonder, where it is not just about thinking, pondering or simply asking questions but where it is to be taken aback and to nurture the sense of always becoming able to be surprised. 'The wonder is of the event's capacity to create a bodying that is in excess of its-*self*, altering the very field of what "I" might be' (Manning, 2014: 166).

It is at the point that it seems apt to engage this conceptualisation of madness as methodology as affect in terms of what it can actually do. To continue with the Spinozist question 'What can a body do?' it becomes necessary to consider *all* bodies in terms of this question. It might be lazy or even tempting to ask this question of human bodies. Such an approach would sit comfortably within traditional conceptualisations of humanist and phenomenologically inflected research, but within a posthuman and, indeed, a post-qualitative mode of inquiry, this is not the case. Using Deleuzian theory and practice to engage in practices of conceptualisation and contextualisation involves research in making shifts away from textual fields of representation and movement towards ontologies of realism and materiality. With an eye to increasing complexity, when we allow affective, process-based and posthuman approaches to come to the fore, we are in 'situations which we no longer know how to react to, in spaces which we no longer know how to describe' (Deleuze, 1989: xi). Using the Deleuzian 'body-without-organs' suggests a possibly posthuman approach to doing (education) research. In considering modes of inquiry that are of posthuman character and inclination it might be possible to argue that our approaches are, therefore, not simply post-qualitative and also post-methodological. The possibilities of a 'post-methodological approach' continues to lead me to thinking about and beginning to practise this non-methodology as methodology here. I have invoked Deleuze elsewhere in this book when I have pointed to him saying that 'The phenomenological hypothesis is perhaps insufficient because it merely invokes the lived body' (2004b: 44) and I want to use this as a means of providing a specific example of where even quite radical and forward-thinking approaches to research practice in humanist qualitative inquiry can be seen to be lacking in quite fundamental ways.

I recently read a book about George Whitman who, in 1951, was responsible for re-opening and giving new life to the famous bookshop, Shakespeare and Company at 37 Rue de la Bûcherie, on the Left Bank in Paris. The bookshop was originally opened by Sylvia Beach in 1919 and played host to many great writers over the years such as James Joyce, Gertrude Stein, Ernest Hemingway and many others. Famously, Beach was responsible for originally publishing Joyce's *Ulysses* in 1922 at a time when no other publisher would entertain such a venture and, perhaps somewhat apocryphally, is reputed to have been forced to close her shop in 1941 during the German Occupation because she would not sell her last copy of *Ulysses* to a German officer who wished to purchase it from her. The spirit of the bookshop is perhaps best epitomised in a quotation from W. B. Yeats that is painted on the wall of the shop: 'Be not inhospitable to strangers, lest they be angels in disguise.' In line with this quotation, the bookshop is, therefore, not simply a place to go to purchase a book, but also one in which the visitor is encouraged to read, browse the shelves, engage in some writing and perhaps even stay for a while.

As a young man in the late 1930s, Whitman embarked on what he referred to as a 'hobo adventure', which involved him hitchhiking, walking, and train-hopping across Mexico, Central America and the States. The following passage, written in Los Angeles in 1938, not only offers a telling manifesto of a young adventurer living in the world during frighteningly volatile times but also eloquently speaks to ways of becoming and doing in the world that whilst somewhat humanist in inclination are, nevertheless, relevant to the account being offered in this book:

> The highest quality of an individual is to be human. The phrase 'to be human' means to follow life wherever it may lead, up and down, down and up, from the bottom of the world to the top, from darkness into light, through each degree of good and evil. As the circle widens, life grows more beautiful and heroic. We are part of everything – men, women, books, cities, railroads – all made from the same atoms and molecules, all living together and dying together, joined into one imperishable unit that can never be divided.
>
> *Whitman in Halverson, 2016: 68*

In this passage Whitman not only offers his somewhat universalistic thinking about human qualities and ways of being but also alerts us to forms of becoming in a world which to him is not simply human. Although he talks about the qualities of 'an individual' it is clear that he is both humble and observant enough to place his understanding of his position in the world not simply in human terms. In writing this book I sense more than anything else the importance of engaging with my work in these kinds of ways. I have engaged in forms of qualitative research and inquiry now for over twenty years and, as my vigour for this kind of work continues unabated, I sense that some of the inquiry with which I have been engaged has avoided some of the complexity that researching in the affective, the processual and the posthuman necessarily entails.

I think that doing autoethnography is a case in point and, in the last few years, I have begun to write into and against much of what autoethnography stands for and does, not because I think that what it does is wrong of itself, but rather that what it does is not enough. In its relatively short lifespan, autoethnography has been hugely successful in asking questions of conventional forms of humanist qualitative inquiry. It has also been successful in promoting research-based practices that have troubled the prevailing and over-determining prescriptions of Positivist thought in qualitative inquiry to the extent that it has become possible to talk of qualitative inquiry in post-Positivist terms. However, in terms of the madness as methodology that is being offered in these pages is concerned, what autoethnography might have achieved in the past, particularly in the ways in which it problematised and challenged the ethnocentric characteristics of its predecessor, ethnography, now needs to be seen in the light that is offered by those inquiries that have, in recent years, been described as New Empiricist and New Materialist and which have emerged through, what Clough (2010) describes as, the 'affective turn' and the growth of posthuman approaches to research in short, in terms of what St Pierre (2011, 2015) and others have referred to as 'post qualitative inquiry'. From this it seems clear that the 'auto' in 'autoethnography' tells us that as an inquiry genre and modality autoethnography is about the individualised 'I' of Cartesian Dualism. Its concerns are with, in the majority of cases, an essentially phenomenological engagement with human selves and subsequent constructions of subjectivity in relation to their situatedness, contextualisation and participation within cultural and social worlds. It is not that autoethnography intentionally, consciously or necessarily excludes attention to and a focusing upon the nonhuman or, what Barad describes as, the 'entanglements' between materialities and the discourses that often construct them in particular ways, it is more that it doesn't seem to notice them. It is in this lack of noticing that the autoethnographic 'I' does not 'see' beyond human existence and its concomitant and exclusively human relationality and hence appears to demonstrate a partiality to creating a metaphysics of being. In this sense, therefore, autoethnography can be seen as an approach to research and writing that describes, analyses and critically engages with the 'auto' of personal experience as a means of working towards an understanding of cultural experience (Ellis, 2004; Holman Jones, 2005). As Ellis herself says in the recently published *Handbook of Autoethnography*:

For most of us, autoethnography is not simply a knowing about the world; it has become a way of being in the world, one that requires living consciously, emotionally, and reflexively. It asks that we not only examine our lives but also consider how and why we think, act and feel as we do. Autoethnography requires that we observe ourselves observing, that we interrogate what we think and believe, and that we challenge our own assumptions, asking over and over if we have penetrated as many layers of our own defences, fears, and insecurities as our project requires. It asks that we rethink and revise our lives, making conscious decisions about who and how we want to be.

Ellis, 2013: 10

It is clear that what is said here, in such an important space by one of the most well-known scholars in the field, places the emphasis of autoethnography clearly and firmly on the human. It appears to do this within a metaphysics of being that excludes reference to all forms of sentient relationality other than the human. Whilst this is not to set up a binary relationship between the human and the nonhuman, it would appear that a level of complexity is taken from autoethnographic approaches to research when relationalities that can be seen to exist between human and nonhuman becoming are overlooked. The approach to research taken by autoethnography will find it difficult to avoid the criticism that might be directed to it of human-centrism, in similar ways that ethnography, its epistemological and methodological predecessor, was accused of ethnocentrism in earlier years. The autoethnographic 'I' appears to be one that is full of emotion and feeling; it is one that can make conscious decisions about the world and that is able to think and act reflexively about and in relation to its own engagement with the world. It is an individualised and individualising being that 'sees' the world through the lens of its gender, its class, its ethnicity and other representational generalisations; its thinking and feeling are produced by the experience it has of the world within which it is situated. In strictly Kantian ways, it is a *thing-in-itself* and, as Heidegger's (1962) phenomenology has shown, this *thing-in-itself* cannot be thought of outside of *dasein*, outside of its (social) situatedness or its *being-there*, this is the very nature of its (human) existence. Consciousness, emotion, reflexivity all seem to reflect and consolidate the arborescence and individualism of this (autoethnographic) 'I', in its reaching up and out for light, in its digging down to establish foundational roots, and, all the while, in the perpetuation of its dominant and dominating will to exist as a being in the solid individuality of its arborescence and trunk-like form.

The concerns expressed here about what I see as the limitations of the body of inquiry that is described as being autoethnographic is that the majority of the work appears to overlook the affective turn that many forms of inquiry in the Humanities and Social Sciences have taken in the last two decades. In this respect, it appears not to have engaged with the valuable and incisive work that has been carried out in posthuman forms of inquiry and to have ignored the important work carried out by theorists who have suggested the need for a post qualitative approach to inquiry in ontological, epistemological and methodological terms. The choice of the quotation from George Whitman's writing at the beginning of this section was meant to be apposite. The kinds of approaches that now threaten autoethnographic forms of inquiry in hugely fundamental ways are not *anti*-humanist; in many respects, the thinkers and researchers who are taking the lead in this work are providing us with *pro*-humanisms in their writing and inquiry. There is a strong sense in which what they offer is of absolute necessity for the survival if the arborescent roots, trunk and branches of autoethnographic inquiry are not to wither and die. In this respect the argument being made here is not anti-autoethnographic in intention; it is designed to encourage autoethnographers to become aware of these 'posts' and 'turns' and to work to avoid the anaesthetising tendencies that appear to be dulling its sensitivities at the moment and in threatening its survival as the radical, cutting-edge modality that it began to offer to qualitative inquiry when it first appeared twenty or thirty years ago.

The madness of Whitman's writing, as he senses 'life (growing) more beautiful and heroic', passionately advocates the human. From his biographies, his writing and the way he lived his life it is clear that his belief in, and commitment to, humanity was immense but crucially he was also fully aware of, and a strong advocate of, the view that '(w)e are part of everything – men, women, books, cities, railroads – all made from the same atoms and molecules, all living together and dying together, joined into one imperishable unit that can never be divided' (Whitman in Halverson, 2016: 68). I sense here in Whitman's writing all the posthuman sentiments, inclinations and interests that have driven the affective and processual thinking and practices of the new materialisms and empiricisms emerging at the present time and that require us to think carefully and practically about post qualitative approaches as we advance and enhance our inquiries in the ongoing emergence of the current century.

In my more recent work with Jonathan Wyatt (Wyatt and Gale, 2013a and 2013b), we have begun to open a space for such an approach to begin to take place. By using Deleuze and Guattari's (1987) assertion that 'the smallest unit is the assemblage' and not the 'individual', that is the concern of the orthodox forms of humanist, phenomenologically inclined autoethnographic practice being examined here, we have offered the notion of 'assemblage/ethnography' as a means of attempting to trouble representational constructions of the self within the context of the entanglements of discourse and materialities that are relevant to our own inquiries. In this work we have offered criticism of the humanist orthodoxies of conventional humanist qualitative inquiry generally and traditional autoethnography, in particular, by suggesting that there is a need for engaging in a Foucauldian 'getting out of selves' (ibid.: 2013b) as a means of animating and activating such approaches. What has been helpful as we continue to make inquiries in this field has been our engagement with Deleuze and Guattari's notion of 'agencement' which Massumi, in the introduction to *A Thousand Plateaus*, and others have translated and used as 'assemblage' and which is the more common translated form in use at the present time. 'Agencement' suggests the relationality that is present in the fluid dynamics of

Spinoza's claim that all bodies possess the capacity to affect and be affected. In her use of the term 'agentic assemblages', Bennett offers a mode of thinking that resonates with that of Whitman cited above and that needs to be brought into play in relation to the future of autoethnography being suggested here. She says:

> Spinoza's conative encounter-prone body arises in the context of an ontological vision according to which all things are 'modes' of a common 'substance.' Any specific thing – 'a shoe, a ship, a cabbage, a king' . . . or a glove, a rat, a cap, and the human narrator of their vitality . . . is neither subject nor object but a 'mode' of what Spinoza calls '*Deus sive Natura*' (God or Nature).
>
> *Bennett, 2010: 22*

The term 'agencement' is really helpful in bringing together the contingent, heterogeneous, ad hoc diversity of what Bennett refers to as 'agentic assemblages' (ibid.: 21) because for her it is important to engage with the vibrancy of matter by acknowledging and working with the claim that all 'things' have power, 'thing power' (ibid.: 4), and that agency is, therefore, distributed through and across all elements or singularities of assemblages. It is, as she has been quoted elsewhere in this book as saying, in the writing 'what is at work here on the page is an animal-vegetable-mineral-sonority cluster with a particular degree and duration of power' (ibid.: 23). Therefore, 'agencement' brings alive Deleuze and Guattari's notion of the 'smallest unit' through its necessitation of relationality and through its animation of the view that nonhuman 'things' are agentic and not simply social constructions and that human agency is also imbued with vital materiality.

Notes

1 Elvan is the Cornish name used for a form of dark igneous rock commonly found there. Elvan was popular as a building stone, with local names such as Pentewan and Polyphant designating its origins. The stone is now quarried, crushed and used as the basis for road building aggregates.
2 Killas is a Cornish mining term used to refer to the sedimentary rocks mainly to be found around the high granite moorlands that are a major feature of the Cornish geological landscape.

MADNESS AS A COLLABORATIVE PRACTICE

I spent the summer of 2003 travelling with my family around Italy. We visited the Italian lakes, Como, Garda and Maggiore. With my children we swam in their warm waters, the Swiss Italian Alps creating a beautiful, awe-inspiring backdrop to our pleasures. We travelled to Venice and spent a week wandering in wonderment absorbed in the busy hustle and bustle of the shaded alleyways and the crowded canals, watching Reuben and Phoebe feeding the pigeons in St Mark's Square, becoming immersed in the scintillating mysteries of living, lost in a world of tourists-becoming-ants in the spectral shadows of the historical immensities of religious iconography and architectures of bygone empires. In those wanderings I remember the insidious haunting presence of Nicholas Roeg's film *Don't Look Now*;[1] I remember constantly and nervously watching out for my children in the crowdedness of those busy streets, living with the fleeting recognition of certain buildings and thoroughfares and the frightened awareness of the lurking persistent infection of grief slowly growing in my bones.

We visited the Guggenheim Museum on the Palazzo and I found my lifelong love of art being given new energies amongst Peggy Guggenheim's personal collection of Picassos, Ernsts, Miros and Magrittes. I became fascinated by the details of her life and her affairs with the painters Yves Tanguy, Max Ernst and others. In the gallery bookshop I stumbled across an edited collection of chapters detailing the lives, loves and relationships of a number of celebrities and famous people, drawn mainly from the fields of literature and art, entitled *Significant Others* (Chadwick and Courtivron, 1993). At that time in 2003 I had yet to embark upon my doctoral studies and my collaborative writing practices were limited to written correspondences in the form of exchanging letters with a few close friends and lovers. The idea of writing collaboratively as a means of inquiry had not yet gained any kind of presence in the turmoil of my life. Despite this, my brief scan of the contents list and of some of the dark, grainy images scattered through its pages led me to buying the book[2] and, to what seemed like at the time, the voyeuristic practice of reading about the private lives and intimacies of a range of artists, musicians and writers whose work had already impressed themselves upon my life. In those initial browsings I found myself being seduced by many of the chapter titles; of the author's description of Sonia and Robert Delaunay as 'living simultaneously', of Vanessa Bell and Duncan Grant's 'left-handed marriage', of the 'tinder-and-flint' of Virginia Woolf and Vita Sackville-West and the 'beauty to his beast' of Frida Kahlo and Diego Riviera (ibid.: 5–6). Something in the idiosyncrasy and the hinted complexities of these titles reeled me in; I felt drawn by the intensive relational spaces that these titles seem to suggest and an emerging need to inquire more fully into the lives that were thinly veiled by them. I have a strong sense that the allure of the title of this book, *Significant Others: Creativity and Intimate Partnership*, and my early readings of the different chapters within it helped to prepare me for a great deal of the thinking and doing of my writing practices at this time. Whilst the notion of 'significance' which energises the book's title tends to reside within practices of representation and discursive construction, I have nurtured a knowing, from my reading of the various chapters within the book, over a number of years, of the intra-active intensities and dimensional multiplicities that energise and animate the embodiments and complexities of human and posthuman spatio-temporal relationality.

Examples of this can be drawn from almost all these chapters clearly exemplifying the tension, instability and, yes, certain forms of madness that can be seen to exist in these relationalities, within the intense frisson and seething creative exchanges of each 'intimate partnership'. These examples can help to bring to life the constant rhythms of representation and reality, materiality and discourse in the relational spaces which they create through their description. It is within the vivid play between these exposed elements that the immanence of life is to be found and the deconstructive force that challenges these mind-matter Cartesian forms is at its most energetic.

So, for example, the bride's parent's description of the marriage of Kahlo and Riviera in 1929 as being 'between an elephant and a dove' (ibid.: 119), the tense and complex nature of political life in Mexico at that time, the different working practices of both artists, the nature of gender relations and the intensities of their social, political and cultural relationalities, makes it possible, even necessary, to have a sense of the significance of their 'partnership' that can only be emergent from the deeply entangled imbrication of its material substantiality and its many discursive constructions that work to describe and embody it in both time and space.

I already knew that Max Ernst and Leonora Carrington had spent time in Cornwall with friends and various members of the Surrealist movement for a short period immediately prior to the onset of the Second World War. As Susan Suleiman says in her contribution to the *Significant Others* book, 'We are in June 1937, the civil war is raging in Spain and a sense of impending catastrophe hangs over the rest of Europe.' Of the love between Ernst and Carrington she says it was 'mad love . . . tempestuous, irresistible, sweeping all obstacles before it, a melding of souls and minds as well as bodies' (ibid.: 97). Within these tumultuous settings their relationship veers wildly with the tides of war and their own instabilities; there are affairs, seemingly irrational bouts of travelling and prolonged periods of grief and separation but all the time 'he continues to work on his paintings of her, and she continues to write about him and to paint pictures like the ones she did when they were together' (ibid.: 99). It is a relationality that fuelled its own mad energies and that produced many reminiscences and much writing and painting of the highest creative quality: the 'Bird Superior' and the 'Bride of the Wind' were an 'intimate partnership' that together produced a creative body of work that is unlikely to have been surpassed if their long, stuttering and passionate affair had not come to be in the intra-acting circumstances of the space and time in which they both lived and that their living actively helped to create.

In a recent email to Jonathan I offered a personal and deeply ontologically grounded sense of how I see collaborative writing working in its most vibrant, visceral and creative form. In studying and then drawing upon Deleuze and Guattari's work on 'minor literatures' (1986) and which I have developed in another plateau of this book, I have tapped in to a wellspring that is fuelling my writing energies in ways that I am still not fully conscious of and that are becoming manifest in many streams, tributaries and capillary veins that surprise and excite me as I become more and more aware of their directions, flows and intensities. I write more about this in this other plateau, likening the constantly changing transmutational energies of the rips, currents, eddies, flows and tides of the sea to the flux and creativity that always seems to be the becoming of (collaborative) writing as creative practice and method of inquiry.

On 8 January 2015 I wrote on the contents page of my copy of Deleuze and Guattari's book on writing minor literatures:

> I am getting my head around this: I am so magnetically drawn to the idea, the poetics and the practices of minor literature: it is where I always have been. I never studied English grammar, no-one told me about meter, or iambic pentameters or rhyming couplets – I just wrote – love letters to Alice Carpenter, newsletters to my Mum and Dad, great newsy philosoph- ical letters to Danny and then stuff and more stuff in my diaries – diaries which now at the age of 69 I would like to do something with but don't know how.

This is the kind of writing that synergistically both fuels and creates this madness as methodology. This is the kind of writing that, when left to my own whims and undisciplined devices, I have always done and this is the kind of writing that I (like to) do now, it is the kind of writing to which I am committed and it is the kind of writing that I am ontologically disposed to engaging in within these inquiries and experimentations and which is at the moment firing me up to write what I hope will be the becoming of this book. In this respect I see the best and most creative forms of collaborative writing also coming alive and working in these experimental and creative ways and so I said to Jonathan on 20 August 2015:

Our writing comes alive when it is in and of immanence; when its processes are immanent, when the emergences of the writings both shine through, from and are in the animation of the crystalline presence of multiplicities. At least for the self that I am calling 'me' at the moment, the writing is about the *this* of *thisness*, it is about the creation of those movements and moments of haecceity where the writing does, where it acts and where it lives in the fragility of its creation and its effect: the rhythm between these two is always immanent, it always diffracts, it cannot survive on reflexivity alone, this is the 'co' of the labour we do, this is what makes it work, this, for this 'me', is collaboration.

This co/labour/ation is relational and it is posthuman and in being so, becoming so, it embraces and lives with the human, it is not anti it, in its *withness* it simply goes beyond it. Our struggle with the 'auto' of autoethnography has been our collaborative struggle with collaborative writing and our embodied and discursively constructed identifications with it, both of which are not separately identifiable but which are deeply imbricated in the intensive multiplicities of their entanglements. This is the immanence of our work, our co/labour/ation, this is where it lives, as a minor literature, stuttering within, around and about the major literatures which will always attempt to gobble it up in the conveniences of discourse and models of practice, taking it on, re-forming it, asking questions of it, troubling it and so on.

In working with and from Laurel Richardson's hugely influential claim that writing is, or at least can be, a method of inquiry, it became a part of the logic and the narrative of my early work with Jonathan Wyatt that the collaborative writing with which we were engaged in our so-called 'between-the-twos' and with the work we were increasingly engaging with others was collaborative writing as a method inquiry. Something in the processual flows and the rhythmic play of this emergent work began to lean more and more heavily upon an increasingly incessant creation of concepts as events and in using our theorising *as* practice, always in the play between discourse, materiality and the emergence of a tentative associational and increasingly radical form of empiricism. Such an approach offers inquiry into the conceptual, affective and ethical sensitivities that are opened up within the constantly differentiating relational spaces that emerge when engaging in collaborative writing.

In exploring the human and posthuman dimensions of writing (auto)ethnographically and collaboratively for a period of over ten years, the remaining section of this plateau will further examine entanglements between and within the representational discourses and materialities that are constitutive of, creative within and responsible for the activation and animation of these collaborative practices.

How else can one write but of those things which one doesn't know, or knows badly? It is precisely there that we imagine having something to say. We write only at the frontiers of our knowledge, at the border which separates our knowledge from our ignorance and transforms the one into the other.

> Only in this manner are we resolved to write. To satisfy ignorance is to put off writing until tomorrow – or rather, to make it impossible. Perhaps writing has a relation to silence altogether more threatening than it is supposed to entertain with death.
>
> *Deleuze and Guattari, 2004: xx*

Whilst there might be evidence to suggest that collaborative practices are increasingly expected and encouraged within social scientific and qualitative inquiry (Gingras, 2002; Gale and Wyatt, 2014; Wyatt and Gale, 2013), substantial questions need to be asked about the nature of these practices and how they can be created and problematised. An important way in which this can be carried out is through an engagement with the entanglements between and within the representational discourses and materialities that are constitutive of, creative within and responsible for the activation and animation of these practices. A consideration of the constant play in collaborative practices generally, between and within 'concept, affect and percept' (Deleuze and Guattari, 1994: 163), is a necessary condition of critically engaging with such forms of newly emergent writing as well as in perpetuating future creative pedagogic and inquiry-based practices.

The existence of collaborative writing as method of inquiry and pedagogic practice is currently unusual, unexpected and largely unwritten. So, for example, doctoral research and writing, particularly within the Humanities and the Social Sciences, is, with rare exceptions (see, for example, Gale and Wyatt, 2008c), a solitary practice and, in the USA and possibly elsewhere, so-called single-authored work is required and collaborative work discouraged for tenure. Further, there is a sense in which it could be argued that, collectively, academic discourses construct collaboratively written work as somehow seamless and, as has been suggested:

> the joint-authored work written as if from nowhere in the first person plural, with apparently no 'gaps' between its disembodied and immaterial authors, and with assumed theoretical understandings of what it means to be a 'single' author—an 'individual'—and, in turn, what it means to be two or more authors.
>
> *Wyatt and Gale, 2013: 345*

The challenge to the creation of such (non) space provides the impetus for the inquiry-based tenor and intentions of collaborative inquiry-based methodologies generally. Such a challenge is initially charged by Deleuze and Guattari's claim that concepts always need to be created and, in so doing, they exist as events. Following Nietzsche, they argue that this creation of concepts involves not simply accepting concepts as they are, refining them or tidying them up but, rather, through what could be referred to in Nietzschean terms as a methodology of mistrust, of actually making them, creating them, presenting them and making them convincing.

Deleuze and Guattari employ and direct this challenge to the establishment and foundation of categories of difference and their setting up of the presence and differentiating practice of 'becoming' (1987). In this respect, therefore, 'collabora-tion', 'collaborative writing' and 'collaborative writing as a method of inquiry' exist within the play of processes of conceptualisation and contextualisation as concepts as events. So Deleuze and Guattari bring concepts as events into play by using conceptualisation and theorising *as* practices and, as mentioned elsewhere in this book, they describe this active process as one of 'plugging in', whereby writing, perhaps more specifically within this context, writing with concepts, as an active creative process. In this vein, Jackson and Mazzei offer the following description of their collaborative writing practices and methods of inquiry:

> We were confronted with multiple texts . . . interview data, tomes of theory, conventional qualitative research methods book that we were working against, things we had previously written, traces of data, reviewer comments and so on, *ad infinitum.* That is we had a sense of the ceaseless variations possible in having co-authored texts that relied on a plugging in of ideas, fragments, theory, selves, sensations. And so we moved to engage plugging in as a *process* rather than a *concept*, something we could put to work.
>
> *2012: 1*

It will be of value to consider the ways in which conceptualisations of collaborative processes and practices can be theorised, used and 'plugged in'. Such an approach can be used to provide a basis for suggesting ways in which their future conceptualisation and activation can be animated within what Barad (2007) has referred to as the 'entanglements' existing between and within human and posthuman dimensions of such practices. Working within and at the same time performing these 'entanglements' brings into affective and ethical existence questions that have been asked before of the ontological complexities of collaborative writing: 'Does this matter? What is this materiality we share? How do I live within the shifting skein of our spatial collaboration and co-existence? How does this connect with my other worlds?' (Gale et al., 2012b: 165)

Between-the-two: between the many?

Addressing questions of this kind not only brings to the fore many ethical and affective considerations of what might be entailed by writing in collaborative ways but also tasks the collaborative writing practitioner to mobilise the conceptual dimensions of such practices and to work with the complex matrices that bring these dimensional considerations together. Collaborative writing involves collaboration with multiple human and nonhuman bodies always in affective play, one with the other. In an interview with Claire Parnet, one of his former students, Deleuze talked about working with Guattari:

> We were only two, but what was important for us was less our working together than this strange fact of working between the two of us. We stopped

being 'author'. And these 'between- the-two's' referred back to other people, who were different on one side from on the other. The desert expanded, but in so doing became more populous. This had nothing to do with a school, with processes of recognition, but much to do with encounters. And all of these stories of becomings, of nuptials against nature, of a-parallel evolution, of bilingualism, of theft of thoughts, were what I had with Felix. I stole Felix and I hope he did the same for me. You know how we work – I repeat it because it seems to be important – we do not work together, we work between the two.

Deleuze and Parnet, 2002: 17

The significance of Deleuze's description of the ambivalences and indeterminacies of his positional stance in relation to his collaborative work with Felix Guattari cannot be underestimated and is central to the conceptualisation of collaborative writing that I am offering here. Their engagement with the concept of 'faciality' (Deleuze and Guattari, 1987: 167–192) and applied here in the plateau of this book dealing with the conceptualisation of madness as process offers a powerful exemplification of the kinds of intensification and potentiation that the intra-acting becoming of two seemingly different bodies can emerge. 'Faciality' can be understood as the point of intersection of two axes, signification and subjectification, described by Deleuze and Guattari as 'the *white wall/black hole* system' (ibid.: 167), the former being the surface from which signs are projected through reflection and the latter being the unknown aspect of the face in which the intensity and potential of affect resides. Elsewhere Deleuze (2005) talks of how the device of the cinematic close-up brings the intersection of these two aspects of 'faciality' together. The history of the collaborative becoming of Deleuze and Guattari has elements of the close-up which offers further exemplification of the intensity of their coming together, what Deleuze describes as their 'between-the-two's' (Deleuze and Parnet, 2002: 17). Of this he says,

Felix was working on black holes; this astronomical idea fascinated him. The black hole is what captures you and does not let you get out. How do you get out of a black hole? How do you transmit signals from the bottom of a black hole? I was working, rather, on a white wall: what is a white wall, a screen, how do you plane down the wall and make a line of flight pass? We had not brought the two ideas together, but we noticed that each was tending of its own accord towards the other, to produce something which, indeed, was neither in the one or the other.

Ibid.

What emerges in and from this 'between-the-two' is, for Deleuze, 'a multiplicity with at least three dimensions, astronomical, aesthetic, political' (ibid.: 18). It was not planned, it is not representational and it offers a deterritorialisation, a line of flight from what was there before, an entrapment, a fixity in the substantive politics of being. So, as Deleuze describes, the collaborative writing practices of Deleuze and Guattari were creative, it produced ideas that were not there before, the emergence of an assemblage potent and intense with heterogeneity and contingency, in his words, 'we don't work together, we work between the two' (ibid.: 17).

And so, in my own early collaborative work with Jonathan Wyatt, the conceptualisation of 'between-the-two' became a *leitmotif* for the emergence and transmutational becoming of our collaborative practice, providing the central theme and title of our collaboratively written doctoral thesis and our first published book (Gale and Wyatt, 2008c, 2009). Also, and in conjunction with this Deleuzian mode of thought and practice, we therefore began to build upon Richardson's (Richardson and St Pierre, 2005) highly influential claims for 'writing as a method of inquiry' and to begin to posit, what we tentatively at first began to conceptualise as, 'collaborative writing as a method of inquiry' (ibid.).

We talked of our collaborative practices at the time in the following way:

> We have grown into this writing. Increasingly we have found that our writing is both a method of inquiry (Richardson and St Pierre, 2005) where, as we write between-the-two's, we discover and construct new meanings and sensitivities, and a lived, embodied experience: writing becomes us.
>
> *Gale and Wyatt, 2010: 5*

Reading these words over six years later and considering their weight in terms of the representations of collaborative practices that I am attempting to offer in this plateau encourages me to consider how significant posthuman modes of thought and practices were, at that time, in relation to the emergence of the conceptualisation of collaborative writing as creative practice being offered here. 'Between-the-two' lives then and now, as mode of practice, activates and animates it: it makes it work and brings it to life. Whilst our engagement with this early writing, greatly influenced by that of Deleuze and Guattari, was using a phrase highly suggestive of the 'betweens' and 'amongs' to be found in the use of the prefix 'inter' and the relationality of 'interaction', what in fact we were beginning to formulate and work with at this time was a mode of theorising and practice much more akin to working with the 'inside', 'within', 'interior' and 'during' to be found in Barad's (2007) more recent and highly important use of the prefix 'intra' and the relationality of 'intra-action'. The shift of attention and emphasis we were trying to make at that time, away from the extensive (inter) relationality of bodies, *qua* categories of difference, towards the intensive (intra-) relationality of bodies in terms of materiality and discourses, *qua* differentiation, remains a major energising force of the theorising *as* practice of collaborative writing that I am offering here. The play within concept, affect and percept that such collaborative practices entail seems to generate relationalities within assemblages.

> It is as if the extensive frontiers of our bodies, matter as skin and flesh, threaten to dissolve as the flows and intensities of performing ourselves through these

writings wash around us. These intensities that come and go, that inspire and expire, that melt inside and outside, become the multiplicities and connections of our performative selves. In this flux I sense our beliefs, our values, our emotions intermingling: I feel warmth in the folded spaces that we create.

Gale et al., 2012b: 166

When we referred, at this time, to working on a 'molecular level' with a Deleuzian 'logic of sense' (Gale and Wyatt, 2010: 5), we were anticipating the ways in which the theory and practice of collaborative writing can now be conceptualised as a posthuman mode of practice and method of inquiry; what St Pierre (2011) aptly refers to as 'post qualitative research'. Working within and actually creating posthuman relationalities of space and time has the tendency to offer greater complexity and richness to the ways in which collaborative writing might be conceptualised as both pedagogic practice and method of inquiry. Within such shifting contexts of plurality, contingency and heterogeneity it no longer seems appropriate or sufficient to be working within the limits of sociological, biological and psychological constructions of the 'individual' and the 'group', 'male'/'female', 'agency'/'structure' and other binary framings of this kind. Through the use of posthuman lenses, these binary constructions of difference appear to offer somewhat simplistic, rather convenient and ultimately highly generalised characterisations of the complexity of Barad's 'entanglements' of materiality and discourse. At this point it seems apposite to question the structuring implications of talking of these 'between the two's'. Surfing the waves of these posthuman forms of theorisings leads me to making sense of the multiple, of deep complexity and of intensity with all its potential in ways that disallows the adequacy of 'between the two'. So whilst we still, perhaps less frequently, use this term to describe relationality, it feels that it is becoming more of a convenience and less of an accurate account of the complex multiplicities of what are involved here. Perhaps it is a form of structuring that can now begin to escape from itself.

Therefore, Deleuze and Guattari's bringing together of concept, affect and percept within their active conceptualisation of 'assemblage' provides an excellent basis for extending and intensifying the way in which collaborative writing practices might be understood. Deleuze's use of 'assemblage' is exemplified in the following passage:

It is a multiplicity which is made up of many heterogeneous terms and which establishes liaisons, relations between them, across ages, sexes, and reigns – different natures. Thus, the assemblage's only unity is that of co-functioning: it is a symbiosis, a 'sympathy'. It is never filiations which are important, but alliances, alloys; these are not successions, lines of descent, but contagions, epidemics, the wind. Magicians are well aware of this. An animal is defined less by its genus, its species, its organs, and its functions than by the assemblage into which it enters.

Deleuze and Parnet, 2002: 69

By approaching collaborative practices within the fluid and transmutating context of an assemblage suggests the need to take into consideration not simply the affective and ethical aspects of human engagements and manifestations but also those possibly unrealised posthuman vectors, forces and energies which have remained latent because previous conceptualisations have not brought them into representational space. With Barad we can begin to look at collaborative writing practices within the context of assemblages and as coming to life by working as emergent, (intra-) activating the 'mutual constitution of entangled agencies' (2007: 33). Talking of the materiality of his writing experiences Jonathan says:

> There is more though: I am questioning why it is not only the writing by hand but the setting in which I am writing. I enjoy writing – I am unable to write in any other context, it seems – in 'in-between' places, mostly cafés but also at, say railway stations, airports. These public, in-between places are settings where people are passing through. Here, there is the noise of people talking – the students discussing their music lecture – and there is movement as people arrive and leave; buses pass, babies chatter, milk is being steamed. So I wonder about this need to write in such settings – amongst movement and transience – and think that these features are perhaps echoes of my internal writing world.
>
> *Gale and Wyatt, 2008: 376*

In this respect, agency is not located within the person who 'has it' and 'uses it' in relation to structure, perhaps as an expression of 'individual' will working within the constraints and dynamics of a 'group', rather agency is seen as being distributed in assemblages which exist in intra-acting multiplicities of material and discursive energies and forces. As we have seen, Bennett suggests that we can talk about 'agentic assemblages' (2010: 21) in which capacities and capabilities are not simply located in human bodies but across an 'ontologically heterogeneous field'. In her work she provides simple graphic illustrations of how Deleuzian assemblages might be seen and, in the context of this plateau, how they might be constituted and of how, at least by inference and implication, collaborative (writing) practices might be seen to be animate within them.

As a consequence of thinking about collaborative writing as a method of inquiry in these posthuman ways and of also beginning to enact a new empiricism, that through association and metonymy, causes us to think, feel and perceive collaborative intra-actions very differently, it also becomes necessary to think of 'who' is engaging in these collaborations, how that 'who' is represented and how its materiality can be seen to exist within the multiplicities and becomings of these distributing and highly intensive spaces.

In response to this and within the context of recent collaborative writing activities, the practice involved in conceptualising 'assemblage/ethnography' (Wyatt and Gale: 2013a, 2013b) pays attention to the kinds of posthuman proclivities outlined above. In so doing, such an approach also draws upon the influence of

Foucault and, more recently, Patti Lather in activating material and realist ontological practices that extend beyond the energies and forces of the simply human. The genealogical methodologies of Foucauldian theory and practice argue for the need to 'get free of one self' (1992: 8) as a means of resisting the constraining ethical and affective technologies that discursively situate selves in particular ways. Such a 'getting free of one self' can be seen in relation to the Nietzschean concept of *entstehung*, or emergence, where movement and inquiry shifts from a descent into the body into a confrontation and struggle with new beginnings and with the play of forces that 'always occurs in the interstice' (Rabinow, 1991: 84). In using the work of Nietzsche in this way, Foucault suggests an approach to the self, to subjectivity and, I would argue, to notions of collaboration and collaborative writing that shifts it away from its humanist and phenomenological modes of theorising and practice towards encounters and becomings that pay much closer attention to the influences, energies and forces of material events and circumstance. Lather's (2007) proposal of employing 'getting lost' as a methodological approach within her 'double(d) science' also adds energy to this movement away from a concentration upon essentialist notions of the self as a category of being existing as somehow separate from the differentiating energies of selves always becoming in the entangled play of materiality and discourse. Animating these practices of 'getting free of one self' and of 'getting lost' are crucial to the problematisation of ontology offered earlier in this book. Here Manning's use of Simondon's notion of 'ontogenesis' is taken as a means of describing and bringing to life bodies on the move, bodies in the moment, bodies as worlding and bodies in relational space as becoming other always in the moment of their creation. Massumi's use of the concept of 'immediation' is also extremely useful in this respect as it brings into focus the literal, finite immediacy of change, of always being on the move. The genesis of the onto cannot be encapsulated within its becoming as it is always happening. Massumi talks of these processes in terms of 'wave-like amplification and propagation' rather than in terms of 'point-to-point transmissions' and then asks what happens in these fields of immediacy:

> It seems to me that rather than personally positioning each individual, it braces them into a kind of differential attunement with others. We're all in the event together, but we're in it together differently. We each come with a different set of tendencies, habits and action potentials.
>
> *Massumi, 2015: 115*

Putting these theoretical energies in play in relation to collaborative writing as a method of inquiry inevitably raises further methodological questions regarding the status and potency of the whole autoethnographic agenda that has gained force within most forms of narrative inquiry in recent years. The construction of this important and increasingly significant research genre and methodological form is, however, charged by a particular view of the self that the rhetoric that I put forward in this book is designed to challenge and inquire into. In the highly respectable field of ethnography, stretching back as far as its early twentieth-century anthropological roots, the emergence of autoethnography has offered a sustained challenge to the objective claims of Positivist science and has helped to bring into realisation Nagel's (1986) claim that there can never be a view from nowhere. We are positioned, we have a stance and, to use an appropriate optical metaphor, we therefore look at the world through particular lenses. This is illustrated in the following, well-known and often quoted passage taken from an important early essay by Ellis and Bochner:

> Auto-ethnography is an autobiographical genre of writing and research that displays multiple layers of consciousness, connecting the personal to the cultural. Back and forth auto-ethnographers gaze, first through an ethnographic wide angle lens, focussing outward on social and cultural aspects of their personal experience; then they look inward exposing a vulnerable self that is moved by and may move through, refract, and resist cultural interpretations.
>
> *2000: 739.*

Such an approach is emphasised by Ellis (2004) herself in the positing of the 'ethnographic I' in her humanistic and highly personal account of what she presents as an autoethnographic methodology. In this work she effectively blurs genres moving from the 'fictional' to the 'factual', and in so doing always places the 'I' and the 'eye' of the individual observer, the 'auto', the prefix of her approach, at the centre of her methodological stage. Whilst such an approach has been highly effective in shifting the Positivism of ethnography into the post-Positivism of autoethnography, in so doing it has also helped in the manufacture of a metaphysics of being that serves to establish and sustain the ascendancy of the human over the physical and the materialities, which, by its very positioning, it attempts to order. Therefore, in proposing 'assemblage/ethnography', Jonathan and I have used the work of Deleuze and other posthuman and geo-philosophical theorists to challenge this metaphysics and to employ notions of 'becoming' and 'multiplicity' as a means of mobilising and making animate the diverse particularities that exist in what Bennett refers to as 'the agency of assemblages' (2010: 20):

> Nothing is fixed, there is always change. With assemblage/ethnography . . . there is a living with the intensities and senses of selves and others that in multiple and diverse settings of time and place coalesce and conflict, confer and differ, and sometimes reflex and also, inevitably diffract. In the not yet known of these always collaborating diffractive possibilities there will be a subsequent and creative interplay of matter and discourse, body and words.
>
> *Wyatt and Gale, 2013a: 144*

Following from this our conceptualisation of collaborative writing practices has to be seen in relation to ethical and affective practices that are not designed, through moral coding and rule making, to establish difference between, rather to bring to the fore, through a realisation, a making real, of the co-implication of all subjects, human and nonhuman, that it is necessary to work beyond the limitations of the individual and the group, to take lines of flight and to always think, feel and act in multiple ways, allowing difference to always precede forms of identification and representation. It is in this way that we can conceive of collaborative writing as a relational, ethical and affective practice that functions in the posthuman, on a plane of immanence (Wyatt et al., 2011: 111) and of a form that is always in play with the infinite vicissitudes of space and time. In this respect the ontology of 'between the two' will always be troubled by the 'differential attunements' and 'immediations' that exemplify its always ongoing 'ontogenesis'.

Collaborative writing and conceptualisation

As previously asserted, central to the philosophy of Deleuze and Guattari and how it is related to collaborative writing is a sense of 'becoming', where talk is of the process of creating concepts in ways which are fluid and open, where closure and working with a fixed approach to meaning and knowledge are to be avoided. In such an approach difference and 'differential attunement' precedes definition, identification and representation and is not locked into binary constructions of difference that follow from a Kantian philosophy of establishing noumenal categories of things-in-themselves that somehow have an existence that is independent of the mind. For example, the categorical imperative to follow rules that is incumbent within Kant's deontological approach to morality would be seen as judgemental and limiting within the affective and ethical sensitivities of the kinds of collaborative writing approaches of the kind being proposed here.

From this it is clear that approaches to collaborative writing as method of inquiry always need to encourage the taking of a diffractive stance in relation to attempts at establishing or founding representations that might precede or hamper creative processes of becoming. 'Concepts are not waiting for us ready-made, like heavenly bodies' they exist in their ongoing creation. Concepts are always in encounter in their existence as events. As Massumi says, 'A concept is a brick. It can be used to build the courthouse of reason. Or it can be thrown through the window' (1987: xii). Collaborative writing practices can be used in similar ways to nurture and promote affective and ethically sensitive engagements in processes of active, fluid, experimental and transgressive conceptualisation. Having an idea of something, raising questions, taking nothing for granted, means working with and within the not yet known, linking such ideas with affect and percept in an ongoing creative and collaborative method of inquiry. Within such a mode of inquiry processes of concept making, therefore, involve conceptualising and theorising *as* practice. Within practices of conceptualisation, putting concepts to work, contextualisation *as* practice, if you will, is also very important. Using the curious and troubling query 'What if . . .?' has the tendency to generate innovative and invigorating approaches to work by placing such ideas within diverse spatial and temporal settings as a means of setting up further and future transformative and transgressive ways of thinking and practising. The practice of 'plugging in' advocated by Deleuze and Guattari (1987: 4) and others involves an active, experimental and ultimately creative mode of practice where concepts as events are actually put to work. 'Writing has nothing to do with signifying. It has to do with surveying, mapping, even realms that are yet to come' (ibid.). This involves a formative, geo-philosophical approach which always emphasises process over product and which promotes an ethical and aesthetic sensitivity over a technical rational formalism. When Nietzsche says that 'we must no longer accept concepts as a gift . . . but first make and create them, present them and make them convincing' (1968: 409), he is talking about worlding, about putting them to work and about making them do something.

In building conceptualisations and attempting to invoke a methodology of madness, Nietzsche's persuasive stance, which encourages a mistrust of concepts, has the potential to enliven collaborative approaches to writing as a method of inquiry. By looking at and using concepts in such writing practices within a fluidity of process that challenges and reconceptualises fixities of product, the pedagogical and inquiry-based implications of such practices become substantial. Concepts as events exist in multiplicity, are always becoming and are both part and generative of new and active assemblages of practice. In this respect concept forming through collaborative writing practice helps to present a radically new form of difference and differentiation in the empirical world. Such an approach offers substantive challenge to the established foundational strategies of a great deal of Positivist and post-Positivist qualitative research because it can be used to promote and promulgate an altogether more radical empiricism than those which rely on the abject figuration that in the qualitative 'data' is some *thing* or some collection of things which can be somehow *collected* and then in a later time and space be *analysed*, interpreted and then used to represent and identify. The discourse of data collection and analysis that dominates the material practices of much of contemporary post-Positivist research does much to limit the effectiveness of that research.

In his re-working of Hume's approach to empiricism, Deleuze, in his early work *Empiricism and Subjectivity* (1991), argues that empiricism can be metonymic and associational and not about these forms of collection and analysis which can be used as a means of providing findings, evidence and interpretations in relation to particular truth claims. Rather, the associational approach that Deleuze recognised in his monograph that largely focuses upon the work of Hume avoids the traditional analytical approaches of discovery, condensation and analysis and instead promotes approaches of displacement and diffraction that invariably involves processes of articulation, of making connections, links and associations. In this sense, therefore, the notion that 'data' can somehow make claims to capturing the moment and that can be used in some way as providing 'evidence' of something that is relational in simple cause and effects terms and used to provide the basis for what might be said or done in the future is placed under erasure. In Borges' world of Tlon, the people there do not conceive that the spatial persists in time and so for them, '(t)he perception of a cloud of smoke on the horizon and then of the burning field and then of the half-extinguished cigarette that produce the blaze is considered an example of association of ideas' (Borges, 1970: 34). Traditional cause and effect approaches can be destabilised and continually threatened by practices of inquiry that always encourage the taking of lines of flight, of making associational linkages, of then seeing them dissolve as new and exciting conceptualisations emerge and take shape. The inter-acting and intra-acting possibilities of such a potentially zigzagging approach to inquiry are often deeply imbricated within the to-ing and the fro-ing of participants in the collaborative writing research process.

In a related vein, Deleuze's work in conceptualising the 'fold' (1993) similarly relates to the processes of flux and transmutation, of always 'becoming' that might be visible in the articulations of these collaborating practices. He talks of the way in which

> [t]he organism is defined by its ability to fold its own parts and to unfold them, not to infinity, but to a degree of development assigned to each species. Thus an organism is enveloped by organism, one within another (interlocking of germinal matter), like Russian dolls.
>
> *ibid.: 8*

In these respects it is possible to think of engagements with collaborative writing practice as involving the constant play between endogamous 'foldings in' and exo-gamous 'unfoldings' where, in the writing, revelation and emergence share an alchemic dance with differentiation and diffraction, always making the familiar strange. Elsewhere I have described these processes using the example of my mother as I remember her working in our little kitchen many years ago:

> I share a memory of my mother with her mixing bowl, her sleeves rolled up and her arms bare, gradually adding flour, butter, water and other ingredients in a growing and sweet smelling cake mixture; I remember that she used to talk about 'folding in the butter' and it is this image of folding in that begins to allow the idea of the fold to unfold for me. As the butter is folded in, from the outside so to speak, some richness, some new quality begins to emerge in the mix, something is unfolding. In the work of Deleuze (1993), the fold relates to processes of individuation, of literal becoming; the process of 'folding in' adds richness, multiple layers and intensification, the process of unfolding opens out, reveals and makes the familiar strange. In this respect, the unfolding can be seen not only as an emergence, but also as a synthesis or a synthetical moment, part of a process, where, as new elements are added or folded in, new relationships and connections are made or folded out.
>
> *Gale, 2007: 477*

Deleuze describes the fluidity and transmutational nature of these rhythmic processes as the constant play between decreasing and increasing, reduction and growth: 'enveloping-developing, involution-devolution' (ibid.). As with the Deleuzian figure of the rhizome, there are a multiplicity of interconnected shoots going off in all directions; as it grows, folding in and unfolding occurs, an assemblage of ideas, data, impressions, interpretations and notes connect in pluralistic ways which defy totalising exposition. Collaborative writing as a method of inquiry within these rhizomatic flows and lines of flight reflects a sense of becoming, of changing interpretations and of a qualitative flexing where the process of the research not only provides insights and critical judgements but also moments of evocation, excitement, response and drama.

So in these newly emergent collaborative writing practices, by engaging in a Nietzschean methodology of mistrusting concepts, I am also proposing, paradoxically perhaps, an ethics of sensitivity and care. 'What we are interested in, you see, are modes of individuation beyond those of things, persons, or subjects: the individuation, say, of a time of day, of a region, a climate, a river or a wind, of an event' (Deleuze, 1995: 26). By continually placing the practices of collaborative writing as a method of inquiry into these planes of immanence where concepts, affects and percepts are always in play one with another, where multiplicities, lines of flight, contingencies and heterogeneities are always made present through the practices of writing, as collaborative writers we are actively involved in 'defining writing as always the measure of something else' (Deleuze and Guattari, 1988: 4). In this methodology as madness, as newly emergent collaborative liaisons are broken and made, these nomadic inquiries into the not yet known involve ethically informed cartographies of practice that carry with them substantive shared responsibilities for all the agentic elements of the assemblage. The singular particularity of each concept as event will reverberate through networks, connections and matrices, constantly setting up further differentiations and practice possibilities. The energies of these vectors, forces and lines of flight set up cartographies of practice that themselves imbricate these new forms of empiricism.

Collaborative writing and empiricism

In *Empiricism and Subjectivity*, Deleuze provides a very telling quotation from Hume when he says, 'Men [*sic*] are mightily addicted to general rules . . . Where cases are similar in many circumstances, we are apt to put them on the same footing, without considering, that they differ in the most material circumstances' (1991: 55). There is a strong and highly Positivistic sense in which this addiction to general rules involves what Deleuze and Guattari refer to the practice of 'tracing', which they are at pains to distinguish from cartography or 'mapping'. They suggest, perhaps somewhat ironically, that 'accountancy and bureaucracy proceed by tracing' (1987: 15) and, in many respects the empirical approaches of Positivist science and, indeed, much of post-Positivist social science can be described in similar ways. According to Deleuze and Guattari, 'tracing' has a tendency to resist the vagaries of trans-formational possibilities. So, in a great deal of qualitative research, under the guise of the discursively accepted, binary construction of the 'data collection and analysis' signifier, the empirical use of quantifying strategies of coding, in order to structure, thematise and generally organise 'data', is common, generally acceptable and wholly resistant to creative diffractive practices. Cartographic practices, however, can be used to bring into creative operation forms of empiricism that can pay attention to the particular and that resist attempts to calcify events within carefully drawn pre-existent modes and categories of practice. In an example that could be drawn from a number of contemporary education contexts Deleuze and Guattari offer the following:

> In the case of the child, gestural, mimetic, ludic, and other semiotic systems regain their freedom and extricate themselves from the 'tracing', that is, from the dominant competence of the teacher's language – a microscopic event upsets the local balance of power.
>
> *1987: 15*

In this new empiricism there is a resistance to and a mistrust of the molar coding of the moral, which attempts to fix inquiry-based practices within the defined parameters and rigidities of Kantian deontology. In this respect, the ubiquitous use of the ethics protocol in a great deal of formalistic research activity and report writing, by its very presence, presents tendencies of resistance to future diffractive possibilities for the research practitioner who is institutionally governed by its strictures and parameters. Rather, within the context of a 'creative evolution' (Bergson, 1911) of such inquiry-based practices, there is an encouragement of the emergence of molecular differentiations which are based upon ethical sensitivities that are always attuned to the possibilities of transmutation, fluidity and flux. Deleuze offers what he refers to as 'the secret of empiricism' when he says:

> Empiricism . . . undertakes the most insane creation of concepts ever seen or heard. Empiricism is a mysticism and a mathematicism of concepts, but precisely one which treats the concept as object of an encounter, as here-and-now, or rather . . . from which emerge inexhaustibly ever new, differently distributed 'heres' and 'nows'. Only an empiricist could say concepts are indeed things, but things in their free and wild state, beyond 'anthropological predicates'. I make, remake and unmake my concepts along a moving horizon, from an always decentred centre, from an always displaced periphery which repeats and differenciates them.
>
> *2004c: xix*

The subtle and nuanced energies of the kinds of discussions and exchanges that can take place within collaborative writing practices always have the potential to produce ethically charged concepts as events which themselves work to produce the molecular energies of inquiry. The constant shifting of intensities, the fluid interplay between concept, affect and percept that this involves is redolent of what Davies and Gannon refer to as *mo(ve)ment*, a term that I have used frequently in this book to animate thought in active and creative ways. They use the elision of this complex term to describe the spatial and temporal transformations that occur within the 'ethical reflexive research practices of collective biography' (2006: x). So the ethically informed processes and practices of collaborative writing as a method of inquiry work in conjunction with 'assemblage/ethnography' to destabilise the molar by paying attention to and incorporating the molecular and intensive practices of new and emergent empiricisms.

As suggested above, these reconfigurations of empiricism that inform the kinds of collaborative writing as method of inquiry that have been discussed in this plateau can be characterised by the metonymic principles of association to be found in the philosophy of Hume and through the articulations of Deleuze in his early monograph *Empiricism and Subjectivity*. In this respect, Deleuze talks of an associational empiricism that involves 'habits of thought, everyday notions of good sense, current ideas, and complexes of ideas which correspond to the most general and most constant needs common to all minds and all languages' (1991: 103). Difference precedes fleeting thoughts, loose conversations and hitherto unnoticed gestures; their connections can be observed and be brought together in what Bennett describes as 'agentic assemblages' (2010: 20). These observations of what Stewart (2007) describes as 'ordinary affects' might make connections, they might offer what Deleuze (1988) describes as 'haecceities' and contribute to the shifting fluidity of 'bodies-without-organs' (ibid.). As Stewart points out in the introduction to her book,

> *Ordinary Affects* is an experiment, not a judgment. Committed not to the demystification and uncovered truths that support a well-known picture of the world, but rather to speculation, curiosity, and the concrete, it tries to provoke attention to the forces that come into view as habit or shock, resonance or impact. *Something* throws itself together in a moment as an event and a sensation; a something both animated and inhabitable.
>
> *Ibid.: 1*

I wish to emphasise the previous point that this form of empiricism is not one that is about a Positivistic quantifiable collection of data. Nor is it about a post-Positivistic qualitative analysis of that which has been collected. The approach being offered here suggests that the orthodox binary convention of data collection and analysis is a methodological artifice that conveniently homogenises and effectively disguises the messy complexities of collaborative writing as a method of inquiry and, more generally, of doing research in the posthuman. A new empiricism does not seek to capture through collection and analysis, rather it attempts to offer, through engagements with the perpetuities of emergence, a sense of the processual heterogeneities and contingencies that are always present in fleeting moments of transmutation and flux. In response to this, in my own work, I have described the possibilities and practices of empiricism as 'vignetting' which is discussed in some detail in another plateau in this book. In short this practice can be understood in its literal or natural form as something that is written on a vine leaf. In this sense it is temporary, its capture is momentary, its force is in an instant; connections and associations are made as all the while the vine leaf, in its physical form, might be withering and fading away. In the assemblage of collaborative writing, 'vignetting' offers a methodological form in which the everyday is brought to life, shared, connected with, passed on and given further life and vitality through multiple metonymic intra-connections.

An example of this can be found, perhaps, in the practice of 'collaborative writing in real time' engaged in by Speedy and colleagues (Gale et al., 2012a) and which is used to provide a sense of the immediacy of movement in the moment that gives energy and intensive potentiality to the emergence of a new empiricism. Also Speedy and colleagues have developed a methodology which they refer to as 'riffing off' to describe the ways in which collaborative writing uses associational practices in these new empiricist ways. Of their work together Speedy says, 'One striking effect of this experiment was the cumulative sense of continuous cycle, not only of inner and outer worlds but of both the mundane and profound that makes up our everyday/extraordinary lives' (Speedy and Wyatt, 2014: 24). In its original form, 'riffing off' involves groups of jazz or blues musicians improvising, perhaps on an original theme, and allowing the solo contributions of the group members to inspire further extemporisations or experimental lines of flight which then, in turn, open up new forms, offer new interpretations and add multiple layers to the emergence of the performance.

These nascent collaborative writing methodologies work creatively and productively to blur the certainties and findings to be found within the orthodoxies and customs of quantitative and a good deal of qualitative inquiry. The urgency to be able to work with the ontological realities and the languages that might be used to express and invent them is extreme. The beauty of the following quotation from Virginia Woolf also illustrates the complexity of the challenge facing the kinds of research that are being proposed and tentatively engaged with here:

> It was as if it became altogether intelligible; I had a feeling of transparency in words when they cease to be words and become so intensified that one seems to experience them; to foretell them as if they developed what one is already feeling . . . no one could have understood from what I said the queer feeling I had in the hot grass, that poetry was coming true. Nor does that give the feeling. It matches what I have sometimes felt when I write. The pen gets on the scent.
>
> *Woolf, 1985: 93*

Therefore, within this plateau, in thinking with singularity and subjectivity and their related practices as events and in using theorisation and the creation of concepts as a mode of practice, I want to argue for a form of collaborative writing as method of inquiry that can be effectively used to engage with the constant play that enlivens the always changing space that continually comes alive in the relations that exist between discourse and materiality. Such an approach to inquiry is one that troubles the so-called 'gap' between theory and practice and, as has been suggested elsewhere in these pages, offers a theorising *as* practice as a means by which metonymic and associational research practices creatively promote data emergence in fluid, experimental and constantly transmutational forms.

If, as I am arguing, there is a sense in which madness as methodology can take a collaborative form, then it is constituted as a form of writing as method that celebrates living and always inquiring into the not yet known. It can be understood as providing and engaging in strategies for performing and dissolving selves as a constructive ethics and aesthetics for affective research and investigation. The madness in such collaborative methodological intent can also be to perform notions of imagined and corporeal collective selves in an attempt to open up multiple spaces of creative inquiry. Such an approach is further offered as a means of challenging the naturalising intent of those hegemonies of humanistic and phenomenological perspectives that act to create autonomous notions of the self that are sustained and perpetuated through prevailing discourses that always operate in resistance to reflexive intent and imaginally driven lines of flight and escape.

In the following plateau, which deals with the notion of friendship and attempts to displace that notion from an explicit and exclusively humancentric and phenomenologically oriented axis, I have drawn upon Deleuze and Guattari's idea of the 'conceptual persona' (1994: 61–85) as a means of offering new forms of sense making in relation to how friendship might be more fully understood and engaged with. In many respects the idea of 'conceptual persona' has some relevance to the foregoing discussion about collaboration and perhaps in further promoting an inquiry into collaboration with who or what. I will briefly touch upon this here as a means of bringing this plateau into a new and slightly differently inflected beginning and ending.

As quoted in more detail in the following plateau, Deleuze and Guattari conceptualise 'conceptual persona' in the following way, 'I am no longer myself but thought's aptitude for finding itself and spreading across a plane that passes through me at several places' (1994: 64). Although sometimes disputed, *What is Philosophy?* is generally regarded as Deleuze and Guattari's final collaboration, so it is interesting to set this conceptualisation against the opening introductory lines of *A Thousand Plateaus* where they say: 'The two of us wrote *Anti-Oedipus* together. Since each of us was several, there was already quite a crowd' (1987: 3). Here we see another expression of 'conceptual persona' in operation and in each case we are given the opportunity to sense the concept working in multiple ways. I want to set this in play in relation to the concerns of this plateau with collaboration and the subsequent plateau that deals with friendship. The concept and the doing of the concept of 'conceptual persona' troubles those binary constructions of presence/absence, subject/object, real/imagined and so on; those dualisms that frame and institutionalise difference into fixed categories of being, that give us psychology and sociology and somehow think that that is enough in the enabling of comprehension. Although there was clearly a powerful collaborating friendship between Gilles Deleuze and Felix Guattari, it was a relationality that did not begin or end with the palpability of their human bodies. In the introduction to his book on their intersecting lives, Dosse says:

> Four-handed. The work of Gilles Deleuze and Felix Guattari remains an enigma, even today. Who was the author? One or both of them? How could two such different men, with such distinct sensibilities and styles, pursue their intellectual agenda together for more than twenty years (1969–1991)? How could they be so close – yet so distant that they used the formal *vous* to address each (though both used the informal *tu* quite easily with others)? . . . It is often difficult to determine what belongs to whom in their writing, but at the same time . . . both writers maintained their own identity and went in distinctly different directions, even as they collaborated on a common enterprise.
>
> *2010: 1*

The rhetoric of Dosse's questions leads to an engagement with the concept of the 'conceptual persona'. Their writing together is a plane of immanence which is constituted in, through and by the intensities and multiplicities that are present in the contradictions, complexities and compositions that Dosse's questions offer. And of course, the desert is made more populous by the presence of Spinoza, Foucault, Hume, Nietzsche, Lacan and many others: these 'conceptual persona' are also in and constitutive of this plane of immanence and, in its becoming, it would not be what it is without their presence within its processual world making.

I offer this as an exemplification, an example, which, in the words of Massumi, always 'harbours terrible powers of deviation and digression' (2002: 18) and which talks to always shifting conceptualisations of the multiple and always mutating 'conceptual persona' that is the plane of immanence of Deleuze and Guattari's writing. I want this 'example' to offer a new form of sensing in relation to the preceding discussion of collaboration and the following discussion of friendship. This writing about collaboration and collaborative writing, as indeed with the writing about friendship in the following plateau and in engaging with any writing with and about human others, will be troubled by its anthropocentric tendencies and intentions, 'with reason and affect centred on the human and on human modes of thinking, feeling, and being' (Wyatt et al., 2017: 753). However, this madness as methodology sees these tendencies, not in epistemologically grounding terms, and rather as starting points for the making of lines of 'deviation and digression' into domains of processual potentiation and territorialisation that are not yet known.

And so this plateau has hopefully offered a sensing of a (collaborative) madness as methodology which offers and revels in its transgressive engagement with writing and researching in a wide variety of collaborative and performative genres. These could be seen as always working in the temporal and spatial construction of the perpetually contingent and ever incomplete embodiment of the always curious and tantalisingly knowing unknown self. Reading of this plateau is designed to encourage diffractive participation in multiple approaches to the construction and presentation of collaborative and performative writing as a method of inquiry by placing selves always under erasure, in providing methodologies of narrative inquiry that refuse to be categorised or named and that work subversively and creatively in the fractures and crevices of deliriously differentiated space–time territorialisations.

Notes

1 *Don't Look Now*, a film directed by Nicolas Roeg, adapted from a short story by Daphne du Maurier and starring Julie Christie and Donald Sutherland, was released in October 1973.
2 Not long after purchasing the book, mysteriously it disappeared from my bookshelves. I have a history of losing and finding books, records and CDs and, after a number of years of absence, it was such a pleasure to receive a new copy of the book from Katy my eldest daughter who had seen it in a bookshop whilst on her travels in Australia and bought it for me as a Christmas present a few years later.

FRIENDSHIP, MADNESS AND THE POSTHUMAN

[B]ecause the only people for me are the mad ones, the ones who are mad to live, mad to talk, mad to be saved, desirous of everything at the same time, the ones who never yawn or say a commonplace thing but burn, burn, burn like fabulous yellow roman candles exploding like spiders across the stars and in the middle you see the blue centre pop and everyone goes 'Awww!'

Kerouac, 1972: 11

He [Guattari] is an 'intersection' of groups, like a star. Or perhaps I should compare him to the sea, he always seems to be in motion, sparkling with light. He can jump from one activity to another. He doesn't sleep much, he travels, he never stops. He never ceases. He has extraordinary speeds. I am more like the hill: I don't move much, I can't manage projects at once, I obsess over my ideas and the few movements I do have are internal. Together, Felix and I would have made a good Sumo wrestler.

Deleuze, 2007: 237

My friend, colleague and long-standing collaborative writing partner Jonathan Wyatt once said of Jane Speedy and I:

As I watch her now, up there ahead leaning against the café frontage, I reflect that it's her edginess (she refers to herself as 'mad' sometimes; Ken writes about his 'madness' too) that I love, that I've been drawn to all this time, that sense of wildness, her passion, her willingness to live dangerously (as I see it). I trust these experiences of her, and trust her. I find that she cares, for me, for us, for the work (see Acker, Hill and Black, 1994; Deuchar, 2008). I feel a little wary, though. It's because I feel staid beside her, and beside both of them. Beside Jane and Ken I feel, well, a little colorless. A girl I liked once watched me play rugby, a game I've hardly ever played. She told me afterwards that she worried for me because I looked like I might snap. (That rugby game was the end of her interest.) Alongside these two I sometimes feel brittle though I have another knowing, which is that they seem to recognize a *daemon* (Cavarero, 1997/2000) that they appreciate. By definition, I don't quite get what they see, but I trust their knowings.

Gale, Speedy and Wyatt, 2010: 25

In our book *Between the Two* in a chapter that we identified as 'Writing space three: The inhabitants of this book', Jonathan Wyatt and I describe walking up Park Street in Bristol in the rain, heading to a favourite haunt of ours that has retained both its significance and the allure of its comforts for us over a period of ten or more years. The Boston Tea Party is a little café which we described in the book in the following way: 'The lighting is low, indie music emanating from the walls; people are milling, relieved to be dry. They look around. This is familiar territory; they have spent many good times here talking and writing' (Gale and Wyatt, 2009: 25). We used our description of this location as a kind of trope for the development of the main idea informing this chapter, this 'Writing space three', that our writing was made up of numerous 'inhabitants'. We go on in the book to mention many of these; citing names that identify members of our respective families, our many friends and a growing body of theorists, philosophers and writers that were animating our work together at that time. I like this plateau. Now that I read it again, probably for the first time since we wrote it, I realise that I like it. I like its innocence, the story that it tells me of how we were at the time; it is like reading a section of a diary that has been hidden from view. It is deeply imbued with affect and I want to draw into play the effects that are writing me into this here and now space and time in the emergence of my becoming.

In the opening section of this chapter of the book we also refer to Deleuze and his description of his early work with Guattari, likening it to an expanding desert becoming ever more populous. Quoted and used in the previous plateau, the following description has been a constant echo around the corners, corridors and walls of our collaborative practices for all this time:

> We were only two, but what was important for us was less our working together than this strange fact of working between the two of us. We stopped being 'author'. And these 'between-the-two's' referred back to other people, who were different on one side from the other. The desert expanded, but in so doing became more populous. This had nothing to do with a school, with processes of recognition, but much to do with encounters.
>
> *Deleuze and Parnet, 2002: 17*

Whilst we confidently used this reference to help us to talk about what we referred to in this chapter as our 'inhabitants' and in appropriating the term 'between-the-two's', ultimately, as the title of our book, I now recollect having a sense of uneasiness at the time about using the word 'desert' in the development of our thinking. What was Deleuze talking about here? Why desert? Did it have something to do with nomadic inquiry, nomads wandering in the desert? I don't think that we addressed questions of this order at the time and I think it is important to do so now: I feel more at ease about bringing these terms and their associated figurations into play in the emergence of these writings. I want to talk in this plateau, this plateau, this desert perhaps, about people; not simply the 'collaborators' who are cited, somewhat impersonally and obliquely in the previous plateau but about family, friends and the people I read and read about in the dynamics of relational time and space as I conceptualise it now. I continue to enjoy the encounters that the use of 'writing space' in the title of that previous plateau generates; I want to disturb the use there of 'inhabitants' and I want to work with Deleuze's desert and its expanding population in ways that make sense to me here and now in the emergence of this book.

And so I begin by wondering if the word 'inhabitants' works or, more precisely, works in ways that I want it to work with me here and now. At the time it felt OK; no, it felt right, I think we both felt that we wanted to talk about people, people who were inhabiting our space, helping to constitute it in certain ways. As I said about them at the time, '(t)hey give a different, but very profound sense to the notion of "inhabitants"; our "habits" emerge from them, we perform our selves in what we do today in part because of what we have habituated from being with them' (Gale and Wyatt, 2009: 26). It feels to me now that we were not sufficiently open to or critical enough about the ways in which 'habituation' and becoming 'habituated' can be part of a discursive construction of identity, a productive modality that can be seen to resist reflexive engagement with such constructions. The etymology of these words clearly connects them with 'habits'; the behaviours and practices that we engage without thinking about, the things that we do that are often used to characterise us and represent us in particular ways. We find in the originations of the cultural reproduction theorising of Bourdieu (Bourdieu and Passeron, 1990) the use of the term *habitus* to provide energising force to his concept of 'cultural capital', which he uses to describe the normative capabilities of those who attempt to engage with the heterogeneities that social mobility or the institutionalisation of practices might attempt to bring about. 'Having' or not 'having' 'cultural capital' becomes indicative of ability, skills and the agentic possibilities of human development in a world of increasing social change.

The associated practices of 'habituation' and becoming 'habituated' work to essentialise the ability, the willingness and the need to be culturally adaptive in a changing world. In a Foucauldian sense such modalities of habitual practice are simply the micro-political forces of control that are animated through a lack of reflexivity. In such processes of theorising, the individual who possesses and employs 'cultural capital' is the docile body, lacking in reflexivity, who, through a care of the self, is identified through discursive construction and adherence to the dominance and determining forces of the regime of truth. I have a sense that the conversation that I would have with Jonathan today about this usage would be very different to the one that took place on that rainy morning in Bristol back in the late 2000s. Now I understand that habit, custom and traditional authority describe significant powers of affect that somehow were overlooked in my earlier thinking. So, although I said at the time, 'I think that our writing has made me more reflexive about that', it has taken a long time for that reflexivity to impact upon the somewhat benign representation of 'inhabitants' that I offered then. My seething and emerging malevolence now takes me into thinking that any form of inhabitation is a form of control and colonising behaviour which locates so-called individuals into so-called groups in ways that overlook powerful and potent affective forces that are not simply located in the so-called social and cultural forces of the simply human. As Deleuze says to Claire Parnet in the quotation above 'This had nothing to do with a school, with processes of recognition, but much to do with encounters' (ibid.).

Are we not men?[1]

In those heady days of doctoral study and book and journal article writing with which Jonathan and I engaged, senses of our collaborative selves, our between-the-two's, our workings together slowly and gradually fuelled a sense of friendship. I say with confidence now, without asking for his views, that these senses of friendship were mutually imbricated, they were foldings in, unfoldings; they were what was happening. They were to do with, in Deleuze and Parnet's words in the quotation above, 'encounters'; they occurred mainly through the ether, through email contact and when we met in Bristol or at conferences and the writing retreats that we held with our colleagues there. These gradually fuelled senses of friendship were never articulated in the sterility of rational conversation but in some of our writings, both published (Gale and Wyatt, 2008a, 2008b) and unpublished, the intensities of these encounters were deep affective currents in the emergence of what we began to refer to as *Becoming-Ken-Jonathan* and, more specifically perhaps, as 'JK Assemblage' (Wyatt et al., 2011: 4). There seems to be a powerful onto-genetics in these comings together that is not decipherable in simple categorical terms. As Bronwyn Davies said in the Foreword to our first book:

> Jonathan and Ken escape, through this work, all the constraining, containing categorisations that might have held them fixed. They cannot be read within any of the old clichés of gender, or nationality, or age, or sexual preference. Their lines of flight dismantle these narrow categories, and in their place offer an ongoing *differenciation* of themselves-in-relation, not just in relation to each other, but to those they encounter, including the readers of this book.
>
> *Davies in Gale and Wyatt, 2009: ix*

And this is how it felt. I hadn't yet read Spinoza at this stage of my scholarly inquiries but as I look back on the emergence of the notion of 'JK Assemblage' some ten years on from its nascent becomings, the energising forces behind, with, on and through, what I have to refer to as, our 'friendship' are these capacities to affect and be affected. I have recently been reading Erin Manning's paper, published in the same year, 'What if it all didn't begin with containment? Toward a leaky sense of self' (2009) and feel a sense of, what I will clumsily perhaps refer to as, the *selves-belief* that animated and activated those early *Becoming-Ken-Jonathan* encounters. We have written about (2008a, 2008b) how members of Jonathan's family thought, perhaps with degrees of thinly veiled suspicion, that perhaps our work together might be involving us in something more than the innocent and highly focused practices of reading, writing, study and conference attendance that we were embarking upon at the time. They don't ask those questions any more so I guess their suspicions have been allayed! There is no doubt that the commitment to and immersion in writing at this time, something that continues to sustain itself as I write these words now, are energising forces working beyond the kinds of 'containment' that Manning refers to in her paper. What I have called 'selves-belief' was, and continues to be, somehow collective, always relational and, as it continues to emerge, about friendship. I observe and like it that those 'old clichés', those lazy and oft-used categories of difference and representation that Bronwyn refers to in the quotation above do not work to 'contain' whatever it is that energises the relationality that can be called 'friendship'. I intentionally use inverted commas at this point to activate my concern with the nouning work that 'friendship' does. The fluidity, movement and contingency of the assemblage 'Becoming-Ken-Jonathan' requires a verb if these relationalities are to be articulated without containment: *Friendship-ing? Friending?* These are both being allowed by my spellchecker: I shall allow them both life for the moment until something in affect encourages some new movement.

So much of this book relies upon the making of an argument which sustains concept, affect and percept making as event. Living with the leakiness of 'body-without-organs' is what the non-methodology of madness of this book wants to be about, to live in the becoming of *délire*, the constant de-railing of containment, is the life force of this methodology that does not want to call its self a methodology and so, in putting forward a protracted and committed engagement with something called friendship, I realise that the fragile subjectivity that this is the writerly 'I' of this book, is again brought into focus and taken to task in its writing.

I like it that Bronwyn Davies saw those early Gale and Wyatt writings as offering 'an ongoing *differenciation* of themselves-in-relation'. I like it that she saw that the writings that were taking place at the time were not holding onto solidities, were not dependent upon categorisations of difference to have life. I think this phrase is important in giving life to the processual nature of 'friendship' that I would like this plateau to animate. Deleuze and Guattari's use of the 'body-without-organs' is also central to what I am trying to do here. They ask in the title of plateau six of *A Thousand Plateaus* the seemingly innocent and simple question: 'How do you make yourself a body without organs?' (1987: 149). In the opening passages of the plateau, they then proceed to show in their writing how fundamentally difficult, complex and potentially life changing doing this is. This process of 'making' is full of contradictions, paradoxes and seeming impossibilities and this is the beautiful madness of answering this question, of providing answers that as soon as they are provided require further change, experimentation and inquiry. There are, however, many practical hints in these passages and the poetic presentation of these ensure that picking them out, focusing upon them, plugging them in and putting them to work is part of the rich patina of differentiating multiplicity and becoming offered by this wonder/full writing. So when they say that the 'body without organs . . . is not at all a notion or a concept but a practice, a set of practices', you know you have a job to do, you know that the body, your body, perhaps, 'has had enough of organs and wants to slough them off, or loses them' (ibid.). In the earlier plateaus of this book, in the engagements with bringing madness to life in terms of affect and process, emphasis was given to Deleuze and Guattari's insistence that the body-without-organs is not an enemy of the organs as such, it is the enemy of the way in which those organs are organised, it is the organism itself and how it is given life through its very organisation that creates these enmities. It is at this point that my concerns to do with friendship in terms of madness and the posthuman can be brought life.

Breath
Swimming in wave curdled sea,
tossed as a cork,
in its relentless washing power,
joyous in brief abandonment.

Walking barefoot through fields,
washed in flooding torrents
of warm summer rain,
I sense the salt and sand
running from my body,
mingling with the earth and grass.

Clouds breaking;
my near naked body
glistens in new light;
no need to dry myself
when my friends are
the sun and the wind.
          Porthcothan, 25 August 2011

In sense making I find huge energy in Manning's elision of 'body-as-assemblage' (2010: 125). In this I sense *body* as any body; as contingent, heterogeneous bodies that are in movement, bodies in encounter, bodies that are event/full and constituted momentarily in the thisness of now. In this sensing body is not about individual or group in any kind of humanist or phenomenological sense. I sense this 'body-as-assemblage' in becoming, as part of what Deleuze and Guattari see as movements

> from forces of chaos to forces of the earth. From milieus to territory. From
> functional rhythms to the becoming-expressive of rhythm. From phenomena

of transcoding to phenomena of decoding. From milieu functions to deterritorialised functions. It is less a question of evolution than of passage, bridges and tunnels.

Deleuze and Guattari, 1987: 322

In these movements I sense moments of continual exchange, transmutation and flux; the very processes of territorialisation are all about passages into something else, some other doing, some other affect induced, affect-producing flow. I want to bring this into play in relation to the relationalities of friendship, collaboration and to those of the wider fields of research and pedagogy relationality. I want to do this as it feels to me that the geo-philosophical transversalities that Deleuze and Guattari and others are mobilising here are also about the complex and deeply entangled relationalities of these materialities with those (so-called) cultural, linguistic and discursive forces that can be seen to construct them in particular ways. So in the territorialising movements from milieus to the heterogeneities and contingencies of the constant living and dying of assemblages there are also phases and stages, passings to and passings from. These are about the 'inter', the spaces that are emergent between the one and the other; what we have referred to as the 'between-the-two's, the vibrancy of the 'dialogue' that we read taking place between Felix and Gilles. In complexity these 'betweens' are not just about what occurs when two separate, individual bodies come together and interact and inter-relate in ways that might be explained by a sociologist. These 'betweens' are about the kinds of intensities that exist within and around this relationality in ways that can be described using Barad's neologism 'intra-action'. In this usage difference is always emergent within and of individuating space making and not some thing that is understood in terms of what is brought to a prescribed space of interaction by bodies that might described through differences between them, say, in terms of gender, class, ethnicity or some other generalising categorisation. As Deleuze and Guattari say of the complexity of such movements in relation to assemblages and processes of territorialisation:

> We could not describe the infra-assemblage (posters and placards) without also discussing the intra-assemblage (motifs and counterpoints). Nor can we say anything about the intra-assemblage without already being on the path to other assemblages, or elsewhere.
>
> *ibid.: 323*

I feel the need to bring complexities of this kind to my understandings of friendship and to consider how these understandings help to inform the ways in which I might go about bringing concepts to life in this theorising and inquiry. It seems that, in the main, understandings of friendship exist within the parameters of humanist forms of thinking; friendship is imbricated with and informed by feelings, emotional dispositions, ethical substance and obligatory demands upon the each and others that are constitutive of that body known as 'friendship'. In the day to day this seems OK. This seems to be part of the getting on with it that is grist to the life mill. However, if with Deleuze and Guattari we can only understand concept forming in close relation to and with affect and percept, if, in the spin of the affective turn, we are to move away from and beyond the sense in which emotions are somehow seen to be owned by individualised and individualising bodies and if the human can be better understood in relation, not only to itself but also to the nonhuman within consideration and animation of the turn to posthuman ways of thinking and doing, then the explanations and practices that inform traditional notions and customary habits of friendship and friendship making have to be questioned and taken to task. Deleuze and Guattari's notion of the 'conceptual persona' that appears throughout their (supposed) last collaborative writing in *What is Philosophy?* provides a very helpful means of doing this.

Conceptual personae and processual world making

In the first instance and in line with the overall rhetoric and processual ontological emergence of this book, Deleuze and Guattari's notion of the 'conceptual persona' can be understood as events, emanating from the multiplicity of encounters and always and only existing in processual becoming. They offer an indication of this through a linking with Pessoa's (2002) literary concept of the heteronym which he used to create imaginary characters and different writing styles:

> Conceptual personae are the philosopher's 'heteronyms' and the philosopher's name is the simple pseudonym of his personae. I am no longer myself but thought's aptitude for finding itself and spreading across a plane that passes through me at several places. The philosopher is the idiosyncrasy of his conceptual personae.
>
> *Deleuze and Guattari, 1994: 64*

And therefore, through this usage, I can think about, say, not writing with *someone* but rather in terms of writing to and with *the concept I have of someone*. This concept is not fixed, it is not a product of representation or identification, nor a cipher or signifier, rather it exists in fluidity, in constant event/ful transmutational (non-)form and in these respects is about individuation and the constant relationality of becoming. It is possible to think about Deleuze writing to and with Guattari in this way, of Gale and Wyatt producing their 'between-the-two's' and of the whole dynamic multiplicity of friendship as a method of inquiry. I see this as a kind of madness that also works to free engagements with selves from what Manning might refer to as 'containment' and in so doing always allows for 'leakiness' in the concept forming of these selves. This leakiness and lack of containment can be found in the detail of the following passage from Pessoa where 'conceptual personae' can be seen to emerge from the heteroronymic play of people and styles emergent in his work. In a letter written to Adolfo Casais Monteiro on 13 January 1935, Pessoa writes:

> How do I write in the name of these three? Caeiro, through sheer and unexpected inspiration, without knowing or even suspecting that I'm going

to write in his name. Ricardo Reis, after an abstract meditation, which suddenly takes concrete shape in an ode. Campos, when I feel a sudden impulse to write and don't know what. (My semi-heteronym Bernardo Soares, who in many ways resembles Álvaro de Campos, always appears when I'm sleepy or drowsy, so that my qualities of inhibition and rational thought are suspended; his prose is an endless reverie. He's a semi-heteronym because his personality, although not my own, doesn't differ from my own but is a mere mutilation of it. He's me without my rationalism and emotions. His prose is the same as mine, except for certain formal restraint that reason imposes on my own writing, and his Portuguese is exactly the same – whereas Caeiro writes bad Portuguese, Campos writes it reasonably well but with mistakes (. . .), and Reis writes better than I, but with a purism I find excessive. . .).

Pessoa, 2002: 487

So in no longer being *my* self and sensing 'thought's aptitude for finding itself and spreading across a plane that passes through me at several places' (ibid.), I feel that I am doing selves differently, in differentiation: by engaging in this thinking, by forming and re-forming these 'conceptual personae' I am always in the process of producing movement and as Manning says 'a body is always alive across lives' (2010: 118). Therefore, in thinking about friendship and in thinking about writing in friendship to and with others whose presence exists in the transmutational fluidity of 'conceptual personae' and who, therefore, exist in the kinds of heteroronymic play described in the passage from Pessoa above, in the individuation of becoming-writing-as-research, it seems more apt to conceptualise madness as methodology as friendship in these terms. Rather than thinking about bodies as essentialised noumenal beings that say and do things in specific contexts and situations, that interact one with the other in modalities of individualisation and group behaviour, it seems better to think about creative processes of intra-relational concept, affect and percept (in)forming on and through planes of enunciation. As I work at this here and now in the dance of now you see me now you don't, as this writing pulls me away from those discursively inscribed, phenomenologically inclined processes that serve to name and individualise me and takes me in its flow of becoming and possibilities of individuation, the persistence of Manning's question, 'where am I in this turbulence of movement?' (2014: 167) sets in play a lively and creative unease which pushes me to this table, this keyboard and forces me to write. In the turbulence of this movement, where each time I write this 'I' this body shivers with concern about this usage; I find myself drawn to the way in which Deleuze and Guattari work with the creative conceptual ambiguity of the French word 'milieu'. I love the way that their working takes my reading in fluid, almost indiscernible flows from one sense of the word to another, so that, whilst at once we are thinking and feeling with the notion of temporal and spatial connections and surroundings, we are also imbued with a sense of becoming, of somehow being in the middle, a middle that is always associated with and deeply imbricated by an outside. And so when I think about 'body', my body, any body, in relationality to other bodies, say, as in relation to the concerns engaged with in this plateau to do with (the body of) friendship, then the play to be found in this conceptualisation of milieu, in terms of these intra-active shifts between 'middle' and 'surroundings', is hugely creative. It is a dance where the imperceptibility of the dancing, folding of one into the other is the immanence of *a* life. The knowing beauty of the dance is indistinguishable from the movements and moments that make it what it is. And so, at once, 'body' and 'body-without-organs' energise one another, where we are in the constantly changing play of bodies in flow, always becoming something other than what they might have been in the movement and moment that preceded their individuation. Of this use of the two meanings of 'milieu' Massumi says:

> To put the two meanings together without falling back into an outside/inside division that calls for a subject or object to regulate it, you have to conceive of a middle that wraps around, to self-surround, as it phases onward in the direction of the more of its formative openness.
>
> *Massumi in Manning, 2013: xii*

In these ways we can think of friendship in the madness of these non-methodologies, not within the constraints and containments of the metaphysics of being but within the multiplicity and capillary fluidities of processes that, in the encounters of their always event/ful creativity, dilute and dissipate those substantialities that have diminished them for so long. Again, Simondon's notion of 'individuation' and Whitehead's process philosophy are intimately wrapped up in the flows and transmutation that make these sensings of bodies of friendship more than possible. Deleuze and Guattari also clued us in to this kind of thinking in their introduction to *A Thousand Plateaus* when they talked about their writing of *Anti-Oedipus* together:

> Why have we kept our own names? Out of habit, purely out of habit. To make ourselves unrecognisable in turn. To render imperceptible, not ourselves, but what makes us act, feel, and think. Also because it's nice to talk like everybody else, to say the sun rises, when everybody knows it's a manner of speaking. To reach, not the point where one no longer says I, but the point where it is no longer of any importance whether one says I. We are no longer ourselves.
>
> *Deleuze and Guattari, 1987: 3*

And so, whether we meet them face to face, observe them through (auto) ethnographic lenses, engage them in post-Positivist modes of inquiry and interview them, interpret and analyse them in, so-called, critical reviews of literature and write with them in collaborative writing practices of friendship and creativity we are always forming and in-forming them on a plane of immanence of individuation and always thought becoming. It seems, therefore, that the constant movement of these 'conceptual personae', making and re-making this plane of immanence are agentic in the processual making of what we call research and of the methodologies with which we mobilise our inquiries. Friendship is an animate part of this processual life which, in and of itself, is about life making. It seems that once we have thought about these thought makings, these in-formations, then to turn our back on them is to allow once again for the operation of heretical forms of being in the world that take place with senses dulled and minds firmly closed and locked up.

Richter, smearing, blurring . . .

Last night I watched a documentary film about Gerhard Richter.[2] I like the fact that Richter's art troubles the concept of the artist's obligation to maintain a single cohesive persona and a recognisable 'individual' style and that his work offers all kinds of different approaches to art practice. It is as if the artist and his work are restless, always in formation, never fully formed with the theory making and practice demands of a particular genre or style. I found this film offering a rare insight into the relative secrecy and privacy of Richter, his studio and, in particular, of the way in which he worked on his well-known 'smear' paintings.

Of this experience, this morning I wrote in my diary:

23rd November 2016

There was a point towards the end of the film when he stood back from the painting, appearing to be looking at the way in which the yellow smear he had just completed was working, at what it was doing in the painting. He seemed almost dumbfounded, bewildered perhaps and almost a little sad. Hesitantly, looking from his work to the camera and then back to his work again, he began to talk about not knowing what he was doing, about not being sure where the painting was taking him. That is so important. I love that. Although he was doing things to and with the painting, intentionally mixing colours, 'smearing' them on the canvas with two squeegees, so much of it was unknown to him, always processual, always merging and affecting, multiplying and diminishing with intensity as the painting flourished and grew.

In those moments, watching his elderly grey, stubbled face up close to the camera, seeing the bewildered look in his eye, feeling those eyes make contact with mine, I loved him, he was my friend. He was something to me that was not simply the vapid virtuality of an image on a flickering screen, he was actualising in my presence with him there: the seeming softness of his smile touched me and, as I think about it now, for me to be able to somehow touch him back with my affection in those briefest of moments was about intensity and palpability that did not depend upon any body to body interaction to be alive. Manning talks about '(t)he body, not individual but haecceity . . . (n)ot individual but individuation.' (2010: 117) and her thinking here helps me to make some sense of the affective space that engaging with Richter at this moment has prompted. This is how I begin anew to make sense of friendship.

Exemplification of individuation?

A well-known methodological approach and research practice used in traditional post-Positivist research in the so-called Humanities and Social Sciences employs the case study method. According to Cohen, Mannion and Morrison the case study can be used as a means of providing,

> The single instance . . . of a bounded system, for example a child, a clique, a class, a school, a community. It provides a unique example of real people in real situations, enabling readers to understand ideas more clearly than simply presenting them with abstract theories or principles.
>
> *2000: 181*

The authors continue by arguing that case studies 'can establish cause and effect' and that 'one of their strengths is that they observe effects in real contexts, recognising that context is a powerful determinant of both causes and effects' (ibd.). I intend to use the following section of this plateau to provide an example of how friendship can be understood in terms of this madness as methodology, conceptualising it as encounter and event and, in so doing, to trouble the kinds of methodological thinking displayed in the preceding sentence of this section. Rather than describing the following, within the orthodoxies of traditional post-Positivist research, as a case study, I wish to follow the thinking of Massumi and suggest that what follows is an 'example' (2002: 18). For Massumi and in direct contrast to the traditional case study model described above, the 'example' is not simply illustrative or representational, rather it is used to open up and trouble such strategies of fixity and establishment. As I have tried to show elsewhere in this book, Massumi says that the use of 'example' and processes of exemplification invites 'the risk of sprouting deviant' and 'requires using inattention as a writing tool' (ibid.) thus offering fundamental challenge to the limitations of context-bound cause and effect theory and the use of the case study method in traditional qualitative inquiry.

Therefore, the following 'example' is used here to open things up, to be both experimental and to offer experimentation as a method. I want to use this 'example' to also exemplify madness as a methodology of the event and to offer means by which, in this conceptualisation of friendship, new individuating relationalities can emerge and affective creativities can be animated. Further, this 'example' also continues the discussion of the question that has been raised elsewhere in this book about how it is possible to write with and about friendship in relation to concerns to do with the containment that the use of the noun requires and in relation to the leakiness of the selves that the term inevitably includes.

This 'example' is based upon an online exchange between two people; two people that know each other, two people that might call each other friends, colleagues, acquaintances, mates; the possibilities are many and within the politics of naming and identification they are all unnecessary for what takes place in the following pages.[3]

It's in the eyes: how do we make our selves visible and invisible?

How is it possible to find selves in the always becoming of friendship and of making the other visible in the shaded murkiness of differences and repetitions? There is always the ever presence of difference in the always shifting reel of now you see me, now you don't, in the always finding of new rhythms in the dance of swing and in the disharmonies of growth and the rhizomatic politics of the riff. How might friendship emerge, be created, live and die through the fluid affective relationalities of doctoral supervision, passages of long distance, unrequited love, red wine and engagements with near–death experience.

This morning I woke up with your email, in bed, beside me . . .

And so living with these persistent premonitions of death I am driven into the arms of my friendship and I write: it is all I can do. The lump in my throat is both figural and physically present; in affect it brings tears to my eyes and in its always recurring physical presence it quietly aches and causes me to cough. As I try to tap these words into coherence I am both drawn by and driven by presencing, presencing you in intonation, mood and flavour. Presencing is sensing; it is about intensity and the potential of the next relational shift. It is about antennae and the animation of a quivering, shimmering body. Elusive moments; wondering about movements: friendship is my/our/your methodology? You live with me as a figure, as a temptress, as oft time muse, as a body whose hug will lift me to the sky . . . and more.

In always becoming you stroke me with your presence: the evocation that this word sets up in me in relation to you is immense: its power tears me apart, my tears flow and my body convulses. As you are stroked my sense of you strokes me, this stroking plays a tune that is never wholly harmonic; the medley of composition is both resonant and dissonant; John Cale, John Cage, Stockhausen, Can[4]. These could all be at our gig as the play is always with the unexpected; in relationality moods always surprise, *affectus*, *affectio*. Sense making, touch, frustrations and the fires that burn fiercely and erratically in our hearts. This stroking sensitises: it is never simply gentle, it sometimes arouses me from sleep and makes me shout 'Fuck why didn't I think of that before', it sets me up for attentiveness, encouraging me to be alert to something or someone or to a somehow that I had allowed to become lazy, sleepy and approaching old age and death.

Our friendship . . . Can we call it that? Is it that simple? Does anyone know? Do they look at us and distinguish us, whatever us is in those ways? Are we different? I tell the world about you and every time I do I am close to tears, I am full of a form of hyperbole that is actually generated by fun, love, with Eros sitting on my lap. Our friendship . . . is it that? Sometimes I am drawn upright by a nudge, a frown, a quiet space in our correspondence and always the uncertainty about who *we* are, who *we* might be, how *we* are becoming and not. You changed my life: you change my life, life's changes, so you are generative of me, this is animatronic, you are the puppeteer who plays absentmindedly with loose strings that become tense by accident and lift an arm or tickle an eyebrow into life. There are many puppets and in many ways 'puppet' is the wrong word because it opens up a lexical space that evokes control and manipulation and that is not what this is about: it is as if the stroking of the strings is evocative in its becoming, the potentialities for life are always multiple, we don't know where they go, we may not even be aware of them but they are always there.

In affect, in our friendship, it is the increasing awareness of impending death that drives me here, here to this place that you helped me to believe in when I first met you, in that place where writing lives, that place that is created by writing, that is populated by the sense that allows me to say, if only to this one self, 'Yes, I can do this'. It is a place where writing creates life: I have learned that with, from and after you. And yes it is a place, it is a *somewhere*, it lives as entangled material and discursive constructed space; I know I am at this place, right here, right now, in its becoming it is write here, write now. It is 'place' not 'space' because you are here and because it would not be 'place' without you, there is hope in 'place', there is animation, activation and writing in this place, for me this is our friendship as methodology, this is the irreducibility of 'friendship' and 'methodology' into rhizomatic one that is not about unity, arborescence, simplicity and linearity but about becoming in the beautiful labyrinthine, messy complexity that we will describe as 'us', you and me, Becoming-Jane-Ken. So it will be easy to cop onto Deleuze and Guattari and call this 'assemblage'; we can cop onto Jane Bennett and make this our 'agentic assemblage'; that might be more helpful because our multiple agencies are widely spread; in Bennett's words they are distributed, we interfere with our worlds, our world and the worlds of others by always diffracting, always taking those lines of flight, always becoming present in the vivacity of the not yet known. It is here where love is made, where friendship is methodology.

And then . . . I lift my self away from this table, away from these black keys, I look into the mirror and 'I' dies: the transference of self from this place, our place, into the world of my own fragile identification destroys something in me, of me, it always does. The materiality of this still pulsing, always dying body can never escape from the necessary and contingent conditions of its discursive construction . . . I see me *as*, I don't see me. In this harrowing space of identification, where trust is gone, where there is no love and where death is always ever present, there is no me to see, whatever is me is seen *as*, whatever might be 'real' in me, is always represented as, by that me and the me's that are my alterity.

And so as I thought I had lifted this self away from my writing from and with you for what I felt might be an intermission, to do something that takes a break from this writing, I realise in an appropriation of Barad's use of prefix that this is an *intra*mission. Here in these moments of death there are deep and frightening movements of intangibility, porosity and leakiness as my monstrous body morphs into, around and with yours and I find this self becoming able to deluge/write in these distressing and de-stressing moments. The reality of the representation of this mirrored self cries with the physical pain it engenders. This lump in my throat is my presence with you and I wonder if I will ever not write this again.

In another email she writes:

I have you in my sights. We make each other visible. Paul Klee says that drawing does not reproduce the visible but rather makes visible . . . so here is my mind's eye, with a way of seeing you, attached. We are attached. I am making us visible to each other with charcoal marks on paper. . ..Jxx

And in reply . . .

I have been looking at your eyes. They have been looking at me. They are on my wall. They are around me. I am taking them in. They are taking me in. You say: 'I am making us visible to each other with charcoal marks on paper'. This is not to trace, to transfer or to code; it is not mimetic, it is not what Deleuze and Guattari call 'decalcomania' (1988: 12), a representational process which lifts an image from one place to another, it is more of a cartography and a kind of creative mapping of the self which is always living with the volatility and ever changing nature of a 'body without organs' (ibid.: 149). There are no stable properties; there is no equilibrium in 'Ken', in 'Jane', in 'becoming-Ken-Jane', in . . . whatever. Your 'charcoal marks on paper' work as a cartography of intensities, always shifting, always marking anew: now you see me, now you don't. I look up and you are looking at me but it is not the 'you' of traced representation that does this, it is the 'who' of the always differentiating repetition of the self that is always becoming-Jane. You are always visible to me in invisibility; we are always de-stratifying our bodies. The passage from Artaud in *A Thousand Plateaus* rings in my head: 'The body is the body. Alone it stands. And in no need of organs. Organism it never is. Organisms are the enemies of the body' (1987: 158). This feels like us. Well, it feels like us to me. 'Jane' does not exist, is not visible to me as a category of difference, I might trace her sometimes when someone asks, when I talk about her or try to identify her in some ways and then . . . and then I start to laugh . . . no, often I cry, as this tracing becomes its inevitable cartography, in differentiation you are always becoming something new to me, I am always reconfiguring, recreating the intensive processes of our becoming. This is my friendship with you: this is our friendship? It is as if affect continually produces and reproduces the animated, schizoid 'body-without-organs' that is us. Spinoza's affective bodies affect and are affected; this is defining, it is defining through rhythm and the dance: our harmonies and tempos are swing jazz, are pulsing techno, are lilting sad songs and with the tone and tenor of each our body/bodies grow. As Deleuze and Guattari say:

> But the rhythm, precisely, is caught up in a becoming that sweeps up the distances between characters, making them rhythmic characters that are themselves more or less distant, more or less combinable (intervals). Two animals of the same sex and species confront each other: the rhythm of the first one 'expands' when it approaches its territory or the centre of its territory: the rhythm of the second contracts when it moves away from its territory. Between the two, at the boundaries, an oscillational constant is established: an active rhythm, a passively endured rhythm and a witness rhythm?!
>
> *Deleuze and Guattari 1987: 320*

In these refrains it is always about rhythm, it is about rhythm and touch, it is not being aware of rhythm and touch as conscious organised things, it lives in extemporisation and movement, in experimentation and moment, it is always improvisational in intensity, it lives in potentiality. It is about friendship that is lived, is always being lived, and is always alive.

Email from Jane, 15 November 2014:

> There is a space in this park tonight that is the shape of my dead brother/ I feel his absence wafting up the hill like I always do at Abereiddy / beside the blue lagoon/ he has never been here to this park / this house/ except that his death still hangs over my life/ like a lintel/ I think of ken / another kind of brother / a brother in arms/lives/ times/ the stones in the park – another park /Hyde park/ken's shape wafts in a different way – not so clear to me not so complete/ a life being lived/ loved elsewhere leaves less trace here

And Ken's response, 5th December 2014

> And I had a brother too.
> A brother who lived,
> Struggling to leave my mother's body
> And who was dead on arrival in this world.
> That's how I knew my brother
> Through the grief that my mother then carried with her for the whole of her life.
> What would have been his love became mine
> And I have struggled living with that love
> All of my life.

So I don't really know about brothers.
I was seven years old when he died into the world,
And all I knew of him was my mother's tears,
And the grey sadness on my father's face.
And I carried on playing with my toys,
A little scared to look up,
Frightened of what I might see.
So I don't really know brothers.
I hear people talk about their friends as their sisters, their brothers,
I haven't found myself able to do that.
Affect has not allowed those alliances to struggle into my world.
So I guess that the names that I use for those others are friends and, yes, lovers
And I know that as soon as I begin to put names to them
They are lost from me.
I much prefer to use the verbs,
It is what I do with those others and what they do with me that counts.

So:

Jane is not my friend, she is more than that; she is not my lover, we don't do that; she is not my sister, I haven't learnt to do that.

We do things. We don't define it. That wouldn't be right because as soon as we did, as soon as we tried to, something seismic would shift, we would refuse our selves and we would find those selves doing something else which would overturn what we said we were before the earth moved.

So, we do things.

She bosses me around . . . I can't get over that. She finds the things that I am rubbish at and really lets me know it. She gets angry with me. I hug her. She gives me the brightest biggest smile and I melt. We tell each other we love each other and write kisses on the tails of our e-mails.

When I first heard that she had her stroke, my heart raced, I cried, I didn't know what to do, and cried a lot more. My red All Stars and my black skinny jeans were in the back of her van and that seemed to be all that was left of me in her.

We get drunk together and giggle a lot. I want more of this. In restaurants when I have drunk too much I can only put my head on her shoulder: there is nowhere else to be.

And we write . . . and we write . . . we seem to write in ways that tells secrets . . . does she think that?! Oh really!? Shall I tell her this? . . . no I don't even think about it, it just comes out; I know I can eviscerate all over the page and it will be OK.

She says we kissed at the Stones gig at Hyde Park in '69: if we did I would have known it, though if you remember the 60s apparently you weren't there so maybe we did . . . yes, maybe we did and maybe we have been looking out for each other ever since.

This is not meant to be a form of case study in which friendship can be understood and given meaning, rather it lives here, to use Massumi's reasoning, as an 'example'. It is not here to represent, it is here to exemplify, to suggest, perhaps, and most of all to do something. I am with Massumi when he says, '(t)he idea of positioning begins by subtracting movement from the picture' (2002: 3) and so the foregoing is not meant to fix 'Ken' and 'Jane' as 'friends' and to position this writing as some form of case study of 'friendship'. Movement is always happening here, what goes on is about fluidity and transformation, it is the dance, it is about rhythm and the refrain, it is about now you see me now you don't: as Massumi says, '[w]hen a body is in motion, it does not coincide with itself. It coincides with its own transition: its own variation' (ibid.: 4). So to talk perhaps of *Becoming-Ken-Jane* is to talk of the politics and the ecologies of movement where things are always being done, being done differently, where relationalities shimmer and stutter in their movement and where the intensity of each moment has the potential to be somewhere, something else. In this respect Manning talks of a 'moving-toward friendship', not in abstract conceptual terms but of how

> It is in and of the body, it is a movement toward sensing an other, a movement where I reach out to touch you, acknowledging the implicit violence in my act of crossing time and space, an act that can never be present in position, but only in passing, an engagement of our bodies in their indeterminacy.
>
> *2007: 23*

This piece of writing, this 'example' within this plateau which is 'in-formation' (Manning, 2007, 2013) in its talking about and with friendship, madness and the posthuman offers a thinking with what a body can do. This thinking is not about the stable, established, individualised, bodies of Cartesian rationalist thought; in its creative conceptualisation it lives as an event in which there is a sensing of movement towards a body-without-organs where this always re-assembling body is living and doing in difference. The body of friendship is not to be signified and seen in the modalities of representation, it lives in the elusive mercurial rhythms and creative patterning of the dance. 'Friendship' or, perhaps, more appropriately, more incisively, 'friend/ing' or 'friendship/ing' is more easily understood in terms of what it does. Deleuze and Guattari's notion of 'agencement' talks to these fluid and transmutational heterogeneities and contingencies and can also be keyed in to Bennett's (2010) conceptualisation of the agency of assemblages as always in the constant play of re/distribution. And so this body of friendship, these 'friend/ings' never stop, their positionality is as fleeting as the 'example' that brings them to life for a moment and never attempts to signify or hold them down and in these active resistances to repetition and generalisation lives the forceful productive energy of their ability to do.

Notes

1 *Q: Are We Not Men? A: We Are Devo!*, the debut studio album by the American new wave band Devo, was originally released in August 1978 on Warner Bros. and Virgin and produced by Brian Eno. The band took the phrase *Are We Not Men?* from a book by H. G. Wells, *The Island of Doctor Moreau* (1896), and is part of a litany of law used in the story by a mad doctor to invoke, through rhetorical chanting, solidarity and awareness amongst a group of surgically force-evolved creatures: are we not men?
2 *Gerhard Richter Painter* (2011) a documentary film, directed by Corinna Belz.
3 This section of writing is an adaptation of a paper that was presented as part of a panel on Friendship as Methodology at the 11th International Congress of Qualitative Inquiry at the University of Illinois, Urbana-Champaign, Illinois, USA in May 2015.
4 The name of an experimental German band from the 1970s/1980s.

WRITING MINOR LITERATURE: WORKING WITH FLOWS, INTENSITIES AND THE WELCOME OF THE UNKNOWN[1,2]

- - - - - - - - - - - - - - -

Something in the world forces us to think. This something is an object not of recognition but of a fundamental encounter. What is encountered may be Socrates, a temple or a demon. It may be grasped in a range of affective tones: wonder, love, hatred, suffering. In whichever tone, its primary characteristic is that it can only be sensed.

Deleuze, 2004a: 176

There are always millions of tons of dust in the air, just as there are millions of cubes of air in the earth and more living flesh in the soil (worms, beetles, underground creatures) than there is grazing and existing on it.

Ondaatje, 1992: 17

- - - - - - - - - - - - - - -

Deleuze and Guattari's (1986) writing on minor literatures, which has its most detailed account in *Kafka: Toward a Minor Literature*, is of central importance to the conceptualisation of and arguments for the madness as methodology that is designed to energise the writing of this book. As Dana Polen says in the translator's introduction to the book and of the authors' approach to its writing and presentation,

Even the key words of the Deleuze-Guattari procedure, words like rhizome, lines of escape, assemblage (agencement), become battle-sites for a process of deterritorialisation as the authors violate their own proprietary authorship of terms and make the words, tremble, stutter.

Ibid.: xxvii

Throughout their writing project together Deleuze and Guattari return and return again to the use of powerful pronouncements in support of the writing of minor literatures, in engaging with forms of writing that work within and against majoritarian writing forms as a means of challenging, of offering lines of flight and of breaking through the hylomorphic structures and frameworks of these major forms as a means of working away from fixities, strategies of representation and all those modes of signification that frame thinking and writing practices in static arborescent rigidities of practice. So, for example, in their analysis of 'faciality' they make powerful arguments for breaking through the representational and reflective 'white wall' of the signifier. They argue for the writing of Hardy, Lawrence, Melville and Miller in terms of its ability to 'get away. To get away, out! . . . To cross a horizon' (1987: 186–187) in sensation and movement to be always reaching towards.

In his conversation with Claire Parnet about the 'superiority of Anglo-American Literature', Deleuze (2002) talks of the need for literature 'To leave, to escape . . . to trace a line' and in quoting Lawrence 'To leave, to leave, to escape . . . to cross the horizon, enter into another life' (ibid.: 36). He goes on to berate French literature because for them 'fleeing . . . is something rather sloppy because we avoid our commitments and responsibilities' (ibid.), 'The French are too human, too historical, too concerned with the future and the past. They spend their time in in-depth analysis. They do not know how to become . . . they are too fond of roots, trees, the survey, the points of arborescence, the properties' (ibid.: 37). And so, Deleuze, in this conversation, seems to talk of a writing of minor literatures that invokes a kind of madness as methodology, a kind of delirium, a going off the rails, an engaging in writing that revels in saying absurd things, and of stuttering in one's own language:

> You can always replace one word with another. If you don't like that one, if it doesn't suit you, take another, put another one in its place. If each one of us makes this effort, everyone can understand one another and there is scarcely any reason to ask questions or to raise objections. There are no literal words, neither are there metaphors (all metaphors are sullied words, or else make them so). There are only inexact words to designate something exactly. Let us create extraordinary words, on condition that they be put to the most ordinary use and that the entity they designate be made to exist in the same way as the most common object.
>
> *Ibid.: 3*

Of this and in specific relation to the conceptualisation of madness as methodology that drives this book, Dosse says of Deleuze and Guattari's writing:

> The schizophrenia that Deleuze and Guattari were brandishing was not the illness of the same name. It was a universalising programme, a limitless process, a constantly reiterated ability to transgress limits, to carry out a release. They believed that this process was at work in Anglo-American literature, which Deleuze in particular appreciated. Authors such as Hardy, Lawrence, Lowry,

Miller, Ginsberg and Kerouac all carried the world within themselves and could be delusional; they could break their moorings and scramble codes to facilitate the flux. Similarly those who could make the language stutter were able to engage in inventing a new style of language that disregarded grammaticality and syntax to let the flux of desire flow and be expressed.

Dosse, 2010: 199

In many respects, therefore, the conceptualisation and writing of this methodology book, a book about methodology, about a non-methodology, about a constantly processual *methodogenesis* is more to do with writing than research. It offers, perhaps, a creative elision of writing and research. In this it suggests that writing, using Richardson's practice of writing as a method of inquiry, is constitutive of the 're' in research, it offers a going back to, not in any sense of reconstituting or putting together of, engaging in re/membering, engaging with some kind of past which can be relational to some kind of present, some kind of future, rather it is writing in relation to worlding, writing as making the world, writing as the creation of concepts as events. This writing is not a writing about, it is a writing that does. Also, as I have pointed out elsewhere in this book, this coming together of writing and research is not a simply human affair. It is as Manning says 'always more than one', it is, as Bennett has pointed out in her account of 'agentic assemblages' to do with 'the confederate agency of many striving macro and microactants' (2010: 123) of both human and nonhuman form.

In writing *Writing Shame*, Elspeth Probyn talks of the shame involved 'in being highly interested in something and unable to convey it to others, to evoke the same degree of interest in them and to convince them that it is warranted' (2010: 72). If writing is done with the intention that it *does*, then there is always the possibility of the human proclivity of wonder in relation to *what* it does. Is it any good? Does it impress? Do people like it? And other curiosities of this kind. The point of these questions is, in an affective, relational and wholly posthuman sense, that they have no point. If we want writing to be operative in and to exist in worlds of representation, interpretation and critique, then these questions take on board a form of importance that is a kind of self-indulgent, self-importance. However, if we recognise, quite simply, that words do something, that, in multiplicity and relationality, they *make* the world, then these questions recede into the vacuum that their stating begins to create. In these respects Probyn argues that 'writing shame is part of an ethical practice. Shame forces us to reflect continually on the implications of our writing' (ibid.: 73). Therefore, writing is a practice that is affective. I understand it working within forms of space making that Barad refers to as space where 'each intra-action matters' where practices of 'knowing in being' create the need for an '*ethico-onto-epistem-ology*' (2007: 185). The ethical, ontological and epistemological aspects of our (writing) practices cannot be separated; to attempt to do so is part of a metaphysics of rationalism and Cartesian individualisation that the current writing attempts to remove its world making from. Writing minor literatures is, therefore, creative of concepts as event, in relationality to, with, from and of human/nonhuman worlds that, in becoming, are constantly affecting and affected.

In this the Deleuzian conceptualisation of becoming is central. So, in the same conversation with Parnet, referred to above, it is clear that, for him, becoming is a kind of madness, a fluid processual engagement with the body in movement in which the body is not a thing in itself, possessing a Kantian status as a category of difference which as a separate being moves in and out of contact with other objects of similar status and kind in the world. Rather, in becoming, bodies are always moving, differentiating, always in play as Deleuze talks of the characters of Thomas Hardy as 'collections of intensive sensations, each is such a collection, a packet, a bloc of variable sensations' (2002: 39–40). These movements are therefore not to do with beings having fixed subjectivities and coming into contact with the world that is somehow separate from them, rather becoming is an always reaching out which is of the world. Manning argues that to 'touch synaesthetically is to appreciate all of the ways in which movement qualitatively alters the body' (2007: xiii). She talks of this as 'worlding' where touch, doing, reaching out are all of the world not to the world. These becomings are an escape, what Deleuze calls a line flight, away from the fixed boundaries and boundedness of the Kantian body-in-itself and towards bodies-without-organs, always moving, always re-organising and always reconceptualising, not in terms of meaning, of what this ever-shifting 'body' might be but, rather, in terms of what this 'body' can do:

> A flight is a sort of delirium. To be delirious (*délire*) is exactly to go off the rails (as in deconner – to say absurd things, etc.) There is something demoniacal or demonic in a line of flight. Demons are different from gods, because gods have fixed attributes, properties and functions, territories and codes: they have to do with rails, boundaries and surveys. What demons do is to jump across intervals, and from one interval to another.
>
> *Deleuze, 2002: 40*

- - - - - - - - - - - - - - -

We were heading for the beach; it was a cold, wet windy day in February 2014. As we left the warm comfort of my house Ella said to me 'I've got my tide tables'. Something about the intended efficacy of her organised ways made me smile.

- - - - - - - - - - - - - - -

I love the way that the rhythms of the sea are prone to the predictions of the clinical chart; the tide table sits there and persistently striates its space.

I love the way that we know to go there to walk the great lengths of rippled sand when the tide table says it is a 0.4 metre low tide at 15.35.

I love the comfort of knowing that in the winter I can put on my walking boots, zip up my leather jacket, abandon my car at the top of the cliff and be off with nothing or no one to clutter my duty to my lover, the sea.

And of course I love the way in which all this is thrown into disarray by the vagaries of the forces that play with the regularity of the moon and the tide; the way that the wind sweeps in unexpectedly from the east and shifts the rips a little to the north, which turns the swells into an unusual diagonal with Rame and suddenly it is all happening differently.

And then the wind returns to where you expect it to be blowing from and the heaving energetic force of those great westerlies throws the early tip of the breakers pounding onto the beach, all with a shore break that creeps up on you and tells you that although it might only be a neap high of 4.2 metres at 16.05, if you don't start moving soon there won't be enough beach left to enable you to walk back and get around that darkening, imposing rocky promontory that lies between you and the steep climb back up the path at Sharrow.

I love the way it messes you up when you are walking the beach in the winter; somehow then you are more conservative, less wild in your heavy clothes, working with the knowing regularities of the charts, comfortable in the confluence of the predicted tide, the moodiness of the weather and the always diminishing light but when it does it in the summer it can kill. There is always something there to surprise you.

I love the delirium of walking the beach in the summer sunshine, in nothing but your shorts, your body burned warm by the day-glowing sun, the ache of your body from the swimming action of your limbs and the ceaseless erosion of care growing with every step you take on that never-ending sand.

And yet people drown in the beatitudes of summerness when care is cast like seeds from the sower's arced arm and deep, dangerous forces lurk ready to do the sweeping away. The tides still live with their idiosyncrasies; rip currents come and go, mums and dads light barbecues, drink cold cheap beer and children from estates in West Bromwich and Ealing, bodies quietly glowing in the pink of the sun that dips down to the darkening shadow of Looe, are fascinated by the race of the outgoing waters and the whipping effect of a new-born rip tide upon their ankles . . . their calves . . . their bodies . . . and then suddenly gone. The days of warm sea and sunshine lull us all into the comfortable rhythmic striations of carelessness and freedom and the sea, without malice and intention, always acts in extemporisation and the unexpected to remind us of its unusual vectors and hidden forces. These reside, come and go, take away and subtract, in always creative processes of evolution; they make us blithely unaware of its smoothing and ever-changing proclivities and calculations.

- - - - - - - - - - - - - - -

I recently went to the cinema to see Mike Leigh's film of the life of Turner. The film upset me in certain ways. I didn't find it easy to watch. Leigh seemed to create a sombre darkness in the film and to find mysterious depths in Turner's life that pitched gloomy counterpoint to the vibrancy and vivid tones of the artist's charged and powerful canvases. I have carried my unease with me like a weight: something about my experience of the film disabled me, I found myself walking slowly out of the cinema burdened by a sense of shadowy depths and unsolved mystery surrounding me. Today, reading *Anti-Oedipus*, whilst engaged in research for another paper, I stumbled across the following passage:

Turner does not exhibit, but keeps secret. It cannot be even said that he is far ahead of his time: there is here something ageless, and that comes to us from an eternal future, or flees toward it. The canvas turns in on itself, it is pierced by a hole, a lake, a flame, a tornado, an explosion . . . The canvas is truly broken, sundered by what penetrates it. All that remains is a background of gold and fog, intense, intensive, traversed in depth by what has just sundered its breadth: the schiz. Everything becomes mixed and confused, and it is here that the breakthrough – not the breakdown – occurs.

Deleuze and Guattari, 2004: 144

It is as if within a milieu of agelessness, within the eternalities of becoming, assemblages are constantly forming and re-forming, bodies repel those hylomorphic tendencies to structure and organise, it is when the 'canvas is truly broken' that the breakthrough is possible in the becomings that it makes manifest. In the film, in the exhibition hall beside the fastidious Constable, intricately crafting and modelling his beautifully representational bodies with organs, we suddenly see Turner provocatively incising one of his dramatic seascapes with a vivid red oil paint scar. In the ambivalence of the mystery of his secrecy and the discourse of the exhibition, the red smear becomes the animation of the painting; in the movement of the moment the breakthrough occurs. The brooding darkness of 'Mr. Turner' that has in sombre half tones colourwashed my own senses seems to find illumination in these moments, in the director's attempts to animate the possibility of breakthroughs to be found in the force of a single brushstroke in relation to the grand organisation of the 'finished' canvas. It is the concept as event that brings new life to the eternal emergence of the 'body-without-organs' (Deleuze and Guattari, 1987).

- - - - - - - - - - - - - - - - -

In delirium, wandering more and more in this life of intensity, world making, my extensive body becomes more and more a mystery; becoming, sensing living with these 'bodies-without-organs'. It is this body with its defined organs, represented, identified, continuing to be difficult to understand. Heart, lungs, eyes, legs – they all work in ways that can be read about in books, in ways that teachers talk about in lessons and yet, as bodies grow in becoming, in their creative sensing of difference, it is possible to feel less and less connected to their machinations in ways that are to do with knowledge and meaning. They are evidently body parts, organs, seething systems of animation but less and less do they feel that they are part of what organises me or of what is my organised self; it is as if becoming-Ken involves losing touch with that being, that denotated and prescribed body with organs. In this sensing, in these transmutations, becoming is a swim, luxuriating in ether, through ethos, with mythos. Bodying occurs through sensing, in sensing the world through intangible essencing of touch, where the separateness of life prescribed by being is suffused by and within flow, fluidity and transmutation. The creative worlding that this animates is never fixed, it is always of potential, its movement in moments potentiates: intensities, flows, molecular shifts of life, in, through, between and around are not simply a part of something that discourse talks of as 'me'; living is in the creation lacunae, where spaces appear in the continuum of self and then fill, live and grow as tissue, blood and touch inhabit that space. Sitting here watching the lava lamp, each movement of the fluids is different, each time as a globe of translucent life lifts and moves, its mass, its shape, its temperature sends it on a different journey through the living space of the viscous fluids, changing its visibility, its balance and the way that it appears through the glass.

– – – – – – – – – – – – – – – –

This morning I was up early
And went walking
By the beautiful sea
The sand cold to my bare feet
A silent, deep grey mist joined sky to water
In a moment
I lost myself.

– – – – – – – – – – – – – – – –

Every stratum is a judgment of God; not only do plants and animals, orchids and wasps, sing or express themselves, but so do rocks and even rivers, every stratified thing on earth.

Deleuze and Guattari, 1987: 44

When walking on the beach there is the energising draw of 'vibrant matter' (Bennett, 2010). 'Me' is dispersed in the becoming that is not simply a surrounding. The 'I' that has to be talked about does and the world in which it lives does; their relative reciprocations are the stuff of life constantly moving in animations of sensation, and so . . .

A billion pebbles,
dried sticks as petrified bones,
sparkling, smooth shards of worn glass,
bright, shining as jewels in the sand.
Shells; mussels, cockles, winkles . . .
some perfect in their abandonment,
others carved and worn by the relentlessness of sea movement,
limpets, their erect nipple tips eroded,
ready to be strung,
then worn, as a necklace around a sunburnt neck . . .
It is the worn-ness that is fascinating,
in the unceasing industry of the beat of the waves,
grinding sharp rock into pebbles,
rubbing smooth pebbles into rough, gritty sand,
rough sand, becoming smooth sand, becoming dust,

always energising, always part/icular, always of molecular constituting
and always, always the changing in/consistencies of the sea . . .
This beach walking is becoming
as absorption, with 'vibrant matter'.
The sea in incessant life forcings,
always creative, sometimes peaceful, sometimes threatening, never, ever
the same, fascinates, no, seduces, with its gradual flows in and out,
in and out,
its passion for the wooing with the moon,
unable to resist the potency of that glowing life force,
flowing together as lovers as the climax of their ebbs and flows
becoming the movements and moments of their highs and lows.
The sensual intimacy of their touching work to surprise
as they inch further up the once dry sand of the beach,
then recede,
further and further
until the wet and shiny wasteland of their withdrawal is the becoming of
the freshly warming beach of their renewed lovemaking.

- - - - - - - - - - - - - - - -

'I love you' is a sound, it is a performance, it lives beyond the words that are used to express it. It is a monad of infinite particularity and exists only in the moment of its expression. Its expression is its materiality and without it it would live in the world of pretentious discourse, false appearances and trite commentary.

'I love you' is resonance, harmony and has its life in the buzzing, fizzing reality of touch; as it performs itself it does so through touch and in reciprocation it blazes into unrecognisable new life.

'I love you' in intensity can be an event that seals the intense multiplicity of 'concept, affect and percept' (Deleuze and Guattari, 1994) within a beautiful felted and entangled knot of vitalism: without its existence in this intensity it is dead.

- - - - - - - - - - - - - - - -

Elsewhere in these writings, Barad (2007) has been found offering 'intra-action' to add the hugely important dimensions of 'between', 'within' and 'around' to the phenomenological and essentially humanistic formalism of 'interaction' and, in so doing, provides richness and depth to the traditional preference for its predecessor. In doing this she also provides an intensity to what she refers to as, the 'entanglements' that animate and activate relations between language and the materialities they attempt to represent. Her work is significant in the way in which she alerts us to the inevitability of complexity that is involved in our ontological engagements with the flux and transmutational nature of the spatio-temporal relations with which we engage. In this I think of talking with friends, students and colleagues and of the animations and multiplicities that working with difference and conceptualisation can bring. The energy and vitality of such complexity is conveyed by Deleuze and Guattari in the following passage:

Here, there are no longer any forms or developments of forms; nor are there
subjects or the formation of subjects. There is no structure, any more than
there is genesis. There are only relations of movement and rest, speed and
slowness between unformed elements . . . There are only haecceities, affects,
subjectless individuations that constitute collective assemblages.

1987: 266

It is in thinking of how writing in the emergence of these flows and transmutations
might help to nurture a living within a plane of immanence whose existence within
and of itself serves to limit and ultimately eradicate categorisations of difference and
the organisation and structuring of bodies into the fixities of existent form. It is like
swimming in the sea and sensing the fierce, heavy insistent pull of the rip current
pulling my body across the regularity of the waves. And in these movements and
flows I am drawn towards Deleuze and Guattari's engagement with 'minor
literatures' and the forces with which they bring to life planes of immanence. And
as this magnetism begins to work I remember Irigaray's accounts of 'parlez femme'
which also suggest such possibilities and vividly portrays the vital potencies and
energies of emergence to be found within the sensual vibrancy and entanglements
of encounters between language and the materiality of the body. She says of 'parlez
femme', they

are contradictory words, somewhat mad from the standpoint of reason,
inaudible, for whoever listens with ready-made grids, with a fully elaborated
code in hand. For in what she says too, at least when she dares, woman is
constantly touching herself. She steps ever so slightly aside from herself with
a murmur, an exclamation, a whisper, a sentence left unfinished . . . When
she returns it is to set off again from elsewhere . . . One would have to listen
with another ear, as if hearing an 'other meaning' always in the process of
weaving itself, of embracing itself with words; but also of getting rid of words
in order not to become fixed, congealed in them.

Irigaray, 1974: 29

It seems that the rhetoric of Irigaray's 'parlez femme' clearly echoes with Deleuze
and Guattari's (1986) work in *Kafka: Toward a Minor Literature* for it is in that work
that they offer an argument that connects writers and writing within collective
assemblages of enunciation, so that when they talk about 'stuttering' in the language
they are not making reference to some form of impediment of speech or
pronunciation, they are describing a way of speaking and writing in the language
that is always emergent, hesitant and taking new forms. Their reading of Kafka
shows that he was offering a 'minor literature' to de-centre and deterritorialise the
dominance of 'major literatures' through strategies of experimentation, mistrust of
traditional idioms and forms and of nurturing collective action. In so doing, perhaps
he was also offering madness as methodology. What seems to be the key to the
potency of a 'minor literature' is that it is performative; it is about *language as action*.

So when poet and radical feminist Adrienne Rich (1975) proclaimed 'This is the oppressor's language/ yet I need it to speak to you', there is a sense in which her statement was a call for a use of language in action that through processes of territorialisation could offer challenge to dominant and dominating existent forms. In this sense, speaking, writing, gesture and intonation all take the form of what Madison (2010) refers to as 'acts of activism'; in the affective play of relationality each action of bodies in movement with one another has the propensity to do something to create change.

The social justice issues present within such solecistic strategies gain force through their transparency: 'major literatures' hold within them the hylomorphic tendencies to marginalise patois and to give preference to *la langue* over *parole*. In this respect, 'minor literatures' *qua* 'bodies-without-organs' (Deleuze and Guattari, 1987) offer challenge to the dominating structural forces of the 'major literature' by offering a world of language usage which Bogue describes as one of 'perpetual variation, interaction, negotiation and contestation, in which language users shape and mould words as elements within shifting contexts, now playing with phrases, altering patterns, and inventing meanings' (2003: 111). The creative and polemical challenge offered here to the imperialism of languages of privilege and methodologies of common sense to be found in the arenas of social class, ethnic diversity and gender relations might be clear to see and difficult to bring into action. Equally, within the context of pedagogical practice, for example, there is a strong sense in which this madness as methodology, in the creation of concepts as events, offers possibility for the highly potent and potentially transformative approach of theorising as practice in the animation of teaching and learning assemblages.

In order to facilitate activation of this kind it feels important to consider the ways in which it might be possible to break down or to avoid the prejudices and rigid binary power relations that might be construed as existing within Deleuze and Guattari's 'major and minor literatures'. When speaking of immanence, Deleuze and Guattari often referred to the fluid possibilities and transmutational becoming of consistency, where striations have been smoothed and where constitutive divisions have been dissolved and eradicated. Deleuze writes, 'It is only when immanence is no longer immanence to anything other than itself that we can speak of a plane of immanence' (2001: 27). In this respect writing towards, within and for a minor literature can also be of this order; stuttering in the language is at the same time the stuttering emergence of the language, it is not an impediment which is measured against the preferences and articulacies of the dominating tendencies of a privileged or major form. In explaining that Deleuze and Guattari's book on Kafka is not just about Kafka, Dana Polan, in the translator's introduction to the book says:

> Rather, writing stands against psychology, against interiority, by giving an author a possibility of becoming more than his or her nominal self, of trading the insistent solidity of the family tree for the whole field of desire and history. The romance of the individual life is exceeded, deterritorialised, escaped.
>
> *Deleuze and Guattari, 1986: xxxiii*

Equally, I think of the heterogeneous and contingent processes and practices of teaching and learning and sense a knowing that they are not about the fixities and foundationalism of categories of difference. The need to focus upon the emergent writings of 'minor literatures' and how they can be used to articulate the operations of bodies and languages in the complex and messy exchanges and entanglements of 'intra-actions' is substantial. When Deleuze talks of stuttering in the language he is offering an invocation to make the language system stutter; he is encouraging a thinking about and a doing of language that will work with the immanent possibilities of difference rather than a rigid transcendence of repetitions. He says that stuttering in the language is not about mixing the two languages, rather it is about inventing 'a minor use for the major language'; he refers to a need to 'minorise language', likening it to music, 'where the minor mode refers to dynamic combinations in a state of perpetual disequilibrium'. In citing the likes of Kafka, Beckett and Lawrence, he talks of the 'great authors' who 'cause language to flee, they make it run along a witch's course, they place it endlessly in a state of disequilibrium, they cause it to bifurcate and to vary in each one of its terms, according to ceaseless modulation'(Deleuze, 1994: 25).

- - - - - - - - - - - - - - - -

In introducing the reader to the rhizome in the opening plateau of *A Thousand Plateaus*, Deleuze and Guattari stress that

> [a] rhizome ceaselessly establishes connections between semiotic chains, organisations of power, and circumstances relative to the arts, sciences and social struggles. A semiotic chain is like a tuber agglomerating very diverse acts, not only linguistic, but also perceptive, mimetic, gestural, and cognitive: there is no language in itself, nor are there any linguistic universals, only a throng of dialects, patois, slangs, and specialised languages. There is no ideal speaker-listener, any more than there is a homogenous linguistic community. Language is . . . 'an essentially heterogeneous reality'. There is no mother tongue, only a power takeover by a dominant language within a political multiplicity. Language stabilises around a parish, a bishopric, and a capital. It forms a bulb. It evolves by subterranean stems and flows, along river valleys or train tracks; it spreads like a patch of oil. It is always possible to break a language down into internal structural elements, an undertaking not fundamentally different from a search for roots . . . a method of the rhizome type . . . can analyse language only by decentering it onto other dimensions and other registers. A language is never closed upon itself, except as a function of impotence.
>
> *1987: 7–8*

And so it seems that if we are to 'minorise language', if '[t]here is no mother tongue, only a power takeover by a dominant language within a political multiplicity', we can use, for example, solecisms in all their different variations, forms and functions to materialise what Deleuze and Guattari are arguing for here. Within the majoritarian force and normative regulation of traditional grammar, a solecism is a phrase that is often viewed as a mistake, something that violates or trespasses the rules of that grammar. However, solecisms not only offer strategies that encourage lines of flight and enable trespass of established genealogical delineations and grammatical boundaries, but also offer, through differentiations of use, improprieties, violations of etiquette, ironies and absurdities which can be seen to materially affect the patterns and arrangements of discursively constructed social relations. If metaphors work to attain a certain cultural consistency and acceptance, and as tropic functionary we find that they often carry with them a certain discursive energy which resists reflexive engagement and contradictory force, then perhaps we need to remember that '[t]here is no mother tongue, only a power takeover by a dominant language within a political multiplicity'. If we employ the forces of Derrida's deconstructive methodology, then we always have to make the familiarity of everyday and traditional metaphorical tropes strange. With Deleuze we need to recognise that with repetition there is always difference. The continuation of practices of similitude, allegory, hyperbole and other accepted modes of comparison and transposition gain their longevity and traditional and customary energies and force, through the politics of their non-reflexive usages; it is only when they are seen to operate in solecistic ways, such as, for example, in the mixing of metaphors, that questions are asked about their status in terms of the meanings that language both provides for us and is given and we can work with a knowing that '[a] language is never closed upon itself, except as a function of impotence'.

In asserting 'That bodies speak has been known for a long time' (2004b: 325), Deleuze offers a transposition which helps to break down the rationalist demarcation and rigid and intransigent delineation of the mind and the body into separate worlds. Again, through his invocation and use of the solecism he provides a means of also understanding the materiality of bodily gestures:

> For example, one arm may be used to hold off an aggressor while the other is held open to him, in seeming welcome. Or the same hand may be used to hold off, but is incapable of doing so without also offering an open palm. And there is also this play of the fingers, some being held open, and others, closed . . . such a gesture is the incarnation of a power which is also internal to language: dilemma, disjunction and disjunctive syllogism.
>
> *Ibid.: 325–326*

There exists in this writing a suggestion of the kind of 'entanglements' that, Barad (2007) argues, animates and activates the intensities that appear to be present in the spaces of 'intra-action' described in her bringing together of the material and the discursive. It seems, as I have suggested elsewhere, that 'when Deleuze sees a concept as an event he is alluding to its interconnected nature that frees it from its purely cognitive or intellectual comprehension and relocates it within multiple affective, ethical, and performative dimensions' (Gale, 2010: 305).

- - - - - - - - - - - - - - - -

And at the back of the club, the rear doorway is highly populated, not with those who might use the door to leave and to enter but with those who seem to prefer to be in limbo, dancing the dance of the in and the out and being both and never one or the other and always one and the other. In the pregnant liminality of this space I sense the intricate entanglement of the vibrant and insistent thump of the dub step, the stench and the heat from the dance floor mingling in indeterminacy with the misty rain falling outside, the orange street lights toning cigarette smoke in hazy and translucent, whirling hues, wafting through the door and dissipating in conversation and sweaty heat and, in so doing, creating this doorway as something more, always something more than its simple, rectangular entry/exit functionality. How beautiful is this space! The talk here is infused with rhythm, the talkers are on the move, not in or out; perhaps back or forward, up and down, always movement in the moment, movement in the creation of the moment, a brief moment in the trance-like infection of the movement of the dance. My sensualism is both part of and creative in this infusion of moment and movement; no language dispels the mythologies and gratitudes that are vitally existent as this space; in this space is the fluidity, potentiality and germinality of organism; bodies wreck and recreate in their intensive reorganisation in this space, this space that is becoming of place and that then moves on again in the next moment of its own creativity. It is in this space that always life begins and ends.

- - - - - - - - - - - - - - - -

And then there are the politics.

In the spatiality and temporality of movement and moment, territory is to do with boundary and distance and can be set in fields and terrains. It can be about marking a boundary, as a dog urinating against a tree, or, through territorialisation, involve being active in establishing an identity and relations between identities. Identities, those frail and translucent indeterminate and singular figures in space and time, apparitions that come and go in the play between the 'me' and the 'you', ghosts that yawn in the doubt that always populates how I see 'me', how you see 'me' and how 'we' see each 'other'. I love the play between materiality and discourse that is so evident when Deleuze and Guattari talk about territory as being 'first of all the critical distance between two beings of the same species' and describe how this is established and re-established in the following way:

> If need be, I'll put my territory on my own body, I'll territorialise my body: the house of the tortoise, the hermitage of the crab, but also tattoos that make the body a territory. Critical distance is not a meter, it is a rhythm. But the rhythm, precisely, is caught up in a becoming that sweeps up the distances between characters that are themselves more or less distant, more or less combinable.
>
> *Deleuze and Guattari, 1987: 320*

Bakhtin's (1981) dialogics of language can be seen to contribute to and be partially constitutive of this rhythmic territorialisation. He uses 'heteroglossia' to describe the coexistence of distinct varieties and forms within a single language. Through this use of language, in both the discursively verbal of our expressions and the materially non-verbal of our bodies, we say who we are, what we like and where we are going. As in the leaps and vortexes of the dance, rhythmically we 'stake out' a territory in relation to the territories of others, establishing harmonies and incompatibilities, resonances and dissonances.

> I finally grasped in a visceral sense why the music was made the way it was: how certain tingly textures goosepimpled your skin and particular oscillator riffs triggered the E-rush, the way the gaseous diva vocals mirrored your own gushing emotions. Finally I understood ecstasy as a sonic science. And it became more crystal clear that the audience was the star: that bloke over there doing fishy-finger-dancing was as much a part of the entertainment, the tableau, as the DJ's or bands. Dance moves spread through the crowd like superfast viruses. I was instantly entrained in a new kind of dancing-tics and spasms, twitches and jerks, the agitation of bodies broken down into separate components, then re-integrated at the level of the dance floor as a whole. Each sub-individual part (a limb, a hand cocked like a pistol) was a cog in a collective 'desiring machine', interlocking with the sound system's bass-throbs and sequencer riffs. Unity and self-expression fused in a force field of pulsating, undulating euphoria.
>
> *Reynolds, 1998: xvi*

The animation of the objective and recognisable categories of difference of extensive bodies, perhaps existing in terms of such specifications as 'gender', 'race', 'sexuality' and 'class' that are to be found in the inadequate usages of 'interaction' and the methodological artifice of, for example, the 'interview', therefore need to be problematised through an engagement with the entanglements and the more complex differentiation of intensities that this book is arguing exists, not simply between them, in terms of affect, value or intuition but rather within and through them in relation to the vitalities and vibrational energies of the milieu of which they are constitutive particularities. The social, cultural and political forces that are involved in the performative institutionalisation of education practice provide a crucially significant illustration of this.

These harmonious, agonistic and recombinant rhythmic moments of terri-torialisation and re/de-territorialisation are described and brought to life in the work of Deleuze and Guattari in rhizomatic forms. As our bodies and words engage in dialogue, in dialogic inquiry, and as our selves, our becoming subjectivities, engage in nomadic circling of texts, narratives and touch we both create and are created by these rhizomatic patterns and flows. As our thoughts, feelings and values, expressed in utterances and the movements of our bodies, are folded in to establish territorial distances, the thoughts, feelings and values of others intra-act, combine and exchange with them in rhythmic response, allowing new utterances to emerge and new meanings to unfold.

In a snowfall
    that obscures the winter grasses
a white heron –
using his own form
    to hide himself away

Dogen

- - - - - - - - - - - - - - -

Engaging in inquiries and random readings as I tried to work a self into the constant becoming of this book, I came across an old diary entry. I read this simple entry through, I read into it the complex anti-linearity in the writing of a life, I sense the emergence of minor literacy, not simply an emergence within a larger structure or organisation but something that stutters and exogamously unfolds from it. I sense minor literacies both emergent within and creating planes of immanence; here there are cartographies that are always mapping, breaking down the certainties of trans-cendentalism and the established categorisations of difference, animating discovery, encouraging experimentalism and activating its own forceful energies and vitalism. I like that this was there then and becomes again now and in so doing dissolves the binary artifice between there and then and here and now.

Little Epiphany – Sitting in Spring Sunshine – 21st April 2007

And after getting the reference to 'the Underground Ones'[3] and realising it was The Subterraneans and picking it up and reading again after all these years, ten to fifteen pages of this my first and still favourite Kerouac book, I realised in that moment that I had also just read one long wonderful sentence that began at the top of page 114 and that finished halfway down page 117[4] and then further realised how with my knowledge, reading and happiness at the discovery of Deleuze, how this sentence in all its ins and outs, ups and downs, forwards and backs is just one fantastic haecceity, an assemblage in a moment, his writing capturing the great rhizomatic wholeness of those moments. I just love it. Love it again, like I loved it so much all those years ago, when, in 1965 I reckon, I read it first. I remember the hardback copy that I borrowed from the old Passmore Edwards library in Launceston[5] which I used to visit with my dad on Friday evenings. Amidst the sensual pleasures of that beautiful old place, its creaking floorboards and the loudly ticking clock, the smell of polish and the startling moment of someone's sudden, inadvertent cough. I remember the excitement of that moment of discovery. Reading the opening pages, I remember being captivated, excited, anxious to live the life of a 'subterranean'. And so I did! I remember those days now as a becoming, as I started to live that whole wacky, intellectual, drunken, raging, laughing Zen life and as I also tried to study, to earn some money and to live my life. Starting then in that middle and now I am here, starting again in the middle.

Reading that sentence of Kerouac's again I fell in love with the way in which it conjured up all those lovely stoned, sensual, often paranoiac apprehensions of love and attraction, of the delirious passionate loving conflict between Leo and Mardou. Finding myself reading it like listening to a jazz solo, absorbed in the flows and the interstices of improvisation without realising that was what I was doing.

As I reconstruct my memories and work with these hopes and conjectures, I also think of Kerouac, of his writing, of his minor literature and of his delirious expression of what is clearly a productive desire,

> because the only people for me are the mad ones, the ones who are mad to live, mad to talk, mad to be saved, desirous of everything at the same time, the ones who never yawn or say a commonplace thing, but burn, burn, burn like fabulous yellow roman candles exploding like spiders across the stars.
>
> *Kerouac, 1972: 11*

In *Anti-Oedipus*, Deleuze and Guattari talk about Kerouac, Hardy, Miller and others within the context of Anglo-American writing as

> men who knew how to leave, to scramble the codes, to cause flows to circulate, to traverse the desert of the body without organs. They overcome a limit, they shatter a wall, the capitalist barrier. And of course they fail to complete the process, they never cease failing to do so . . . Never has delirium oscillated more between its two poles. But through the impasses and the triangle a schizophrenic flow moves, irresistibly; sperm, river, drainage, inflamed genital mucus, or stream of words that do not let themselves be coded, a libido that is too fluid, too viscous: a violence against syntax, a concerted destruction of the signifier, non-sense erected as a flow, polyvocity that returns to haunt all relations.
>
> *2004: 144*

I want the 'men' in this quotation not to be simply men, perhaps I want them to become vagrants who, like Deleuze and Guattari's 'nomads', might live in poverty, who might wander from place to place unsure of their 'small plot of new land' (1987: 161), who, in their constant becoming, are able to break out from the discursive forces that place them within a disabling category of difference. Perhaps with Deleuze and Guattari I want them to 'Go across, get out, break through, make a beeline, don't get stuck on a point. Find the line of separation, follow it or create it, to the point of treachery' (1987: 186–187). And I wonder, as again I am thrown back to starting in the middle, is this the space to create? Is this the place to be?

Notes

1 This plateau was originally published as a paper in the journal *Qualitative Inquiry* with the following reference: Gale, K. (2016a) Writing minor literature: working with flows, intensities and the welcome of the unknown *Qualitative Inquiry*, 22(5) 301–308. I am

grateful to the editor Professor Norman Denzin and to the publishers Sage for giving permission to publish the paper here in this form.

2 I have punctuated the text of this chapter as it was originally published with stuttering lines in a way that is intended to suggest emergence and the potential for non-linearity and idiosyncrasy in the reading of and engagement with its text. In this respect I have tentatively appropriated Deleuze and Guattari's use of 'plateaus' from their book *A Thousand Plateaus*, of which Massumi says in his translator's foreword: 'A Thousand Plateaus is conceived as an open system. It does not pretend to have the final word. The author's hope, however, is that elements of it will stay with a certain number of its readers and will weave into the melody of their everyday lives' (1987: xiv).

3 In Deleuze and Parnet's *Dialogues II* (2002: 51) there is a reference to 'the Underground Ones'.

4 These page references can be found in the following edition: Kerouac, J. (1973) *Pic/The Subterraneans*. London: Andre Deutsch.

5 My hometown in Cornwall.

MADNESS AS METHODOLOGY AS PERFORMANCE

The madness as methodology that is offered in this plateau will promote an engagement with the performative; it will use a logic of sense that will encourage a consideration of Austin's (1962) notions of 'speech acts' and 'performative utterances' and, in so doing, will provide an analytical account of Spinoza's question 'What can a body do?' in terms of the ways in which research and inquiry might be carried out. In this book I have often returned to Deleuze and Guattari's suggestion that once concepts are formed they can be 'plugged in' (1987: 4); this is how these concepts are kept alive; this is how world making is animated and energised. Active processes of conceptualisation create encounters with the world and, in so doing, they make the world and there is also a sense in which they are to be found in the world. The rhythms of territorialisation that Deleuze and Guattari (1987) descriptively invoke when they talk of the play between 'striated and smooth space' is both creative in and of space at the same time and consequently, in similar ways, there will also be some play between acts of conceptualisation and contextualisation. The encounter that is the 'plugging in' of the concept will 'smooth' out preceding conceptualisations and conditions and, in so doing, will 'striate' space in particular ways: the encounter will act, it will do something, it performs, it will, at least in part, tell us what a body can do. It is how Deleuze and Guattari (1987: 320) describe the momentary movement of two animals confronting one another and how their 'territories' expand and contract in oscillational rhythm as the relationality of their 'boundaries' shifts in constantly moving transmutational ways.

These rhythmic exchanges are about harmony, tone and the constant play of the refrain. This play is about the intensification of the micro-political, involving forms of power that are not external to the performance. It is not about one body having power *over* another body; rather it is about the reciprocating play between bodies engaging ontological facilitations which enhance the power of these bodies to act in particular ways and to do particular things. These particularities, the movement in moments of these particles, creates an intensification of onto-relationality involving an aesthetics in which senses are heightened and new languages and concepts can be formed. These processual dynamics challenge the flattening of norms and values of traditional reflexivity which, in the nurturing of consensus and critical cohesion, has the tendency to promote an *an*aesthetics, which works to dull the vitality and vibrancy of these rhythmic forms of world making. So, what I shall refer to and work with here, this *madness as methodology as performance* is part of an aesthetics that is designed to challenge and subvert those performance modalities that work to simply stage, represent and not to give new life. So it is not perform-ance that is about, or of, the representations and character identifications of mimesis that is in operation here, it is the space which is created when speech *acts*, when a body *does*, it is,

> [A] pure becoming without measure, a veritable becoming-mad, which never rests. It moves in both directions at once. It always eludes the present, causing future and past, more and less, too much and not enough to coincide in the simultaneity of a rebellious matter.
>
> *Deleuze, 2004a: 3*

It is as if the rhythms produced in these performative movements and moments are constantly in play. As Deleuze says elsewhere, stuttering takes place in the language, it is not an impediment of the language, it is what the language does in its always becoming, it is the immanent nature of language constantly making itself, and world making in so doing. The schizophrenic plays that Deleuze and Guattari offer in *Anti-Oedipus*, for example, move from one enunciation to another, from the use of one language code to another, in the writing of the minor literature that always works within for and against the major literature that it might be seen to be a part of. In their use of Artaud's 'body-without-organs', they talk about the 'schizo' having 'his own system of co-ordinates for situating himself at his disposal', he has 'his very own recording code which does not coincide with the social code, or coincides with it only to parody it':

> he deliberately *scrambles all the codes*, by quickly shifting from one to another, according to the questions asked him, never giving the same explanation from one day to the next, never invoking the same genealogy, never recording the same event in the same way.
>
> *Deleuze and Guattari, 2004: 16*

- - - - - - - - - - - - - - - -

As I write, on this day, Tuesday, 11 October 2016, it is nearly four in the afternoon. The sun is struggling with the onset of autumn. I share the efforts it makes: autumn heralds winter and darkness takes over from light. It is becoming less and less comfortable to walk out of my little house in my T-shirt, shorts and worn-out flip-flops, a towel, my swimming things, a book and some writing materials under my arm and take the simple five minute journey down to the beach. I swam in the sea early yesterday morning, the sun was a glazing shimmer on the water; apart from a few curious oyster catchers, I had the beach to myself – I was lost in the beauty of the moment. Later, as I walked up the cliff on my way home, dark clouds covered the sun, a sharp cold breeze suddenly blew in from the east and increasingly heavy spots of rain turned my warm salt-stained body into a damp chill as my leisurely walk home turned into hurried strides and thoughts of a warm, comforting bath to revive my dampening spirits.

Liz, my partner, recently bought me a copy of Joyce's *Finnegans Wake*. Having recently read *Ulysses*, I felt excited about carrying on with the kinds of adventures and experimentations that Joyce's writing had evoked in my reading of this amazing book. And there, in my warm bath, hot coffee by my side, my brand new copy of *Finnegans Wake* in hand, I decided to venture into Joyce's night, hoping to continue experiencing the enjoyment and pleasure I had gained travelling with him through his day. I am drawn by the following sentences taken from the opening pages of Seamus Deane's introduction to the book:

> The first thing to say about *Finnegans Wake* is that it is, in an important sense, unreadable. In order to pay it the attention it so impertinently and endlessly demands, the reader must forego most of the conventions about reading and about language that constitutes him/her as a reader. The advantage to be gained from doing so is considerable, the conventions survive but they are less likely thereafter to dwindle into assumptions about what reading or writing is.
>
> *Deane in Joyce, 2000: vii*

And later, '[t]he book is written in the English language and also against the English language; it converts itself into English and perverts itself from English' (ibid.: viii). It seems to me that the 'unreadability' that Deane refers to here in relation to Joyce's writing is its very readability, it is how the book performs its self and how, as readers, selves are performed in the reading of the book. These are the performances of touch, of the book reaching out, touching us as readers, its self wanting to be touched, readers being touched in different ways, the movements and moments of touch immanent upon and with selves in always differentiating relationality. Manning talks about this in terms of a 'politics of touch' and suggests that '[a] gesture interrupts language in the moments when language attempts to convert itself to actuality' (2007: 8). It is clear that when Deane talks of the 'unreadability' of *Finnegans Wake*, he is suggesting that, at least in part, Joyce is also doing something of this gestural kind in his writing. Deane does not literally mean that the book is 'unreadable', rather that it is unreadable only to those readers who can only read in one particular way. In this sense *Finnegans Wake* is hugely gestural, it performs itself in ways that throws open challenge to the representational modalities of signification that construct language in highly normative, customary and authoritarian ways. As

Manning says,

> a gesture acts as a force that renders palpable language's instability . . . [it] reinforces the fact that communication is not linear, that language cannot be concretely symbolised, that the words that 'reach' an other cannot be completely comprehended.
>
> *Ibid.*

What is crucial to this discussion of the performative nature of texts, and of how they might be both constructed and read, is a consideration of Spinoza's direct and hugely important question, 'What can a body do?' In short and in terms of a *madness as methodology as performance*, bodies, both human and nonhuman, perform selves in different and always differentiating ways. Manning's gestural interruption of languages attempting to move to convert themselves to actuality is a performative intervention that gives life to bodies. In worlds of gestural sense making, unreadabilities, unsayabilities, undoabilities offer energising life force to the intensity and potentiality of always becoming, that in spatio-temporal relationality, is the vital force of world making.

Sense can further be made of *madness as methodology as performance* through engaging with language in the ways in which Deleuze himself talks about reading a book. In moving the reader towards an engagement with 'bodies-without-organs', a conceptualisation that is highly relevant to this discussion of performance and which I address elsewhere in this book, Deleuze tells us that reading a book involves treating it as 'a little non-signifying machine' where explanations, interpretations and critical engagements are not necessary. Rather, he says, it is about asking questions like: 'Does it work, and how does it work?' 'How does it work for you?'

> This intensive way of reading, in contact with what's outside the book, as a flow meeting other flows, one machine among others, as a series of experiments for each reader in the midst of events that have nothing to do with books, as tearing the book into pieces, getting it to interact with other things, absolutely anything . . . is reading with love. That's exactly how you read the book.
>
> *Deleuze, 1995: 7–9*

St Pierre uses her reading of this quotation to offer an 'undoing' of the subject, processes and practices of education. She says, 'I was happy to come upon this description of reading and be granted permission to give up the pretense of signifying and "making meaning" in the old way' (St Pierre, 2004: 283). Her work in this paper suggests that through practices of 'undoing' the subject (of education) the subject can be 'done' in different ways; just as the 'unreadability' of a book is, paradoxically, in practice its 'readability', what bodies do is done in different ways, this is how they perform (selves) in different ways. In these performances, difference is immanent to its self, the very practices of differentiating and differentiation makes difference.

This plateau is designed to promote an active use of concepts that does not use contextualisation and the consideration of what a body can do in simply reflexive ways. Reflexivity emerges from reflective practices which claim to somehow provide a mirroring of reality: the representation that is the resultant of such thinking sets up practices of signification, identification and intentionality which are resistant to the realist ontological strategies and claims of this inquiry and the practices of performance outlined in this plateau so far. Such approaches provide the conditions of possibility that Foucault referred to in his engagements with discursive constructions of selves, knowledge and meaning. Rather, and with Haraway (2000) and Barad (2007), this plateau involves itself with the 'interferences' that are possible if concept forming, the Deleuzian practice of 'plugging in' and encounters as living performance are engaged with 'diffractively'. The insidious pervasiveness of the reflective trope in the humanities and social sciences, through the use of strategies of representation, attempts to displace selves elsewhere and to produce sameness and established categories of difference. In contrast, Barad's diffractive methodology presents challenge to this by offering 'patterns of difference that make a difference' (ibid.: 72). In these respects diffraction takes the encounter and differentiates it through bringing to light the multiplicities of the event and the entanglements of materiality and language that are constitutive of it.

Engagements of this kind with *madness as methodology as performance* will also enable a return to some of the earlier themes and practices of the book and will encourage diffractions that will raise questions about what work do practices of concept forming and plugging in actively achieve in taking research and inquiry forward in positive ways. This plateau is written with some degree of structural tidiness in mind (!) as it has the potential to lead the reader to considering practices of resolution, conclusion forming and recommendation making. So when methodology is considered as the thinking behind what is done or what is to be done, there is a sense in which those methodological thoughts and considerations are situated as embodied actions entangled with discursive constructions and which are realised, *made real* in ontological terms, through performance.

Butler (2006) has famously argued that we *do* gender; that somehow the gendered self emerges through and because of gender constructions that are culturally or societally inscribed: it is performative. The work of Pelias (1999, 2005), Pineau (2011) and other performance scholars might consider the act, the performance, in terms of what it might do or what it does; in this sense the self offers a performance in which mimesis, poesis and other forms are engaged to inform, evoke and bring something to life in different ways. Standing back from this performance demands a reflexivity and Pelias asks of the action of his performance students, performing selves in particular contexts and situations, what work does it do? What work does it do? The rhetorical presentation and the critical engagement of the performance scholar and, indeed, the performer, is both deeply troubled by and structured around this hugely axiomatic question. It is also a question that can be approached in more than one way.

In the context of the relational space that is animated, or not, by the dramatic act, the question is critically motivated and is, therefore, largely interpretive. The person who intends to act in a particular way, who then acts and then in reflection considers the energy, efficacy and effectiveness of the act is performing self in such a way that is critical, interpretive and ultimately judgemental. We can, for example, visualise the dedicated teacher who constructs a lesson plan from a given curriculum structure with the intention of satisfying, through the various strategic pedagogical practices of the lesson, certain preconceived and explicitly stated learning outcomes. This behaviourist model deeply inscribes many aspects of teaching and learning where the designed action of the learners is overtly or covertly informed by the prefixing phrase 'At the end of the learning experience the students will be able to . . .' which is followed by the relevant verb. In this respect the teaching and learning 'performance' is brought sharply into critical focus through the use of the question: 'What work does it do?' The post hoc, technical rationalism of Schon (1983, 1987) and others clearly describes such practices through the use of the notional practice of 'reflection-on-action', which is used to look back, retrospectively, on that which has been done to see if, *in fact*, the prescribed learning outcome has been achieved. Whilst such an approach shifts the emphasis from propositional forms of knowledge to those of action and the performance, there is a deeply worrying consequence of engaging in such an approach. As Usher, Bryant and Johnston have pointed out about practice that is centred on action:

> This, however, is a particular kind of action, it is neither random behaviour nor behaviour predictable from a body of theoretical knowledge. Rather, it is appropriate or right action – and what is appropriate or right depends on the context or situation. Every context of practice has its own distinctive features which provide possibilities and impose constraints on what can be done. Here, then, action is conceived as being inseparably linked with, indeed constituted by, contextual knowledge.
>
> *1997: 126*

And so the question 'What work does it do?', whilst possibly very well intentioned, can never be wholly dislocated from the identifications of its representational context and, therefore, as we see from the work of Foucault, the operations of power are understood as being inextricably linked with the constitution of subjects. The reflexive nature of the critically reflective eye interprets practices in terms of their worth, their efficacy and, through reflecting on action, the self-regulating practitioner either becomes praiseworthy or penitently confessional and, in so doing, is constituted in particular ways. Within the apparently benign panoptical context of the critical appraisal of the performance, the question 'What work does it do?' operates, through the discursive constructions of the curriculum, the lesson plan and associated assessment procedures and the subsequent confessional processes of embodiment as a technology of self, inscribing practices that are not only signified but also embodied. In these respects the effect of the question 'What work does it do?' is to flatten the affective nature of relational space by working to achieve agreement, consensus and standardisation of practice.

However, and as suggested earlier, there is another way in which the question 'What work does it do?' can be asked, and it is worthwhile to turn again to Foucault as a means of providing a means of reconstituting the approach to this question. As has already been offered here, selves are situationally constituted through the operation of power and whilst in certain aspects of Foucault's writing dealing with notions of governmentality, the all-seeing gaze of panoptic technologies, docile bodies and the disciplining of selves, this can be seen as an extremely deterministic and malevolent view of power, in his view there is no single locus of power. Foucault consistently offers the view that power is in everything, it is not simply about the hylomorphic impositions of power originating from outside and above and designed to bring about order and control according to previously constituted rationalities and procedures:

> I wouldn't want what I may have said or written to be seen as laying any claims to totality. I don't try to universalise what I say, conversely what I don't say isn't meant to be thereby disqualified as being of no importance. My work takes place between unfinished abutments and anticipatory strings of dots. I like to open out a space of research, try it out, then if it doesn't work try again somewhere else. On many points . . . I am still working and don't know if I am going to get anywhere. What I say ought to be taken as 'propositions', 'game openings' where those who may be interested are invited to join in; they are not meant as dogmatic assertions that have to be taken or left en bloc.
>
> *1991: 90–1*

The work done by such an approach is very different from that required by the interpretations of the question offered above. What Foucault offers in this passage is an acknowledgement that the world is a very complex place. The world that is offered here is one which cannot be reduced to or flattened by forms of interpretation, critique and persuasive rhetoric that attempt to locate the performance within the representational strictures that attempt to make that which is different more like itself. The work of Augusto Boal (1993) whilst largely embedded in humanist practices and emancipatory critical inquiry has the potential to offer a move towards the kinds of performance practice suggested in this passage of Foucault's. In Boal's *Theatre of the Oppressed*, rather than simply being spectators watching the drama unfold on the stage the audience are encouraged to become active and to actually engage with these unfoldings, to offer challenge and to suggest other approaches to the performance. In this way, by attempting to replace the concept of the 'spectator' with that of the 'spect-actor', Boal encourages all the participants to become part of the performance.[1] In this way the binary construction of the actor/performer and the audience/spectator has the potential to be dissolved as all the 'spect-actors' become active in exploration, improvisation and transformation of the reality of the performance with which they are engaged.

Boal's work was greatly influenced by the emancipatory politics of Paolo Freire and the Critical Theorists of the Frankfurt School[2] and hence, like its predecessors, it embodies a strong interpretivist stance and works to subvert and overthrow, what is essentially, a source of power that is external to the dynamics of the performance group and the drama that is being played out. A key enforcing concept of this work is Freire's notion of 'conscientisation', a term used to describe the ways in which individual consciousness can be changed through the processes of 'seeing' and engaging with the world in different ways. Again if we consider the question of what work do these practices do, there is a strong sense in which individualised 'conscientisation' is designed to produce the group solidarity of agreed critique and a consensus of challenge to the dominant oppressive order. The *madness as methodology as performance* that is being offered here is of a very different kind. It is one that offers strong challenge to performance as purely representational. It is one that attempts to shift the focus of attention away from the substance of objects and subjects towards the processual and the eventful. And it is one that concerns itself with world making in terms of encounters and events and in creating difference that continually differs from itself.

Madness as methodology as performance distinguishes itself from more obviously mimetic and dramatic forms of performance through its concerns with the politics of affect. Conventional modalities of performance draw upon historical and cultural reference points to establish a reflective quality in the performative act; a mirror can be held up to the performance and judgements can be made about its quality in terms of its ability to convey, perhaps, a particular character, a given emotion of a set of social circumstances. In affect, however, whilst there is not an intended dislocation from the past or from antecedent constructions and articulations or indeed from possible connections with the future, the emphasis here is more to do with moments of encounter in the present. Massumi in discussion with Manning brings in to play the concept of 'immediation' which,

> offers a way of drawing attention to the event as the primary unit of the real. The idea is that whatever is real makes itself felt in some way, and whatever makes itself felt has done so as part of an event. It has entered in some way into the immediacy of the moment as a factor in the event now taking place.
>
> *Massumi, 2015: 147*

I have an understanding of 'immediation' as an intensive quality that is vitalised and energised by the way in which in the moment of movement, in the movement of the moment, past, present and future have an encounter of coalescence in performance as an event. Such moments and movements can be seen to exist within and to animate time as aeon, their force is not about the measured critical reductions of reflective and interpretive consideration, it comes from the power of affect. Deleuze alerted us to the need to acknowledge time in terms of aeon and not simply in terms of its chronological linearity. This conceptualisation is of fundamental importance in bringing a lived rather than a staged conceptualisation and methodological practice of performance as event to life.

In contrast to the linearity of chronological time or *chronos*, Deleuze offers a conceptualisation of ontological time which he refers to as *aeon*. In this respect *aeon* can be understood in conjunction with a Deleuzian treatment of the virtual, within the sense in which when that which is virtual is actualised it ceases to be whatever it was before in virtuality. For example, in becoming, when bodies can be seen to do, concept forming is affectively performed and displaced in whatever happens in the movement from virtual to actual. Difference, in itself, always produces something new. It could be argued therefore that *aeon* is not perceptible within an individualised Cartesian form of meaning making; it cannot be somehow grasped within the mind of sentient understanding body – if it were it would be something different. As a counterpoint to chronological time, *aeon* can be understood as ontological time and in this respect exists in virtuality, always eluding the making real or realisation that is the energising force of actuality. In a sense *aeon* can never be actualised, it excludes the present. It is for this reason that *aeon* includes a past that is 'always already passed' (i.e. a past that never had the status of a present) and a future that is 'eternally yet to come' (i.e. a future that is never capable of arriving) (Deleuze, 2004a: 165). In other words, *aeon* is constantly peeling away – in both of the above directions – from the present. It should also be clear from this description that *aeon* operates within the sphere of immanence that was discussed earlier.

Performance therefore involves enunciations in which encounters with what is said or what is done are part of the multiplicity of potential affects. The language of the performance and indeed the performance in itself will stutter; it will stutter in its own language and in these respects the performance will exist as a form of minor literature which works within and around those major literatures that might try to encompass it and bring it within the confines of its own limitations and patterns of conformity. Prescription, definition and classification are not a guiding or influential part of this conceptualisation of performance and as Grosz points out, 'It is no longer appropriate to ask what a text means, what it says, what is the structure of its interiority, how to interpret or decipher it. Instead, one must ask what a text does, how it connects with other things' (1994: 199).

In the autumn of 2016 I spent a whole day in Reading Gaol, immersing myself in an event by the experimental group Artangel.[3] I attended Lemn Sissay's reading of Oscar Wilde's *De Profundis*, his long, searching and despairing 50,000-word letter of love, anger and remorse written to his lover Lord Alfred Douglas who, with his father, the Marquis of Queensberry, had been, at least partially responsible for Wilde's two-year period of incarceration. Sissay's continuous reading of the letter lasted over a period of six hours and I found myself moving in and out of the space that his very evocative reading created during this time. As part of the Artangel event, many of the cells in the gaol were given over to installations and exhibitions of the work of writers and artist's such as Nan Goldin, Ai Weiwei, Peter Dreher and others who wished to present this work as a form of engagement with Wilde's imprisonment and the work that he produced during this time. In the event brochure one of the quotations from Wilde's letter describes his cell in the following way: 'Outside the day may be blue and gold, but the light that creeps through the thickly-muffled glass of the small iron-barred window beneath which one sits is grey and niggard. It is always twilight in one's cell, as it is always midnight in one's heart.' Even though as participants in the Artangel event we were able to move freely in and out of the cells, some empty, some with artists' and writers' exhibits, this pervasive sense of containment, entrapment and a dulling of light stayed with me and followed me around for the duration of the day that I spent there. The whole experience was duly imbued with affect and it seemed impossible to live within these walls without being washed with sullen, grey loneliness of this deeply saddening space.

I struggled with my listening to Sissay's rendering of *De Profundis*, I languidly took pictures in the shadows and murky light of those dark caverns and dirty prison walls and felt temporarily lifted by some of the writings I read and the artwork I viewed. Of these one in particular took me into another space. A number of cells contained large rectangular pictures of water, on first observation nothing seemed particularly unusual about these pictures, they seemed to portray the ebbings and flowings of a deep foreboding river and gradually, as I viewed each one in turn and began to read the notes alongside and below the photographs by the artist Roni Horn, I found myself being drawn into the swirls and eddies of the water, becoming immersed in shifting moments, each absorption taking me deeper into folds of skin, then flying over mountain ranges, back to caressing a naked body and then suddenly looking at the undulations of a dark cloudy winter sky. These pictures of water were performing to me, with me, in me and around me; I found myself, temporarily at least, taken from the oppressive confines of the prison and able to float in loose, spontaneous movements with the water in the pictures. My 'seeing' of the pictures did not seem representational; I did not feel as if I was having to 'see' something that the artist wanted to me see – seeing was happening. Seeing in this here and now was an event, just as writing about it now is an event: I am writing, I cannot help that, you are reading, these are encounters, this is eventful. In these movements and moments bodies, human and nonhuman were and are doing. These bodies, human and nonhuman had and have the capacity to affect and be affected: what these bodies do and can do is highly differentiated, this is what they are, they are nothing other than this. The immanence of these encounters that I tentatively describe here are about constant difference; difference producing difference: this is a life, nothing more, nothing less.

I kept returning to the pictures. The same things kept happening. I began to notice very small writing running along the bottom of the pictures. Moving closer and reading the writing I found that they were little numbered passages. Each passage seemed to have a life of its own, with at most limited connection to the passage preceding or following it. I began to be drawn again, this time by the writing, my curiosity about the apparent randomness of the different numbered passages growing as I read and then read some more. What is the writing about? What is this writing saying? What are these numbers? Answering the last question made me jump when I realised what the numbers were and what they were doing. Deeply embedded in the folds and the flows of the water, pulsing above the little numbered passages of writing below the pictures were tiny numbers, seemingly ducking and bobbing about in the movement of water like little plastic ducks. Hitherto, these had been invisible to me earlier when I had been standing back looking at the pictures, allowing what I was seeing to perform to and with me in whatever ways this happened. I moved back to the numbered writings, read, looked up at the picture, found the number bobbing in the water and moved back again to the writing, back and forth, in and out, each time, sensing something new, each time shifting from words to images, from numbers to writing in flows and trans-mutations that seemed to have vitality and life force of its own. I staggered.

Strange. I took pictures of the water pictures, of some of the writing, my intentions felt dispersed in the moments of the viewing and the taking; other people moved in and out of the cells where the pictures were located, I didn't see them and yet of course I did, my seeing of them was diffused in light, colour and intensity, now you see me, now you don't.

I have just picked up my phone and looked again for the first time at some of the pictures that I was taking in those deep moments of affect, those two or three weeks ago. Even on the tiny screen of my phone, now as I synonymously write these words, these flowing transmutations start to work on me again, I feel taken, I feel movement in to a different presence of sensing, my skin is tingling, my head is buzzing. I will write down some of the words, I am trapped by the written text, perhaps the images will follow.

The numbers didn't impose them selves on me, the passages of writing to which they were attached didn't attach them selves to me in any particular representational or significant way. I didn't go back to the pictures to find out which numbered passage connected to which number in the picture and to which part of the picture the number was in and to what was happening in that part of the picture. Nothing in my movements in and out of the pictures, to and fro between the writing and the picture, from number to word to image, was in any way directional or controlled: it felt as if a child, a demented person and an aimless wanderer were all in control of the imaginary cursor that was moving me around. I had a powerful sense then and some thing of the same order now, as I am immersed in the writing of these words that, quite simply, in complex affect, some thing was happening, human and nonhuman bodies doing, performing, without intentionality, without plan and without the rigour of hylomorphic constraint or control.

15   Do you believe that this particular colour (whatever it is) is mainly geology? Just benign muck making the water this foul colour. Maybe you can say it's the foulness that attracts body parts and various other items an individual might want to hide, including oneself. And maybe it isn't. Maybe there's some metaphysical reason for the river's special colour – some rare spiritual coincidence perhaps. Who knows, is it filthy-looking water that attracts the wanna-be secrets of humanity, or is it the wanna-be secrets of humanity that sully the water?

22   Did you see Blow-up? Do you remember the park scene? – and the rustling of the bushes in the wind? And the camera – just watching – wandering over the clearing? The sound of the bushes was dark. The river reminds me of that sound.

29   This water is full of unknown hints – unspeakable, unpronounceable things. Sometimes I console myself by imagining all the things in the water. I console myself with the horror of it. It's not the obvious stuff like rats and condoms and sewage. That's easy to imagine. But I try to visualise the viruses and bacteria as well, like hepatitis and E. coli and the little bacteria, dysentery and cholera and that disease called Weils and, who know, maybe a remnant of the plague, just lingering the way things tend to do near water.[4]

And from my pages and pages of notes from that day I picked out these three; just these three. I have to. And now as I write them in here I try to do this without representational intentionality and it is hard. I claim spontaneity. I imagine Burroughs, Gysin, Bowie perhaps, and tempt the idea that these inclusions are something that arrived randomly, without design from cut-up: that would be dishonest. And so I will save myself from such artifice and allow my description of what happened to me that day to rest amongst encounters with the words above.

So the *madness as methodology as performance* that I have tried to articulate and bring to life here is one that does not rest upon interpretation, critique, identity and representation. Performance is immanent; it does in relation to its self. Like touch, performance does; it exists in the play between bodies and is the indeterminate and indetermining frisson of bodies in action and encounter, each having the capacity to affect and be affected. It is as Manning says of dancing the tango:

Tango is the dance of the impromptu rethinking of the politics of communication. Tango is the dream of the known played out in the night of the unknown. It is the politics of the unwritten, yet the palimpsest on which everything political aspires already to have been written. It is the voice of the immigrant displaced through movement. It is the movement of the stranger, echoing in the distant resonance of a music that has many times crossed the world.

Manning, 2007: 3

In the dance, thinking and doing can never be separated from the self. Dance is the non-representational movement that creates it and that is immanent to itself. In the dance thinking and doing are processual. They are not forms of content, 'thoughts', 'actions', that exist as objects, which can be objectified and represented in particular ways, then interpreted and critically appraised in another space–time. Thinking and doing are transversal and, as such, are always, in Deleuzian terms, 'in between' bodies of all kinds, they are always on the move, to and from, passing through, entering here and leaving there, in these movements always affecting and being affected. In this sense they are immanent, they exist on a plane in which the play of multiple encounters between the virtual and the actual is the always creative production of the event/ful/ual. So, when Manning talks of the practice of 'choreography' she is not describing some hylomorphic force that, in an impositional sense, controls from above or from the outside. She explains 'choreography as a practice that attends to the immanent field of relation that is part and parcel of environments in-forming . . . in Guattari's terminology, a heteropoeisis, a self generating practice of difference' (2013: 76). Therefore, the performance is not a content-specific object that is performed, the performance exists immanently, in this sense, it *does*. The *madness as methodology as performance* that this involves sees dance and choreographic practice as a form of aesthetic creativity in which body/space/time is always a relational composition of sensation, potential and movement. In this sense choreography, in the dance of performance, works to come alive in exploration, creativity and experimentation. It does not use a binary logic to challenge rationality and technique and articulates it within energising forces of sense, serendipity and improvisation, in the creation of new deviating lines of flight and difference. The *madness as methodology as performance* that is being described here is not one that is designed to set up figurative parallels with other modes of practice, which might be carried out, for example, in education, teaching and learning. Rather it is designed to suggest that the conceptualisation that is offered here has the quality and potential to be integral to performance within any modality or setting, as a means of engaging and energising creatively productive practices within such fields.

Notes

1 There are resonances between Boal's work with the *Theatre of the Oppressed* and that of Julian Beck and the Living Theatre, which in many respects epitomised the radicalism of the 1960s by also attempting to disrupt established norms and values and by encouraging the audience to perform. It is possible that in its attempts to shock, to confront and to offer challenge to the establishment that the intentions of the Living Theatre were different from those of Boal.
2 A useful citation and authoritative account can be found at 'Frankfurt School' (2009). In *Encyclopædia Britannica*. Cited from Encyclopædia Britannica Online: www.britannica. com/EBchecked/topic/217277/Frankfurt-School.
3 For over thirty years, and since 1991 under the direction of Michael Morris and James Lingwood, 'Artangel has produced extraordinary art in unexpected places in London, across the UK and around the world. In their words they 'produce art that challenges perceptions, surprises, inspires and wouldn't be possible within the confines of a gallery'. Inside: Artists and Writers in Reading Prison, 4 September–30 October 2016, Reading Prison, Reading, RG1 3HY UK.
4 Quotations taken from: Roni Horn, *Still Water (The River Thames for Example)*, 1999. Exhibited at Artangel.org.uk/Inside, 4 September–30 October 2016.

CONSIDERING (NON)DATA AS EVENT: EMPLOYING INTERFERENCE AS METHODOLOGY

Any work that is carried out on engagement with research and investigation into any academic discipline or field of inquiry must also involve itself in an engagement with the notion of data. 'Data' is a signifier: it represents, it involves identification and, as a consequence of all these constructions, it does. This book claims to engage with methodological approaches. These approaches have been described in earlier plateaus as non-methodological and as being concerned with methodogenetic ways of processually conceptualising and doing *madness as methodology as event*. This plateau is designed to inquire into conceptualisations of 'data' and to offer suggestions about the way that it might be seen to work that trouble and problematise other ways in which the data concept has been formed and used to signify and represent.

Throughout the writing of this book the writerly ontological predispositions which attempt to offer active conceptualisation, fluidity of process and transmutational flux in its writing practice create an active presencing which has to engage with linearity, reason and discourses that organise, structure and form. In writing this book, desiring production should be in alliance with book as body-without-organs; this production should be, at least in part, about challenging the realities of organisation that discursively construct academic books of this kind, perhaps starting with the classification of form and content and the linear development of text that proceeds in orderly, chapter by chapter fashion from the Introduction to the final Conclusion. Indeed, there is a danger that fixing the start of a piece of writing is to fix the self in the metaphysics of linearity which creates illusions of beginnings and endings, causes leading to effects and the diminution of infinitesimality. In thinking of processualism, ontogenesis and of always finding entry points and lines of flight in and out of the rhetoric and affective practice of this writing, holding the writing of this book down for a while and then letting it fly for a while has been an exciting balancing act of movement and sensation, of now you see me, now you don't. Perhaps the desiring production that is energising this book has been circling the 'data' text, unsure of when to pounce and somewhat frightened by the prickling defensiveness of the discursive fence that seems to have allowed it to exist as a given, unchallenged and dominant in many areas of research activity and academic practice.

The following words of Berlant offer a focusing upon how a troubling of the data signifier might be embarked upon and of how new conceptualisations that allow for its entangled existence in worlds of discourse, materiality, encounter and event might be created. She says:

> Then, there remains the question of the *direction* of the repair toward or away from reestablishing a relation to the political object/scene that has structured one's relation to strangers, power, and the infrastructures of belonging. So, too, remains the question of who can bear to lose the world . . . what happens when the loss of what's not working is more unbearable than the having of it, and vice versa.
>
> *Berlant, 2011: 27*

The emergent presence of these 'infrastructures of belonging' and, in particular, of the attachments that exist to them have become fixed and established through generations of essentially Positivistic scientific practices. Discursive constructions of researcher reality, which operate through the resistances they offer to reflexive engagements with their conditions of possibility and their epistemological origins, work to assign researcher roles and practices to the repletion of particular practices, the most common of which emanates in the constructed, constrictive rigours of the data collection and analysis binary. Creative digression and conceptual diversification has the potential to offer highly precarious journeys through the unctuous vapours and cloying mud of the normatively constructed and discursively inhibiting contours of the Positivist swamp.

In the study of geodetics, for example, a datum acts as a starting point; it is a point from which all other measurements can be projected and, thus, as a system of ordinates. It offers a view of the world which is imbued with fixity, stability and the metaphysical artifice of prediction: the datum enables us to know where we (really) are. When the terrain is rocky, treacherous and unpredictable, the datum offers a sense of security which provides the uncertain traveller with something to trust. So, the use of data, in its traditional Positivistic formulation, offers the very seductive and largely non-reflexive practice of data collection and analysis as a means of establishing the basis for the linearities of March of Progress[1] forms of thinking and doing. Hence, in engaging in the kinds of 'struggles to change' that Berlant refers to above, I wish to offer possibilities for the re/de/territorialisation of the data signifier and the binary construction of research practices that emanate from it and, in so doing, offer suggestions for processes of research practice that might help to facilitate what I will tentatively refer to as 'data events' or 'data as event' in productive and enabling ways.

So, for the creative movement of these words in the intensive variegation of this moment, it is again to Spinoza, now inevitably perhaps, within what Clough (2010) has referred to as the 'affective turn', to which it is necessary to lean towards. If all 'things', whatever they might be in the spatio-temporal relationality of this 'mo(ve) ment' (Davies and Gannon, 2006: x), have 'the power to affect and be affected', it is important to emphasise the corresponding position taken by Bennett (2010) and referred to earlier in her assertion that all 'things' have power: 'thing power'. The elision of power and affect is materially substantive in the sense that it brings to life agency, the sense that within and around 'thing power' there is also agency. These 'things' are agentic and, in heterogeneity and contingency, can be understood, in relationality, in terms of *agencement*, or, to use Bennett's own term, à la Deleuze, 'agentic assemblages' (2010: 20). In her work Bennett carefully shifts our attention away from the orthodoxies and traditions of psychologically inflected notions of agency and, in doing this, she points our attention towards spatio-temporal relationalities which inhere a distribution of agency and which can be understood in terms of movement, flux and the energy of transmutational flows. She also helps to shift thinking away from arborescent forms of post-Cartesian individualism towards the Deleuzian claim that the smallest unit is the assemblage. Such an approach helps to encourage a form of affective thought which nurtures a coming to life of these 'agentic assemblages' in rhizomatic patterns of movements and moments and having the modal quality to constantly and, in highly complex and particular ways, undergo modification: 'it is to mod(e)ify and be modified by others' (2010: 22). In the temporal rhythms and constant inventions of these relationalities, where assemblages assemble and reassemble, where modification is processual and tensions produce inevitable intensities, agency can be understood in terms of multiplicity, existing in play, in complex, non-hierarchical ways. Perhaps in the animation of the 'recognition (of) the misrecognition you can bear' (Berlant, 2011: 26) is where and in these ways that 'data events' can come to life.

Reading Barad offers substantive processual interference with traditional forms of data conceptualisation and contextualisation, particularly in relation to her stressing of the importance of what she refers to as an '*onto-epistem-ology* – (a) study of practices of knowing in being' (2007: 185). As she points out: 'We don't obtain knowledge by standing outside of the world; we know because we are *of* the world' (ibid.). This resonates powerfully with the active conflation of 'concept, affect and percept' that Deleuze and Guattari (1994) make in their proposals for a creative philosophy of encounter and event. In bringing this diffractive historical narrative into the movements of these (present) moments, I sense a coming to terms with the creative paradox of knowing/not knowing, with Barad, that 'each intra-action matters' (ibid.) and a tentative sensing of these as 'data as event'. Further, and in relation to this, it is necessary to think and work transversally, to cut across the usual, discursively prescribed categories and procedures and to connect with the politics and procedures of the event.

Thinking and doing with Spinoza works in the intensity of the encounter and the constant spatio-temporality relationality of affect; in this respect the power to affect and be affected is an energising creative and politically potent force. In offering challenge to the interiority of the subject and its objective manifestation in representation and identification, it is important to think and re-think, compose and decompose, always in encounter and event, the influence of affect on the multiplicity of this relationality. Thinking and working with data cannot escape encounters with these forces of attention: a conceptualisation of data has to be re-cast in relation to this. As we have seen elsewhere in this book, working with affect involves taking a lead from Whitehead (1929) in always emphasising and engaging with process over substance. Such an approach enables transversal cuttings, what Barad (2007) might refer to as taking 'agential cuts', across the established orthodoxies of practices of categorisation, classification and organisation, to live with and always re-compose Deleuze and Guattari's 'body-without-organs' (1987: 158). In the fluid assembling/ disassembling movements of the 'body-without-organs' data, in its traditional established form, excitingly and creatively and in complexity, becomes more and more difficult to pin down. If the moments of the movement in and of the body are always in transmutation and flux, then the idea of data as somehow fixed and able to have meaning becomes less and less tenable.

Elsewhere Deleuze says of the 'body-without-organs' that it exists 'Beyond the organism, but also at the limit of the body' (2004a: 44) and within this logic of sense the concept (of data) has to be lived otherwise it is nothing. As previously discussed, Bonta and Protevi have pointed out that the 'body-without-organs' is 'a misnomer', and, as such, is a confusing term which, they suggest, would have been better described by the term 'a non-organismic body' (2004: 62), or in Deleuze's own words 'The body without organs is opposed less to organs than to that organisation of organs we call an organism. It is an intense and intensive body' (2004: 44). So the intensive reality of the BwO is engaged with in terms of sense, enabling us to come to terms with data as event in relation to the allotropic variations of the always shifting movements of constantly transmutating 'bodies'.

It is significant to stress here Deleuze's point that phenomenological thinking and practice does not go far enough in simply invoking and working with lived bodies. This, at the same time, provides a thinly veiled inducement to move in, around and beyond simply human modalities of inquiry. So when Deleuze and Guattari pronounce that 'the enemy is the organism' (1987: 62), they suggest a creative engagement with smooth space, space which is composed of events and haecceities, perhaps of the order described in Virginia Woolf's (1985) term 'moments of being', where sensing and the haptic trouble work to displace the optical and the discursive and to displace the thinking and knowing practices traditionally associated with the individualised and individualising self. St Pierre's conceptualisation of 'transgressive data' in a paper published in 1997 first drew my attention to the orthodoxies exercised as given in the use of data in conventional research practice in the Humanities. In her paper she proposed, what she referred to as, 'uncodable, excessive, out of control, out-of-category' (ibid.: 179) forms of data: these were emotional data, dream data, sensual data and response data. In proposing these forms of data St Pierre offered a challenging problematisation of the discursively constructed, dominating and containing uses of the data signifier which is associated with the orthodoxies of traditional methods of research and knowledge production.

Reading this work some years ago and engaging with the practice-based ideas emanating from it, encourages me to follow an approach to inquiry that opens up complex, new and exciting challenges in qualitative inquiry, shifting research practices away from conventional forms of truth seeking and knowledge construction towards inquiries involving sensing, movement and engagements with the always not yet known.

The opportunities offered by this living processual aesthetics animates spaces of affect and intensity rather than simply those of stratified formation and immediately tangible properties. This territorialising activity of 'smoothing' alters the striations in space afforded by traditional research methods and the 'facts' they attempt to produce and is therefore sensitised to and creative of these data as events. The rhetoric of such an approach suggests that this living with and through these 'uncodable, excessive, out of control, out-of-category' data is the only way in which its immediate and pending mortality can be averted. I read in Massumi's reference to William James' living conceptualisation of 'things-in-the-making' (2015: viii) a volatile and necessary derision of Kant's essentialist and noumenal 'thing-in-itself' and a productive desire to always facilitate becoming in and of the movement in the moment, where multiplicity is always in play and where and when selves are only ever tangible in relation to encounters in and of affect.

This continual processual living with the power to affect and be affected is, creatively and paradoxically, both the death of and the means by which data can have life; it is in the intensive multiplicity of space/time entanglements in which becoming in the event is the only sense in which data as a living, animating concept can give life to the inquiries we wish to make of the world. In an emergent sense, this re-conceptualisation and re-composition of data therefore offers a means of working with inquiry and all its concomitant 'fellow travelling concepts' (Massumi, 2015: x) in radically new, different and ultimately creative ways.

How might this be done? In this madness as methodology how can a productive (re)conceptualisation of 'data' be constructed in ways that help to free it from the constraints of representational discourses and dogmas of signification and which encourages a problematisation and troubling of the established orthodoxies and limitations of the data collection and analysis practice binary? As researchers living with data it may never be possible to escape from the entanglements between materiality and discourse, reality and representation that Barad has alerted us to. When she talks of the possibilities of diffractive methodologies, cracks and fissures in the orthodoxies of traditional approaches to data and research practice begin to appear and it is from these interstices that lines of flight from containment from the judgemental forces of reason can be made. It is this use of diffraction as interference that helps to animate and further mobilise this madness as methodology. She points out that the complexities and multiple interferences of diffractive practices

> highlight, exhibit, and make evident the entangled structure of the changing and contingent ontology of the world, including the ontology of knowing.

> In fact, diffraction not only brings the reality of entanglements to light, it is itself an entangled phenomenon.
>
> *2007: 73*

So in working with 'data as event' the intentionally paradoxical conflation of data/non/data provides a basis for being continually attentive to the possibilities of conceptual fragility and differentiation of practices. This is quite obviously a world in which there are no Kantian transcendental conditions of possibility and where the possibilities of madness as methodology become more and more present as the doors of given and unchallenged orthodoxies swing closed. It is a world in which experimentation is always prior, where the need for interpretation gains fragility, where, indeed, interpretation becomes another artifice in domains of representation. Rather, it is a space in which connections can be made and where associations are always possible. This is redolent of the new empiricism that Deleuze conjures from the work of Hume. Here it seems that the differentiating relations that are always emergent from and with these associational connections are somehow always just beyond the terms used to convey them. In transversality they are always on the move. They are elusive and tantalisingly mercurial in their presence of now you see me now you don't. This is the world in which life is given to the conceptual elision of data/non/data. Hume's associations challenge, by continual effervescent displacement, the violence of social partialities. The new empiricism that Deleuze (1991) recognised and explicated in his reading of Hume is one that is premised upon turning knowledge into belief and in promoting logics of becoming and relational multiplicity. In this respect Deleuze describes multiplicities in terms of the entanglement, connection and bifurcation of lines; for him these lines are 'true *becomings*' that are distinct from unities, fixities and the histories from which these are developed: 'That is the concept exists just as much in empiricism as in rationalism, but it has a completely different use and a completely different nature: it is a being-multiple, instead of a being-one, a being-whole or being as subject' (Deleuze and Parnet, 2002: viii). New and creative conceptualisations of data must emerge from this: relationalities and multiplicities have to be understood in terms of the associational. Associations of the kind that Deleuze develops from his reading of Hume are used to trouble causal, condensational practices where metaphorical tropes attempt, through strategies of representational equation and unification, to attach, distil and rationally establish meaning. Orthodox procedures of, so-called, data collection and analysis animate this process by establishing that data can somehow be comprehended and captured in object form and examined closely like an insect pinned to a display board.

In this associational empiricism, the promotion of metonymic processes which act to displace such condensational fixities by not naming and by offering exploratory and experimental associations in meaning is used to diffractively locate inquiry into and about the always not yet known. Barad might refer to disruptively creative associational engagements of this kind as 'interferences' which can be seen to resemble her 'diffractive patterns' which are composed of 'patterns of difference that make a difference' (2007: 72). Conceptualising data in this way serves to displace the discursively dominating idea that data somehow are objects that can be collected, like fauna from the forest, and then taken to the laboratory and analysed through vigilant exposure under the microscope's lens. Traditional forms of ethnographic research exemplify these practices. An account of this is provided in the following passage; the author, whilst displaying certain ironic characteristics also provides a telling account of the orthodoxies of data collection and analysis procedures that are often employed in qualitative inquiry:

> The conduct of an ethnographic project will result in the accumulation . . . of voluminous notes . . . (together with other data). The second major act of textual construction involves what is usually (and revealingly) called 'writing up' . . . In the first mode, the writer is involved in 'writing down' what goes on: the imagery is that of transcription uninterrupted by self-conscious intervention of reflection. The second phase . . . carries stronger connotations of a constructive side to the writing. In this phase what was written 'down' is treated as data in the writing 'up'.
>
> *Atkinson, 1990: 61*

The domination of the data collection and analysis binary is vividly portrayed in the imagery of this extract and clearly displays the principles underlying the kinds of research practice to be found in most forms of Positivist and post-Positivist inquiry in the Humanities and Social Sciences. The image of the ethnographer as recorder and collector, avidly 'writing down' what is being observed for the purposes of future analysis and interpretation, busily engaging in the 'accumulation . . . of voluminous notes', clearly exemplifies the orthodox and foundational practice of 'data collection' and the production of 'facts'. In this the field notes that are being written down will be used to somehow 'capture' what has been 'seen' and then be used to provide 'evidence' of these observations and then written up. Such an approach is traditionally linked to the application of the conceptual rigours and ethically informed practices of reliability and validity which then, in turn, are used to supposedly give authenticity, veracity and truth value to that which has been faithfully observed and collected. The written field notes that have been recorded now exist in a world of fact as 'raw data' and can undergo reflective examination and be interpreted as part of subsequent data analysis procedures.

In offering an account of what he refers to as the 'ethnographic imagination' in the ethnographer's move from 'writing down' (date collection) to 'writing up' (data analysis), Atkinson demonstrates Nagel's (1986) claim that there can never be a 'view from nowhere' but does not appear to take the opportunity to challenge the representational nature of knowledge production that is inherent in his example. And so we have here an example of the ways in which positionality, stance, viewpoint and perspective have to be taken into consideration alongside representational methods of interpretation, selection, coding, and other analytical strategies of this kind. It is clear that such reflective approaches are agentic in the *generation* and *production* of so-called data, where the ethnographic research practice actively creates objects which are the representational *consequence* of the so-called inquiry. The questions that this raises for the application and use of the practices of data collection and analysis are incisive and highly significant.

In contrast, an empiricism that talks of metonymic relationalities and diffractively sees data as existing as encounter and event offers substantive challenge to the often-unnoticed orthodoxies and proclivities of such research practices. An associational empiricism of this kind recognises the continual rhythms of ascent and descent, of emerging and diminishing 'patterns of difference that make a difference' and revels in the transmutational experimental fragilities that such patterns bring to life. This is how I have come to have a sense, within this madness as methodology, a kind of knowing in constant action, of data/non/data. It is in this respect that Kathleen Stewart's (2007) engagement with the ordinariness of affect provides another dimensionality, a plane on which it is possible to make sense of data as contingent and event/ual and of the creative paradoxical nature of the data/non/data conflation. With Deleuze and Guattari (1994) I cannot shift affect from its close and intensive entanglement with concept and with percept and in this living with sense knowings are made up of continual movement in moments. Increasingly, like Spinoza's conative bodies, in Humean associational multiplicity, sense, space and time only becomes realisable (made real) in terms of encounter and as event, perhaps as Bachelard (1969) might have it, in terms of a 'poetics of space' (and time).

In the opening page of her book *Ordinary Affects*, Stewart says, 'The notion of a totalised system, of which everything is always already somehow a part, is not helpful (to say the least) in the effort to approach a weighted and reeling present' (2007: 1). This sense of 'a weighted and reeling present' is forceful in energising a productive desire to reconceptualise data in terms of constant becoming in space and time. The totalising nature of systems that Stewart refers to bears resemblance to Deleuze and Guattari's challenging engagement with 'hylomorphism' (1987: 408) and the tendency of institutions to conform to structural ordering and systemic control that are projected in advance by external agencies as a means of organising these systems in particular ways. In her engagement with 'ordinary affect', Stewart talks of trying 'to slow the quick jump to representational thinking and evaluative critique' (2007: 4) and there seems to be little doubt that hylomorphic tendencies lean with great imposition and exert pressure upon contingencies, ambivalence, dis/organisation and what might be perceived to be chaotic features of organisational life. Deleuze and Guattari demonstrate that through strategies of 'territorialisation' (1987: 314) these tendencies lean on and exert organising principles and forces that are anathema to the 'body-without-organs' (ibid.: 149) , they attempt to displace, organise and override what Bennett recognises, animates and describes as the 'distributive agency' (2010) of assemblages. In employing the associative and affective qualities of Spinoza's conative bodies, Bennett offers resonating connection with Stewart's 'ordinary affects' by demonstrating in her work 'the power of a body to affect other bodies [which] includes a "corresponding and inseparable" capacity to be affected' (2010: 21). So in sensing with Bennett that agency is always distributed and being distributed, that, as living with the vibrancy of these entanglings of representations and realities, language and matter, Spinoza's conative body is more and more in its becomings a singularity in the heterogeneities and complexities of what she refers to as 'agentic assemblages'. Again, in further highlighting the limitations of the humanistic inclinations of the phenomenological approach, Bennett points out

> Bodies enhance their power in or as heterogeneous assemblage. What this suggests for the concept of agency is that the efficacy or effectivity to which that term has traditionally referred becomes distributed across an ontologically heterogeneous field, rather than being a capacity localised in a human body or in a collective produced (only) by human efforts.
>
> *Bennett, 2010: 23*

And, in this respect, contexts are not benign, simply existing as backdrops to the interactive engagements of human actors, rather, in multiplicity, things, all things, have to be considered in event/uality, they are always in the making, intra-actively engaged in human/non/human, spatio-temporality.

This plateau proposes a madness as methodology which actively conceptualises data as constantly event/ful and that promotes an active and problematising conceptual elision of data/non/data. Such a conceptualisation is designed to offer challenge to orthodox systems and practices of data construction and production that are set up to exist in relation to the essential and noumenal qualities of things-in-themselves, existing as separable categories of difference. In a methodology of this kind data is more easily understood in terms of transmutation and flux, where multiple entanglements of materiality and discourse are the vibrant matter of 'agentic assemblages' and where it is a commonplace to acknowledge with Haraway (2000) that bodies do not end with their skin. These kinds of 'entanglements', which Barad (2007) engages with in her 'intra-active' approach to research and inquiry, are clearly highly complex and brimming with immense potentiality in relation to the intensities with which they are inevitably imbued and to what demands they place upon the researcher who is curious enough to set up encounters with them. To use Stewart's words again, 'the effort to approach a weighted and reeling present' (2007) will be challenging and ultimately extremely rewarding.

In following this point I notice that Massumi, in introducing his 'politics of affect', says: 'Much of the work of the book is dedicated to laying the polyvalent groundwork for this reforging of concepts, transversal to their usual diametric opposition with each other' (2015: x). I use this viewpoint as a touchstone for the rhetoric of this plateau; I want to problematise traditional conceptualisations of data that are grounded in Positivistic modes of thought, I want to trouble and destabilise the tidy and ultimately simplistic dualism of data collection and analysis and to offer processual data modalities that revel in insecurity, experimentation and the troublesome nature of their applications. In this I am with Berlant when she says 'the ritual habit is another route to preserving banality, turning care of the self into a mode of ordinariness' (2011: 62). This methodology of madness is designed to care for selves in ways that will promote experimentation, problematisation and the means to offer challenge to the research practice 'sanities' that have contained and constrained them hitherto.

Returning to the question posed earlier, 'How might this be done?', I read Deleuze and Guattari's following question as a methodological prompt: 'But when one writes, the only question is which other machine the literary machine can be plugged into, must be plugged into in order to work' (1987: 4). I see this 'plugging in' as experimental, productive and hugely necessary. Through all their collaborative practice Deleuze and Guattari work in the construction of space where 'there is no heaven for concepts', where the object of inquiry 'is to create concepts that are always new' (1994: 5) and, in this respect, I am attempting to give some life to this conceptualisation of data as event as a form of mapping and a suggestion of an approach to come.

I have written elsewhere (Gale, 2014) of the possible ways in which an engagement with data can take place outside of the constraining forces and hylomorphic tendencies that totalise and order research practices in particular ways. I keep returning to engagements with the possibilities of 'data as event'. I read Haraway quoting Bergson as saying: 'What is real is the continual change of form: form is only a snapshot view of a transition' (2000: 17). Manning takes this further when she says, 'When form becomes in-formation the body multiplies' and later, drawing on the work of Simondon, 'he liberates (the body) from the pre-supposition of a form, demonstrating how a body is always alive across lives. The body's individuation is its force for becoming, not its end point' (2010: 118). Similarly, in working with a Deleuzian 'logic of sense' the play between concept, affect, and percept offers a highly pluralised, transformative energising force as bodies constantly organise, re-organise and dis-organise in the creative non-organisation of 'bodies-without-organs'. Conceptual, affective and perceptual complexities articulate and connect in the spatio-temporal relationality of shifting moments and movements of the constantly folding flows of discourse and materiality. With Whitehead (1929) again I sense process enabling a problematisation of substance, where these processual movements and moments, transversally cutting across, through and beyond the brief fragility of existing formations offer the 'continual change' referred to by Bergson and the processes of 'in-formation' referred to by Manning in the quotations above.

I read the following and begin to think about tentative methodological procedures that could encourage an engagement with 'data as event':

> 'Vignette' is a word that originally meant 'something that may be written on a vine-leaf'. It's a snapshot in words. It differs from flash fiction or a short story in that its aim doesn't lie within the traditional realms of structure or plot. Instead, the vignette focuses on one element, mood, character, setting or object. It's descriptive, excellent for character or theme exploration and wordplay. Through a vignette, you create an atmosphere.

www.vineleavesliteraryjournal.com/

I wonder about the role of the vignette in providing short, impressionistic scenes that focus on one moment, that trace or instigate a brief movement, or give a particular insight into a character, an idea, a setting, a state of mind, and, in intuition, a tacit sense of knowing in indeterminacy and the fragility of shimmering movement. I sense a connection here with Massumi's (2002) use of the 'example' and the practice of 'exemplification', discussed in detail elsewhere in this book. I sense a connection here with what MacLure says when talking of data that 'glows': 'The glow seems to invoke something abstract or intangible that exceeds propositional meaning, but also has a decidedly embodied aspect' (2013b: 661). There is a sense of something going on here, something intensive, something that is about the intricate, complex and deeply entangled relationality of language and the idea, on the one hand, and the materiality of movements in the moment, on the other. The creation of an 'atmosphere' seems highly relevant in this encounter, this engagement with something in becoming, as data, as event. There is something about the intangibility of these moments and the amorphous nature of these movements that falls within the intensity of sensing a vignette as something being 'written on a vine leaf':

> I suppose, as the leaf shrivels and dies with the emergent and luscious sensual pregnancies of the grape, so does its 'writing' with it. And so it is clear that vignettes, at least in intentional ways, don't explain, or define, or even conceptualise; they just offer a little window, an in/out/sight, a glimpsing of an image that is literally smaller than the original and yet provides subtleties and flavours, nuances, and qualities that might otherwise not be seen, felt, or heard: a sharpening of focus, a heightening of awareness, a touching upon intensity.
>
> *Gale, 2014: 1000*

In reading how Haraway imagines 'how like a leaf I am' (2000: 132), affectively I feel drawn to conceptually mapping a methodological cartography that enables a working with 'data as event' in ways that can effectively make moves away from the abject significations of representational fixity and productively activate a creative immersion in the entanglements of materiality and discourse in practices of (post-) qualitative inquiry. This might be what a madness of methodology can do. Deleuze describes such practices as being involved in 'continually dismantling the organism, causing asignifying particles or pure intensities to pass or circulate and attributing to itself subjects that it leaves with nothing more than a name as the trace of an intensity' (1987: 4). It feels that this continual dismantling of the organism through the rhizomatic working of Deleuze and Guattari's 'principle of asignifying rupture' has the potential for promoting affirmative, transformative practices involving the practices of 'plugging in', of doing something with them and in so doing bringing them alive. As Deleuze and Guattari say, the principle works

> against the oversignifying breaks separating structures or cutting across a single structure. A rhizome may be broken, shattered at a given spot, but it will start

up again on one of its old lines, or on new lines . . . the line of flight is part of the rhizome.

1987: 9

In these respects I have come to visualise a *madness as methodology as event*, a methodology that is always involved in doing; engaging in practices of 'vignetting'. Similar to Whitehead's (1929) concept of 'superject' where emergence is processual in world making not in terms of substantive subjectivity, these practices can be seen as involving a *sensing of things-in-the-making* rather than of *knowing things-in-themselves*. This sensing brings affect alive through beginning to enable a working *through* the world and, as Massumi says, 'It is thought taking the plunge, consenting to ride the waves of affect on a crest of words, drenched to the conceptual bone in the fineness of its spray' (2015: vii). 'Vignetting' can describe active processes of working in and through the world, animating becomings in continual processes of briefly and hesitantly drawing attention and momentary bringing to life.

- - - - - - - - - - - - - - - -

Poem, early hours 18 September 2015:
Now you see me now you don't
Other bodies surge through me like pulsing heterotopic forces.
I am undone with surprise;
the repetition of images of thought
display in always different forms (in/form/ation);
names of past others collide with the mundane industry of the moment,
for the breadth of less than a second time stands still.
I sense another's word,
it might be a body part;
a smell creeps into me, animating bodying
and intensity reels me in, reels me in to life.
In ontological freeze frame I activate my memory and the moment is gone,
the movement into thought holds the image, briefly:
The rationality of forgetfulness.
Now you see me now you don't.

- - - - - - - - - - - - - - - -

The vignette, a singularity, itself a form of data as event, in turn helps to compose an assemblage of associated singularities that, having been produced and that work in certain ways, have their life and then, like the vine leaf, shrivels, desiccates and falls and in its processual composting becomes another vine, another grape another leaf to be written on. And so,

> It makes more sense to me to think of vignetting, of actively and performatively bringing the world into becoming through drawing attention, through blurring the peripheral for a moment to sharpen and clarify the central, through interfering with false binaries to represent in the play of making

temporally and spatially hesitant the real. It is momentary; it lives in the wink of an eye: aeon. The fingers sliding down the fret board, slurring the notes in a Deleuzian-like stuttering, gliding upward or downward in minimal imperceptible action and monumental effect; as the note vibrates in your groin, you sense tears lightly rolling down your cheek. These are the foldings and unfoldings that content themselves in the hesitancy of intention and unintention, when the words are flowing, when the paint is alive on the canvas and the design is awash with the spontaneity of the moment.

Gale, 2014: 1000

I sense this 'glow' of data, with Whitehead, as less than substance and more as process; it is both seductive and productive and, in this sense, as a virtual light it is actualised in processual awareness, not as consciousness but in *event/ful/ness*. I sense here with this conceptualisation of data as event an engagement with Deleuze's (1997) application of 'duration', particularly in relation to his work with Hume. In accounting for and applying Hume's empiricism of association, Deleuze offers that 'duration' not includes but produces difference and in this sense it is about transformation and creativity. 'Duration' is about the multiplicity of tentative associational syntheses that temporarily instantiate connections between events and encounters, such as those brought to life in the processual practices of 'vignetting'. This not only provides for a sensing of data in event/uality but also a sense of durational time, not in terms of the linear longevities of *chronos* but in the always differentiating repetitions of *aeon* (Deleuze and Guattari, 1987). Deleuze's use of 'duration', in relation to the emergence of this associational empiricism, brings together a sense of data as event, as always processual, involving things-in-the-making, not things-in-themselves and 'as lived experience, brings together both unity and difference in a flow of interconnections' (Parr, 2010: 83). As Massumi points out in addressing Spinoza's treatment of affect, the power to affect and be affected 'is to be open to the world, to be active in it and also to be patient for its return activity . . . One always affects and is affected in encounters; which is to say through events' (2015: ix). This openness to the world, the doing of things-in-the-making, what Manning, Massumi, Stewart and others have called 'world making', cannot be carried out and seen through the lenses of scientific research orthodoxies. When Manning (2009) gives the title of one of her papers, 'What if it didn't all begin and end with containment? Toward a leaky sense of self', she provides a rhetorical phrasing which helps to mobilise the point I am making here. The madness as methodology that I am trying to conceptualise here and the processes and practices of 'vignetting' that I am proposing as integral to it are less likely to emerge through, from and with bodies that live with the kinds of containments that Manning is referring to. In Deleuze and Guattari the conceptualisation of 'becoming' can be readily associated with Whitehead's notion of 'individuation' and with Manning's processes of 'in-formation' and those associated 'leaky bodies'. What these thinkers have in common is that notions of containment and leakiness are not simply human constructs to be understood according to the practices of phenomenological reasoning, rather they can be understood, as Manning describes, in the following way:

> When the skin becomes not a container but a multi-dimensional topological surface that folds in, through and across spacetimes of experience, what emerges is not a self but the dynamic form of worlding that refuses categorisation. Beyond the human, beyond the sense of touch or vision, beyond the object, what emerges is relation.
>
> *2009: 42*

In this conceptualisation of data it is no longer simply possible to accept the logic of reason, rationality and the orthodoxies and traditional empiricism of conventional research and inquiry that is practised in the Humanities and the Social Sciences. In the madness as methodology that is associated with this conceptualisation, I sense the multi-directionality and diverse impulse of flows of transversality sustaining me as I move through these moments of creativity. As I use my writing here to inquire into and employ this madness as methodology, I live in the energies of the wash that these impulses generate. Phenomenological suppositions and tangibilities of experience and consciousness erode as serendipity, chance and the play of now you see me, now you don't, create senses of self in flow, where leakiness and containment provide the tempo and rhythms of a dance that is always animate in the gliding, individuating emergence of becoming.

In his song 'Gates of Eden' that was released in 1965 on the album *Bringing It All Back Home*, Bob Dylan evokes a powerful image of his lover, coming to him at dawn and telling him of her dreams. She tells him of her dreams, showing them, describing them, providing a glimpse, the briefest movement in a moment, something that she simply recounts and does not attempt explain. It is clear from Dylan's lyrics that her words are simply there to show him something; she offers no explanation, she does not represent, her words are there, they provide an encounter, they are glimpsed, as an event, and life goes on.

In the beautiful lyricism of this song there is no sense in which she engages in interpretation or draws upon Freud, or Jung, or whoever, to tell us what these kaleido-scopes of the dark night are all about or what they might mean. It is the glimpse that is significant for her: we would be foolish to imagine anything beyond that; any inquiry into meaning, any setting up of a discourse of representation would be an abuse, it would be the coarse vulgarity of shovelling something into a ditch. I imagine her dancing with the images of the dreams still fresh in her body, sharing her colours, her smells, and her vibrant waking vitality with the man she loves. In my imaginings I love that she dances with what is there, her presence in their shared early morning space is brought to life by the vibrancy of her movements and her moments, in the here and now, in instantiation, in this becoming. There is a shimmering creativity, the making of new events that, in their repetition, bring to life events of new, pure life. Her glimpses are haecceities, moments of being, where her movements in thisness bring life to life and, in so doing, move on, not with neglect, abandon or the loss that associates with the vagaries of memory but with the energy of creativity, where living is always in the moment, of not yet, of the always new event. In the powerful poetics of this song it is clear that Dylan is living and engaging with her in worlds of sense. The realist showing of the dreams vibrate in the ontogenesis of their shared moments together; for him, inside the *Gates of Eden*, these are the only words that can give him truth.

Here is a *methodology of madness as event*, here is my 'methodology of madness'. In my weaker moments I worry that I play upon the cusp of a metaphysics that attempts to create a category of practice that is grounded within a particular point of view, one that relies upon a tentative epistemological fabric that could be easily torn and replaced with something much more secure, much more foundational. If that is the case, I gain relief when I say 'Give it a try', 'Plug it in', 'Riff off that'; that is what it is about, it is a new empiricism, it is that Deleuzian re/reading of Hume that concerns itself with the associational, the metonymic and the always becoming absorbed in the wonder of where that might lead to, how it moves affect in the moment and how it might tear me apart.

I have lived with the beauty of this song for fifty years. My vinyl copy of the album has written on the cover '25th December 1965': my mum and dad gave it to me for Christmas. I was 18 years old. 18 years old. I have to repeat that. I want this repetition to do something, I want it to work, I want to sense it's working in affect. I love it that I don't know what this song, this album, has done to me but I know that it is there, it has power, it affects and through whatever is me it also has the power to affect me. *Erewhon*,[2] Fat Boy Slim – it is right here, right now, living, vibrant and vital, in the whatever and the whoever that produces the words that are on this page and that reads them in the simple subtle vibrational fragrance that lives in them now.

Along with every other becoming, every other 'thing' that affects and has the power to be affected, although we might deny it, there is a sense in which we are all subject to the relational capacities of the constant play of all these energetic forces. In my singularity I am at my desk, the sun has just set, the sky in the west is still aglow with the pinks and blues of nightly comforts, the day is putting itself to rest in the gradual retreat of brightness into dusk and then dark. In a brief moment of organisational rationality I need to check the date, it is 29 July 2015, the moon is waxing, it presents itself tonight as a waxing gibbous and I wonder, as always, about its powers, about how it energises me as it glows and grows and then, later in its calendar journey, how it drags me down with it in its deepening, depressing trajectory as it descends into invisibility and darkness.

I have begun to argue here, specifically in this plateau and, more generally, in the book as a whole that the cultural and methodological logic of emergent posthumanisms works to disallow narrowness of thought and practice and to trouble the tyrannies of epistemologies of fixed meaning. As an alternative, I am proposing an approach to practice that I conceptualise as madness as methodology. I have also described this madness as methodology as event as a non-methodology. I have done this, not because it is not a methodology but because I wish to conceptualise an approach to processualism and use, rather than to ascribe substantive meaning to any one method as a means of establishing a category of difference, and, hence, I offer this as a *methodogenesis*.

I understand the research practices that will emanate from this in relation to the conceptualisation of data as event. In this I offer for consideration a practice of 'vignetting' as possibly providing an approach that can work to engage with and indeed creatively and aesthetically produce ontogenetically inclined material and discursive entanglements of human, nonhuman, relationality. So, data is understood in process, as events, where madness energises the 'in-formation' (Manning, 2013) of *methodogenesis* and where the always shifting body of madness as methodology is not simply understood but is made sense of, not in terms of what it means but in terms of what it does. So *doing*, perhaps as 'vignetting', interferes with, it brings this to life through the use of diffractive ways of looking, of looking elsewhere, of settling on this and that, always aware of the intensities and potentialities that can become present in alighting elsewhere, at another time.

> One's always writing to bring things to life, to free life from where it's trapped, to trace lines of flight. The language for doing that can't be a homogeneous system, it's something unstable, always heterogeneous, in which style carves differences of potential between which things can pass, come to pass, a spark can flash and break out of language itself, to make us see and think what was lying in the shadow around the words, things we were hardly aware existed.
>
> *Deleuze, 1995: 141*

This is also how I am making sense of data within the emergences of post-qualitative inquiry. In these inquiries, these always nascent research practices, I am always writing into the not yet known, I am always involved in the practice of 'writing to it' (Wyatt and Gale, 2017), of using transversal approaches in the writing of 'minor literatures' (Deleuze and Guattari, 1986) and of engaging theorising *as* practice in the active animation of creative philosophies of encounter and event. Therefore, it is my hope that these always emergent understandings of data, of actually *doing* data, might offer opportunities for bringing non-totalising modes of sensing to life within the vibrant potentialities of such experimental and creative approaches.

Notes

1 So called 'March of Progress' theories derive from a scientific illustration created by natural history painter and muralist Rudolph Zallinger that was published in 1965. The illustration presents 25 million years of human evolution by depicting a range of human evolutionary forebears from ape-like ancestors through to modern homo sapiens all lined up as if marching in the same direction in a parade. The image has promulgated numerous copies and is largely responsible for the popular emergence of a linear and anthropocentric view of so-called development, civilisation and progress.

2 Deleuze in *Difference and Repetition* and Deleuze and Guattari in *Anti-Oedipus* use *Erewhon*, the title of a Victorian novel by Samuel Butler, to convey multiplicity and difference, not as something fixed but as eternally differentiating. Butler meant the title to be read as 'nowhere' backwards; in Deleuze and Guattari's usage, *Erewhon* is both *no-where* and *now-here*, exemplifying the play between the inside and the outside and the constantly becoming of the assembling/dissembling shifts of bodies-without-organs.

WHAT CAN THIS MADNESS AS METHODOLOGY DO?

So this plateau is the final plateau to appear within the apparent linear structure of this book. If this book has been read according to the discursively constructed conventions of book reading, then this plateau will be seen to contain a few surprises, some ideas that this book production has germinated and it will appear to bring the book to a close, drawing certain conclusions and making some suggestions for possible future practices. If, however, the reader has hopped, skipped and jumped from plateau to plateau in their reading of this book and perhaps in using the index to help them to choreograph the dance of their lines of flight, then it is likely that the reading of this plateau will have been absorbed into the processual animation of concept creation that has been one of the energising features of writing and, I hope, reading this book: this plateau offers another possible line of flight.

I am writing this plateau with still more plateaus to write and to complete. I am not being syllogistic in my presentation of these pages. In this respect my 'conclusion' does not necessarily follow from its 'premises': deductive reasoning has not paved my path to the writing of this plateau. This plateau is emergent in relationality; it grows as other plateaus grow, its life force is deeply imbricated with that of the other plateaus. I sense as I write this plateau, in anticipation and with experimentation, I am likely to re/turn to other plateaus and re-write something that I have already written there. This has been the way throughout the writing of the whole book; it is the way of this always becoming-book, its logic is of movement and sensation rather than of linearity and rationality. All my world making takes these forms: to use Manning's term again, it is always about 'in-formation' (2013).

I have come to a time in the writing of this book that I feel the need to concern myself with, and to focus a little more sharply upon, what this madness as methodology might do and, indeed, is doing as these pages become animate in their processual folding and unfolding. In short, it will involve me in talking about and showing how this madness as methodology can be made, in terms of what it can do, in terms of what it does. So if I focus upon and think about working as someone who engages in something called research and inquiry, who works with other people in institutional settings, universities, engaged in educational practices to do with teaching and learning, then what I feel that I need to embark upon in the writing of this plateau is to talk about this madness as methodology in terms of what it might do in education settings.

I sense that, as the ideas and the writing of them begins to unfold with me here and now, the book and this plateau, specifically, will need to propose an approach to these education practices which involves *doing*. This is a doing that works, not in ways that are prescribed or set, that can be modelled or that represent, but in ways that involve derailment, going off track, engaging in experimentation that is unbounded. It will be about the action of bodies, any bodies, human and nonhuman, in constant engagement with what those bodies can do. It will be alert to the observation that these encountering, pro/active, en/acting, doing and re/active bodies are always also being acted upon and being done to and with, because all bodies have the capacity to affect and be affected.

A few years ago I stumbled across such an approach when engaged in an earlier piece of research with colleagues into the use of action research as a means of inquiring into notions of education and professionalism within a higher education setting (Gale, Turner and McKenzie, 2013). In this research the employment of action research, as conceptualised by Somekh and Zeichner (2009), Carr and Kemmis (1989) and others, was used as a means of animating the processual longevity of the research over an extended period of time and also to allow some creative, evolutionary flexibility in terms of the changing nature and possibilities offered by the research practice. Hence, through engaging all the research participants, all relatively new to working in higher education, in the use of Richardson's (2000) approach to 'writing as a method of inquiry', they not only began to work with the emergence of diffractive possibilities, but also began to allow a new approach to interfere with and encourage a new conceptualisation of the practice of action research to also emerge. In using the flexibility of this diffractively infused, action-based approach to research, as researchers, we also began, through the emergence of the research process, to problematise the highly human-centric nature of action research as it had hitherto been traditionally conceived and employed. The following extract from Richardson's paper suggests how this action-based approach began to emerge, shifting it from its original and substantively human-centric proclivities and intentions towards the appearance and practice of a more processual and assemblage based form of inquiry:

> At first we were drawn by conventional discursive constructions to employ phrases such as 'group dynamics' and 'communities of practice' to describe the flows and intensities that were emergent within the writing practices we were promoting.
>
> How anodyne and flat those terms now seem in respect of the writing and the engagement with professional action we are now experiencing in the

action research. In the emergent nature of this space, there seem to be multiple connections being made within the dynamics of the research, in terms of the participants' interactions with one another, our interactions with them, our own interactions with one another and our growing sense of the intra-active nature of these becomings that, I feel, cannot be captured through the use of these terms. This complexity is reflected in Mary's (one of the respondents) comments when she said:

> The minute you've written something, it almost becomes somebody else's because they put their interpretation on it or their slant on it.

As part of the emergent nature of the action research practice, these movements and moments were increasingly conceptualised within a sense of becoming-professional. Within this we noticed a linked blurring of fixed senses of self and, in line with this, enforced separations of self and other, form and content began to dissolve into mixtures and hybridisations. The various exchanges of writings and readings that took place were clearly significant in helping to nurture this. It is not that the name or the classification, the binary or the dualism is done away with; rather, it is that it becomes other within the active and fluid and transmutating life force of the assemblage.

Ibid.: 12

As mentioned elsewhere in this book, the emergence of this diffractive, action-based practice style within the research process itself prompted an inquiry into the notion of 'assemblage/ethnography' (Wyatt and Gale, 2013a, 2013b) as a means of attempting to promote an approach to, so-called, action research that serves to trouble and destabilise its traditional human-centric and largely phenomenological conceptualisation and practice.

A posthuman-inclined and relationally oriented approach to ways of action-based inquiry and doing that were beginning to emerge in my research at this time involves an always arriving from elsewhere and an always becoming something other than before. Such approaches are embodied in always diffracting moments in movements, movements in moments of persistent and incessant ontogenetic creation of bodies in time and space. These 'mo(ve)ments' (Davies and Gannon, 2006) will be about sensation, they will be embodied in and generative of individuation and the constant living activism of agencement. I shared with my research colleagues at this time, as these new approaches to our inquiries began to emerge, that we were mobilising and engaging what Soyini Madison has referred to as 'acts of activism' (2010). This relational sense of activism, of doing something with, through and to, of sensing these 'mo(ve)ments' of and in intra-acting human/ non/human exchange gave a new intensity to the research practice which I am continuing working with in my thinking, feeling and doing in the space making of this book, at this time. The practice of 'plugging in' (Deleuze and Guattari, 1987: 4) conceptualisations that Deleuze and Guattari promote and bring to life in the early pages of *A Thousand Plateaus*, is integral to this activism.

In these respects, research and inquiry can no longer live in domains of practice based upon those sharpened hierarchies that frame the 'researcher' and the 'researched' as somehow separate categories of difference and that are in relationships that are somehow already formed by their discursively constructed, interactive dimensionality. Rather, these 'acts of activism' are animate in the doing of coming together of human/non/human bodies. These comings together are about composition. Composition is not fixed, it is always becoming. It is the energy and intensity of individuation where the elisions of movement and moments are the processual driving force of life. Linked to these comings together of ceaseless composition, Manning (2013) offers the practice of 'choreography'. As she points out, 'choreography' is not solely and exclusively limited to its alliance with dance. 'The choreographic . . . is a technique that assists us in rethinking how a creative process activates conditions for its emergence as event' (ibid.: 74–75). And so I sense choreographic acts as being relational in the affective space of world making, where bodies can *do* in relation to one another, all having capacities to affect and be affected. Choreography then is about assemblage. It is about the sense of assemblage that is to do with *agencement*, it is about the sense of assemblage that is to do with *arrangement* and involves the coming together of composition where relational time and space in and between bodies is always part of world making. In my reluctance to identify and represent I choose not to talk about the choreographer, just in the same way that I try to avoid talking about the 'teacher', the 'learner', the 'researcher', the 'researched' and other identifications of this kind. Therefore, there are senses in which choreographic acts are *done*, they arrange and involve making forms, in-forming, in particular ways. They might be organisational and impositional and then be accommodating and responsive. They are likely to interfere with preceding acts and to territorialise space and time in all kinds of troubling and disruptive ways. In this sense it is possible that choreographic acts happen. They happen in relationality and they are not owned and of the individual person. In the comings together of choreographic composition there are multiple acts which are constitutive of these comings together. All the senses will be vibrant and animate in their spatio-temporal re/pro/en/actions. The social will vibrate in intensive movement with human/non/human exchange, so that facilitation, enabling, empathy and intervention will emerge in relation to all bodies in these comings together. I sense the madness in the in-forming of such a methodology as involving what Newman has called a 'postanarchism'. This is one which

> emphasises an anarchism of the here and now, unencumbered by . . . revolutionary metanarrative . . . [an] ontological anarchism . . . which entails a form of thinking and acting without an *arché* – in other words, without stable foundations or essential identities to determine its course.
>
> *2016: xii*

I love the politics which emanates from, that is, this activism. In one sense the politics is emergent and for me it is joyfully and happily aligned to the way in which this actively relational world making is also deeply educational in its processual becoming. This 'thinking and acting without an *archē*' offers a highly political and, I wish to argue, a deeply educational approach to practice. It is one which offers challenge, in hugely creative ways, to the very *archi*tecture (my emphasis) of institutional design and practice. It encourages a thinking about what Manning refers to as 'mobile architecture' (2013: 102) and the action of 'architecturing', where the very design, building and enactment of practices are always in play. This seems to carry some resonance with humanistic inflected practice of facilitation where education practitioners, through strategically conceived 'interventions' bring to life knowing, learning and meaning making, where the 'scaffolding' is flexible and enabling and facilitates the growth and emergence of the 'human' (Heron, 1989). In the context of this madness as methodology, the intentions and practices of these humanistically inclined practices are enhanced by paying attention to a more creative and situational ecology in which relationality is not simply human and, within intended complexity, more than human. In the 'architecturing' of these posthuman compositional intricacies, the approach that Manning refers to as 'choreographic' comes into play through world-making practices, bringing to life the always new and the not yet known, through the use of 'a technique that assists us in rethinking how a creative process activates conditions for its emergence as event' (2013: 75). Awareness of and engagement with the relational ecologies and political potentialities that such approaches brings in to play are of crucial importance in the animation of knowing through becoming within the emergence of institutional educational settings at the present time. (Some ongoing and recent examples of this can found at: http://senselab.ca/wp2/ and www.plymouth.ac.uk/whats-on/beyond-words-conference-2017.)

Considering the question that heads up this plateau leads in the pursuit of many inroads and outroads, generating many endogamies and exogamies, through capillary flows that spill in subtle streams and then tumble in raging torrents of enthusiasm and discovery. There are many possibilities that enable starting in the middle; each can be made sense of in terms of intensities, always having the potential to be something, somewhere else. There are many middles, each having always emergent histories of the present. Working from Nietzsche, Foucault talks of genealogy as:

> the union of erudite and local memories which allows us to establish a historical knowledge of struggles and to make use of this knowledge tactically today . . . what it really does is to entertain the claims to attention of local, discontinuous, disqualified, illegitimate knowledge against the claims of a unitary body of theory that would filter, hierarchise, and order them in the name of some true knowledge.
>
> *1980: 83*

I love the politics of this quotation. I have shared it with my students and have asked them what they could make of it, what they could do with it – lovely things always came out. Following some initial hesitations about Foucault's use of language, they begin to open up challenge to the strictures and structures of curriculum, the containing restraints of learning objectives, the narrow prescriptions of assessment procedures and the many codings and framings that control, legitimate and ultimately limit teaching and learning practices. They begin to 'get' Foucault's idea of 'technologies of self' (1980) instrumentalising learning and constructing teacher and learner identities in particular and invariably limiting ways. They begin to challenge the ways in which teaching, learning and the organisation of assessment procedures are created for them and by them through the insistent and all-pervasive modalities of discursive construction present in all aspects of institutionally normative and legislative life. Represented, coded and identified by grades, evaluations and assignment scores, they begin to see, in Foucault's explanation of disciplinary procedures and care of the self, that as the subject *of* institutional and academic discourses they then become subject *to* them.

Extending these pedagogical practices into a consideration of the work of Deleuze and Guattari (1994) and in encouraging them to actively practice concept creation, as exemplified, particularly in their final collaboration, *What is Philosophy?* is designed to assist them in offering challenge to the boundaries set up by these representations. An engagement with the ways in which discourses of this kind can actively striate institutional and pedagogic spaces can be used to mobilise, amongst colleagues and students alike, the use of thinking and theorising as practice in territorialising such spaces in different ways. Further, introducing them to the idea that it makes sense to think of space not as an empty vessel to be filled but as an active living process that is actually created, helps to put into action Soja's (2010) practice of 'spatialising', of actually encouraging a *doing* of space in different ways. Such approaches can serve to promote transformation and in creating spaces that are intensive and animate in potentiality. Active, creative concept making as event/ful process helps 'seeing' and engagement with traditional and customary institutional hylomorphisms that invent and control legitimacy of thinking and practice in highly constraining ways. This is sensation animate within what Manning (2007) calls the 'politics of touch' where movement is always towards, always in thrall of some ceaselessly becoming other. This politics talks to *agencement*, to the vibrant movement of all bodies in dynamic fluidity and exchange. This is the immanence of the ability of education, of educating as processual sensualism, to *do* to promote the always becoming other. *Agencement*, perhaps expressed alternatively by what Bennett (2010) calls 'agentic assemblage', is both the awareness of and the becoming alive that is animated in this 'politics of touch'.

As considered in other plateaus, Massumi (2002) has offered the use of 'examples', in processes of exemplification, as a means of bringing this into the light; where the 'example' is the singularity in assemblage whose movement is brought to light in the educating moment, through illumination and the diagrammatic force of a new becoming. In immanence the 'example' is the past, present, future of these movements, not simply bringing the experience of the past into a present 'thing' but also touching out and beyond, reaching towards in the creation of always something new. We have seen in another plateau how such processual exemplification challenges and seriously troubles the generalising and universalising features and tendencies of the case study so commonly and uncritically used in conventional post-Positivist forms of inquiry. The way in which Massumi's use of 'examples' and processes of 'exemplification' encourages 'inattention' and a bringing to light of digressions, deviations and difference also illustrates the ways in which Barad's (2007) use of 'agential cuts' are employed, in transversality, to rip through and tear existing fabrications and patterns of thought. In terms of the orthodoxies and traditional practices of pedagogy and research in higher educational institutions at the present time, 'exemplification' also offers a healthy antidote to the almost obsessional need to set up representation, interpretation and critical inquiry as a necessity within the frameworks of such practices. As Massumi says of the activity of the example, as, through the use of detail and digression, it interferes with the stability of concepts and reconnects them with other, different concepts, then

> take another example. See what happens. Follow the new growth. You end up with many buds. Incipient systems. Leave them that way. You have made a systemlike composition prolonging he active power of the example. You have left the reader with a very special gift: a headache.
>
> *2002: 19*

The established nature of critical approaches to curriculum and research in the academy has the tendency to limit inquiry within its own self-defining boundaries. By leaving readers with a 'headache' of this kind, the use of examples and exemplification encourages problem making, active practices of problematisation and experimentation and, in all, approaches to pedagogy, research and world making in general that are far more open and creative. The 'headaches' that researchers, teachers and students alike might suffer are also part of a 'politics of touch' (Manning, 2007) wherein capacities to affect and be affected are deeply charged by energies of movement and sensation that come into play through the use of exemplification.

In choreographing the play between the inside and the outside that animates this politics of touch, it is the movements that come to life in the sensing and doing of world making that is so powerfully affective in the making of new life. The capacity to affect and be affective is deeply potentiate in the making of these movements; it is the energies that are always emergent in the dance between the latent and the manifest, the centrifugal and the centripetal, the infusings and those concomitant outfusings that are constitutive of the 'architecturing' and world making of productive and creative living life. It is in these heres and nows that is the becoming of living of what Deleuze calls 'a life',

> a life of pure immanence, neutral, beyond good and evil, for it was only the subject that incarnated it in the midst of things that made it good or bad. The life of such individuality fades away in favour of the singular life immanent to a man who no longer has a name, though he can be mistaken for no other. A singular essence, a life.
>
> *2001: 29*

In thinking about this, in this immanence of a life, I am drawn to the ceaseless individuation of bodies in spacetime. I have spent so much spacetime in education; I have to think about this in terms of what bodies in education can do. *Becoming-teacher* bodies, *becoming-student* bodies, *becoming-classroom* bodies, *becoming-staffroom* bodies, *becoming-curriculum* bodies and so on; I have been writing this book, thinking about these bodies, thinking about sensing what I might say, what these bodies might do, what this *Ken-writing-about-these-bodies-in-education-might-do* will have to say about this, what this contingent, heterogeneous *agencement* might do in these past/present/future spacetimes of writing-reading-book assemblage. I make sense in these becomings with Manning's words of 'a life' when she says, '[a] life is immanence felt in the stirrings of actualisation. Force of potential, force of life' (2013: 44).

I recently read Robert Macfarlane's (2007) book *The Wild Places*. My good friend Jonathan Wyatt gave me this book some years ago and, at that time, I was unable to fully concentrate in or on the reading of it. My life was deeply troubled at this time and there was something about this book that, in that here and now, I was unable to live with in ways that gave me comfort or joy. In the words of its back cover endorsement, the book describes the author's embarkation 'on a series of beautifully described journeys in search of the wildness that remains in these islands . . . *The Wild Places* mixes history, memory and landscape in a strange and bewitching evocation of wildness and its importance.' Something disturbed me in the reading of this book and it is only with the strength that my life has now regained that I am able to read this book. I am drawn to conceptualisations of the 'wild' and to 'wildness' but, in my imaginings, I find the stark possibilities of 'wilderness' somewhat worrying in their suggestive implications of a not far distant, dark and barren dystopia. Macfarlane talks of 'wild places' as places that are being lost in a 'headlong drive into our technological termite-life, the Brave New World of a completely man-controlled environment' (ibid.: 82). He concerns himself that 'wild country' might only be available to us to 'drive to its edge and look in'; he talks of the need for this 'wild country' to provide reassurance 'of our sanity as creatures, a part of the geography of hope' (ibid.: 83). Living in Cornwall, sensing my own 'Cornishness' and seeing the erosion of so much of what has made this a unique and beautiful part of the world, with its tumultuous surf, rugged coastline and dark mysterious moors, by the incessant tides of mass tourism, I share a sympathy for what Macfarlane talks of here: there are few, if any, 'wild places' left on this little peninsula. However, what he is saying is not enough but it does give me an idea about this madness as methodology. First, of all the inner/outer binary that he sets up, with its inferences of subjective and objective realities is inconsistent with the thinking and processes I have wanted to work with here. By talking of 'place' instead of 'space' Macfarlane suggests a politics of space that has to be challenged. 'Place' suggests to me objectification, reification, representation and identification; it is a naming of space that does not pay attention to the conceptualisation of space as always being made. This is a conceptualisation that is in all of us to potentiate; we all have the capacity to make movements that animates the processual differentiation of space. The naming of space as place with which Macfarlane appears to engage in here does not allow for 'architecturing', for choreographing the fluidity of a politics of folding and flow in which strict divisions between inside and outside, subject and object are encouraged to dissolve. If, in Manning's (2007) 'politics of touch', folding is always immanent, where the animations of endogamous and exogamous movements are constitutive of worlding as a constant relational process, then acceptance of the naming of space as place is to lower resistance to the powers of external, hylomorphic, controlling forces. Therefore, in this I want to think and act with the affective force of 'spatialising' (Soja, 2010), of the capacity of all bodies, human and nonhuman, as having the capacity to affect and be affected, wherein 'wilding' is an active form of movement, of reaching out and of doing something in the world, something that is akin to what Stewart, Massumi, Manning and others have referred to as 'worlding'. In this I think of working with others; friends, colleagues and students and not simply engaging in a driving to the edge and looking in but in actively and immediately bringing the world to life in new and different ways. In this respect, 'wild' is not a 'place' to visit, it is a space of becoming where the new possibilities for new life are always present and where the potential for change is always massively charged by the vibrant possibilities involved in 'wilding' in world making, in animating and bringing to life in always new and different ways. Such movement in moments, moments in movement can bring wildnesses to life in classrooms, workshops and studios in ways that can give life new vigour and life to education, to teaching and to learning and to the ways in which it could be researched.

In the whole ongoing process of trying to bring this madness as methodology to life, the question, expressed by others as 'Is "the posthuman" educable?' (Pedersen, 2010) has been present in my mind. In the ontogenetic formulation of these ideas on these pages I ask how I can answer this question in these heres and nows when, in the heres and nows in another spacetime, the questions and answers will be different. In posing this question I take relief in reading Massumi when he says:

> Passage precedes construction. But construction does effectively back-form its reality. Grids happen. So social and cultural determinations feed back into the process from which they arose. Indeterminacy and determination, change and freeze framing, go together. They are inseparable and always actually coincide while remaining disjunctive in their modes of reality.
>
> *2002: 8*

This madness as methodology cannot resist thinking educative practices that work with conceptualisation as event. In this the transversal potentiality of always becoming in the flow involves working within and in the creation of agentic assemblages in which all bodies have the capacity to affect and be affected. With the focus of attention upon what a body can do, education will always be transformative in terms of potential, of turning things in to other things in flow, in movement in layers of space and time making.

My youngest daughter, Phoebe, recently shared with me the most recent edition of the fashion magazine *I-D*, an issue wholly devoted to engaging with creativity and the importance of creative practice in contemporary space and time. I found myself browsing the images, reading the pop-up captions on T-shirts and dresses, 'Stay weird, stay different', 'Gender is a drag', and marvelling at the extravagant challenge offered by many of the clothes portrayed there. I particularly liked a quotation from Tim Walker, the photographer who had been commissioned to compile the photographs for the whole edition. When asked 'Why is creativity more important than ever?', he responded by saying 'It's the weapon against banal, corporate, algorithmic blandness' (*I-D*, 2017: 36). This simple, direct and strongly political statement made by a man whose main weapon is his camera is powerfully relevant to the politics of touch that is integral to the creative practice of concept making as event that has been used to suffuse much of the writing that populates these pages. Concept making as event is about education, it is agentic, it is about creating something new, making it work and then, if necessary, moving on, in transmutation, to the creation of other new concepts and practices of engagement. And so all I can do in the politics of bodies in agentic touch, one with each other, is to continue with concept creation, to enjoy the dance and to revel in the ontogenetic possibilities that each new movement brings to life and to always have a sense of the potential that each new movement brings. As Manning says, ontogenesis 'refers to the capacity to emerge, to invite a moving-off the grid that challenges stagnant organisations of signifying bodies' (2007: 25).

In these emergences, therefore, I think of the way in which other writers, researchers and scholars have offered suggestions about the way in which this might be done. I think of the recently reported example of Finland (www.bbc.co.uk/news/world-europe-39889523) where the school curriculum is no longer based upon specific subjects and where learning is encouraged through the use of cross-subject engagement with topically relevant events. This example encourages me to think of Foucault's notion of discipline and to think of the ways in which the subject, the topic, the academic discipline of, say, Sociology, say Chemistry, actually and actively *subjects* students to the discipline of the subject; the subjects *discipline*. Elsewhere, Sellers and Gough (2010) have engaged in collaborative responses to thinking (differently) with Deleuze in educational philosophy and curriculum inquiry. Malone (2015) in her paper 'Reconsidering children's encounters with nature and place using posthumanism', has drawn on 'place-based research' and 'new materialist and posthumanist approaches' to examine the educational experiences of children in Bolivia. Honan and Bright (2016), working in higher education, have suggested ways of writing a thesis differently, using Deleuze and Guattari and a 'post-qualitative' approach and Done (2013) through what she describes as 'a singular doctoral experience', describes her experience of writing her PhD thesis within a 'supervisory assemblage'. Masny, in her development of 'multiple literacies theory', suggests that literacies are 'an assemblage of asignifying desiring machines . . . [that] actualise as words, gestures, sounds, listening, writing: ways of becoming with the world' (2013: 75). De Freitas envisages 'the classroom as rhizome' and by drawing on 'the work of Latour, Deleuze and Guattari, and Chatelet' shows how 'the concepts of the rhizome, assemblage, and knot are applied to the study of classroom interaction' (2012: 557). Davies and Gannon's collaborative inquiries and their development of the concept of 'pedagogical encounters' sees the space of teaching and learning as an assemblage, where 'space is far more than a passive backdrop to human action', rather, as they see it, space is 'active in shaping what is possible' (Davies and Gannon 2009: 8). In this their use of practices of 'collective biography' (Davies and Gannon 2006) engages with 'pedagogical encounters' 'beyond individualised versions of the subject, toward subjects-in-relation', 'subjects-in-process' (ibid.). Manning's (2010) connecting of 'autistic perception' with 'choreographic thinking' offers, perhaps in more complex ways, a means by which we can begin to avoid a generalising and binarising 'chunking' of experience into fixed categories of subject/object, male/female, fact/fiction and other limiting dualistic fictions of this kind. More recently, in my own work with Jonathan Wyatt (Wyatt and Gale, 2017), the practice of 'writing to it' is offered as a means of creatively engaging with writing practice in and with the not yet known in higher education. 'Writing to it' offers a methodogenetic conceptualisation of writing practice that is creative and inquiry based, where, if a problem is encountered, the simple act of 'writing to it' has the potential to mobilise thinking and practice as event in ways that do not have to depend upon intention and pre-conception. In exemplification 'writing to it' can be used to creatively challenge the discursively constructed prescription that all students, when setting out on their inquiries, must present and have accepted by their tutors and supervisors a fully articulated, rationalised and justified set of research questions, indicating clearly where, how and when the research will be carried out.

All these examples and more show, at least in part, ways in which turning to affect and moving into the posthuman can be 'educable'. By offering a madness as methodology, and in engaging with what I see as the play between this conceptualisation and that of 'madness as (non) methodology', I refer to all these examples as a way of indicating the variety of possible applications and practices that are available to those working in the field of play referred to as education. To do this is not to engage in what Deleuze and Guattari call 'decalcomania', described by Bonta and Protevi as 'the mimetic process of lifting a code, image, or text from one medium, then transferring it to another without transforming it' (2004: 75). Rather, it is, in Deleuze and Guattari's words, to

> [m]ake a map, not a tracing. The orchid does not reproduce the tracing of the wasp; it forms a map with the wasp, in a rhizome. What distinguishes the map from the tracing is that it is entirely oriented toward an experimentation in contact with the real.
>
> *1987: 12*

This cartography is about the immanence of working with practice in, with and to the not yet known; it is the ontogenetic presencing of now you see me now you don't, it is working with the sensing that the territory is always on the move, always being moved, it is about working with experimentation and indeterminacy and the amorphous beauty of the play of affect: 'If you don't understand try to feel. According to Massumi it works' (Leys, 2011: 434).

Working diffractively, as Barad suggests, interferes with and offers resistance to hylomorphism and the kinds of 'ideological stage apparatuses' (Althusser, 2014) that reinforce, consolidate and legitimate normative practices and procedures in higher education research and pedagogy. Engaging with interference involves the creation of transformation and transmutation, in making connections that promote fluidity and capillary flows which work to generate leakages and 'an always more than one' (Manning, 2013) that troubles and is disruptive of those processes that attempt to binarise and hierarchise institutional relationalities.

Originating in the social theory of Habermas, Horkheimer and Weber, the notion of 'scientism' has traditionally been used to describe the means by which the practices of the natural sciences, involving measurement, inductive reasoning and empirical observation and recording, are used to establish a comprehensive, universalising and authoritative view of the world. 'Scientism' promotes such a worldview to the exclusion of other perspectives and practices. As scientific principles and practices seep into and discursively regulate all aspects of life they can be seen, as Sorell points out, to promote them as providing the most valued approach to learning by placing 'too high a value on natural science in comparison with other branches of learning or culture' (1994: 1). Scientism, therefore, is a term that does not simply describe a scientific method, *qua* academic discipline and practice of rigorous inquiry, rather it insidiously and discursively promotes the view that science is the only reliable source of all forms of knowledge. Consequently, as Massumi says:

> Scientific method is the institutionalised maintenance of sangfroid in the face of surprise. Properly scientific activity starts from a preconversion of surprise into cognitive confidence. Science takes off from an a priori posture of recognisability: a knowledge-ready precontextualisation of any and every situation.
>
> *2002: 233*

I have vivid and somewhat disturbing memories of science lessons from my schooldays when having to participate in an 'experiment' actually involved us willing young pupils in engaging in regulated and highly controlled procedures that produced a repetition of some important fact or the establishment and hence an understanding of an item of foundational scientific knowledge. There was no excitement or wonder in carrying out the 'experiment' in the Physics lesson that showed us again and again that acceleration due to the force of gravity was 32 feet per second, per second, thus confirming the veracity of Newton's Laws of Gravitation. And so, I found the following note in my phone recently: I quote it here, as a possible antidote to the previous forms of thinking and practice:

> Understanding is, like madness, a process. It is less a substance or even a condition it is something, after finitude, which is always changing. It is not

something you have, it is something that is, it is a verb, it is something that you do and that therefore what it is is never the same, it is something that is always happening, in flow, flux and transmutation. And therefore understanding is understanding in becoming; if it has an existence it is in multiplicity, it is becoming something other than what it was; if it is described as having been got and, therefore, somehow fixed, then understanding is what it is not. It makes more sense to think of understanding in terms of sense and sensing. As we sense something we move toward sensing it in a different way, our relation changes. In sense making it is more sensible to talk of process and less of substance, to live in world making with verbs rather than nouns. Accepting nouns accepts fixities, asserts belief in substance over processes and, in terms of living, loving and learning, gives up on the world.

Such established scientific normativities present huge challenge because, as the foregoing argues, we are not talking about a methodology of instrumentalism, of getting the job done, we are describing an affective relationality which establishes genealogies, generalisations and practices of totalisation that are discursively inscribed and established, and which function to prevent the flourishing of other more diverse, anomalous and potentially creative approaches. In my earliest encounters with the work of Foucault, Deleuze and others I remember referring to my educational practices as engaging in 'creative pedagogies of resistance' (Gale, 2003: 165). At that time I felt excited about the possibilities involved in encouraging my students to offer challenge to, what I saw as resistances to interference, to the eradication of surprise, to engaging in diffractive methodologies and in challenging the scientistic orthodoxies pervading all aspects of institutionalised educational life. In those electric processual moments Foucault's elision of power/knowledge was becoming in its animation; I sensed a coming to life; things beginning to work. Through the bringing to life of these movements, dis/re/un/coverings came into vibrant becoming, conceptualisations began to be made, work began to be done and the seeds of madness as methodology began to be sown.

In one sense I have built upon and shifted from the practices that I have outlined here without ever entirely abandoning them. From the early 1970s I remember working with what was then called student centred learning, which, at the time, involved practices that were strongly influenced by the humanist philosophies of Carl Rogers (1961), Abraham Maslow (1943) and later John Heron (1989). By placing the experiences and needs of students at the centre of education practices, the teacher-centred approaches of Liberal Humanism and the outcomes-driven practices of Behaviourist-inclined curriculum were challenged through the use of strategies of intervention and practices of facilitation, referred to earlier in this plateau. The shift of emphasis towards the, so-called, needs of the learner that this generated offered greater opportunities for student involvement, expression and, within the context of my own facilitative practices, also of conceptualisation, of actually engaging students by asking them what they thought about the world, encouraging them to be experimental in workshop practices by asking them to actively engage with the challenge, 'What if?'. I enjoyed the disruptive challenge that this offered to the conventional, psychologically inflected cognitivist and behaviourist educational practices that were current at that time. Postman and Weingartner's (1971) book *Teaching as a Subversive Activity* was for myself and a few like-minded spirits hugely influential. With chapter headings such as 'Crap detecting', 'The inquiry method' and 'So what do you do now', this book was a vital catalyst for change in the work that we were trying to do in classrooms at that time. Reading and using this book, whilst I was engaged in my PGCE studies in 1972–1973 in London, pushed me towards working with practices of concept-ualisation that involved me in engaging learners in practices focused upon their learning. Of course, what I learned here was enormous and continues to be hugely influential in terms of what as I do as an educator today, nearly fifty years later. The forceful energies that are released when processual conceptualisation comes into play remain addictively a part of the material/ discursive entanglements with which I want to be involved in the educational practices of my current work. In working with such practices today I feel that the various 'turns' that have impacted upon me and that have taken me into these posthuman, affective, relational and materialist ways of space/time creation have all helped me in moving towards attempting to express this madness as methodology in these current pages.

So, in the writing of what might be read as a concluding plateau, there is a need to talk to what a 'body' of education can or might do. I have asked the direct and enacting question of Spinoza's throughout the making, throughout the 'in-formation' (Manning, 2007, 2013) of this book: 'What can a body do?' What can, if there is such a 'thing', the body of education do? Central to this question and to the asking of it is, of course, what is this body, if it is a body at all? In saying what it is, what it might be, what is its becoming, could involve a bringing together of all the theorising of this book within a practice-based set of recommendations for the future. How would that work? How would that be? What transductions might that open up for future inquiry? What assumptions would be present in the list that might emerge? How prescient could and should this be? In what sense could my list of recommendations live beyond the moment of their creation and translation into writing on these pages? These are questions that have been at play in the dancing emergence of this book and I cannot write these words without returning to Artaud, Deleuze, Deleuze and Guattari and the 'body-without-organs'. It is the work that I have done and continue to do with this conceptualisation that is a major life force in the becoming of this book and the questions that I continue to ask here, at this stage.

Judgement and its attendant connection with critique, evaluation, interpretation and reflection plays a major controlling part in many aspects of institutionalised education at the present time. This is manifest in the intensive, concomitant, relationality of judgement to the active presence of hylomorphic practices of curriculum design and operation, the segregation and hierarchisation of subjects, the setting up of learning outcomes and assessment procedures and the pre-eminence given to, so-called, cognitive development and behavioural change. In these respects, judgement is an integral and embodied feature of the teaching/learning nexus that is active in discursively constructed pedagogical and research-based realities within institutionalised education at the present time. In following Nietzsche, Spinoza, Bergson, Deleuze and others this madness as methodology project involves itself in challenging systems and structures that are predicated upon the disciplinary procedures inherent within the practices of judgement referred to here. As Deleuze says, '[t]he way to escape judgment is to make yourself a body without organs' (1997: 131). In my understanding, in asserting this, he also demonstrates, through his reading of Kafka, for example, how something like, say, the body of education, can be made a 'body-without-organs'. In ways that are similar to how he shows that writing minor literatures can be written into the writing of major literatures, Deleuze also shows how bodies in becoming can have a similar relationality, in terms of their capacities to affect and be affected:

> Kafka . . . makes two worlds or two bodies co-exist, each of which reacts upon and enters into the other: a body of judgment, with its organisation, its segments (contiguity of offices), its differentiations (bailiffs, lawyers, judges . . .), its hierarchies (classes of judges, or bureaucrats); but also a body of justice in which the segments are dissolved, the differentiations lost, and the hierarchies thrown into confusion, a body that retains nothing but intensities that make up uncertain zones, that traverse these zones at full speed and confront the powers in them . . . on this anarchic body restored to itself.
>
> *Ibid.*

In my reading, the first expression of the body-without-organs is to be found in Antonin Artaud's radio play, *To Have Done with the Judgment of God*, first published in 1947, when he says:

> When you will have made him a body without organs,
> then you will have delivered him from all his automatic reactions
> and restored him to his true freedom
>
> *Artaud, 1976: 571*

This is, at the very least, a wonder/ful starting point for considering what education research and pedagogy as a body (without organs) can, might and perhaps, should be. The stanza quite obviously contains dubious, simply human-centric, ethical and political intentions and proclivities and has to be considered carefully in these respects, but it offers a sensing of what that body can do. As well as Artaud's original conception and accounting for it, both Deleuze, in a *Logic of Sense*, and Deleuze and Guattari, in the two volumes of *Capitalism and Schizophrenia,* offer slightly varying conceptualisations of the term. I have used my sensing of these in conceptualising the 'body-without-organs' in my own writing here and, of these, I choose to work with a version offered by Deleuze and Guattari in *A Thousand Plateaus* when they say that the 'body without organs is permeated by unformed, unstable matters, by flows in all directions, by free intensities or nomadic singularities, by mad or transitory particles' (1987: 40). In this quotation I sense Artaud's delivery from 'automatic reactions' and, if not a restoration, at least the possibilising of 'freedom', two qualities so important to the sensing of educational research and inquiry as a 'body-without-organs' being offered here. It seems that Artaud's performative work is a becoming-mad, which is never a being mad; as an experiment in thought and action what he writes and has to say is an affective madness, beyond the qualities of the Cartesian individual and, in this respect, quite believable and do-able in the way that it performs itself in encounters with and creation of the world. Deleuze describes it as

> a pure becoming without measure, a veritable becoming-mad, which never rests. It moves in both directions at once. It always eludes the present, causing future and past, more and less, too much and not enough to coincide in the simultaneity of a rebellious matter.
>
> *2004a: 3*

I need to return to the writing of plateaus that appear earlier in this book. In this I have to ask myself if what is being written here and the questions I have asked in the processual becoming of this book are being addressed and answered in some way. I wonder in what sense is what I am writing here a form of, what St Pierre (2017) describes as 'post qualitative inquiry'? Will these writings come to life and live in, what she describes here as, the 'next generation' of qualitative inquiry? As I have worked to propose this madness as methodology, I have been constantly aware of MacLure's observations about approaches of the kind that challenge many of the established orthodoxies and practices of qualitative inquiry. In citing Deleuze she suggests that

> so long as the iron rule of representation still covertly governs these adventures, we will continue to inhabit a world in which 'one is only apparently intoxicated, in which reason acts the drunkard and sings a Dionysian tune while nonetheless remaining "pure" reason' (1994: p. 264, emphasis added).
>
> *2017: 49*

I have a sensing that what is being said here by Deleuze and tentatively being reiterated by MacLure might well be the case. However, this sensing does not dampen my spirits! I feel committed to keeping my *methodogenesis* in play. I sense that this *methodogenesis* offers transversalities of practice that have the potential to live and promote post-anthropocentric sensitivities. These can be used to animate a cutting across those segregated hierarchies that separate, categorise and disconnect human from animal, man from woman, black from white, subject from subject and so on. Learning from Deleuze's conceptualisation of thinking as doing, as event and as always happening 'in-between' (Deleuze and Guattari, 1987; Deleuze and

Parnet, 2002), I work back over my words and remain sensibly attentive to the practice of thinking as movement in and through and hence of always destabilising the fixities of cultural formations. In this, for example, I think about the rigidities and constraints embodied within the cultural formation of institutionalised education and feel concerns about the effects upon the formalised emergence of subjects. If the posthuman can be conceived of as educable, if this madness as methodology can be put to work, then thinking needs to be done with Deleuze when he argues that,

> personal uncertainty is not a doubt foreign to what is happening, but rather an objective structure of the event itself, insofar as it moves in two directions at once, and insofar as it fragments the subject following this double direction. Paradox is initially that which destroys good sense as the only direction, but it is also that which destroys common sense as the assignation of fixed identities.
>
> *2004a: 5*

Thinking further with Deleuze and through education, it then feels important to attempt a conceptualisation and doing of education, as an 'abstract machine' (Deleuze and Guattari, 1987) where, with the practice of this madness as methodology, the codings, closed structures and hylomorphic tendencies of formal institutionalised education can be troubled and destabilised. Thinking education as an 'abstract machine' will then involve participating in and making connections with other effects, encounters and events in the processual, heterogeneous and con-tingent production of 'machinic assemblages' (ibid.). In this, sensation, movement and gesture will be used to creatively cut across the established objectivities of curriculum, assessment procedures and the representational discursive construction of a reality that says that learning outcomes can somehow be prescribed in advance of the learning that might be taking place. In this madness as methodology I want to shift the focus of thinking and doing, in education and other institutional settings, away from its groundedness in the agentic human subject with its concerns about subjects and objects and the differences that are shaped between them by the divisiveness of binary logics and the thinking that is attendant to them. In doing this I want to shift concerns towards more than simply human processual individuations in which encounter, relationality and difference emerge from the play of multiple agentic forces. In achieving this, the problem appears to be to do with the persistence of forms of representation that work to fix and stabilise thinking and practice within accepted and established boundaries and which ignore those movements and forces which act to generate difference from itself. So, rather than thinking about these subjects and objects, these identified teachers, learners, managers, curricula, subjects, outcomes etc., perhaps this can be achieved through thinking with Deleuze (2004c) and through education about 'larval subjects'; processually unfolding creatures, always 'in-formation', that are always becoming and hence never fully actualised through being fixed in determined positions and roles.

I shall allow this final plateau, what will appear as the 'concluding' plateau in the book, to live within the rhetorical eventfulness of the questions of this kind and that myself and others pose. As I do this I have in mind some of the introductory words in Gregg and Seigworth's (2010) description of their *Affect Theory Reader*. They do not describe their introductory chapter as an introduction, it does not appear as such in their contents list; rather, it emerges as 'An Inventory of Shimmers' in which it is suggested that the various contributions to the book might appear and be engaged with as quivering and vibrating movements in the emerging heat and light of new life. When I first discovered this 'introduction', after having already read and worked with a number of the contributions to the collection, I felt pleased with the discovery and sustained by the sense that my reading of and with the collection was and continued to be fluid, transmutational and continual in its emergence. And, as I begin to write what will be the final plateau of this book, still having a good deal more of the rest of the book left to write, I can associate with and be animated by their engagement with Spinoza's '"yet-ness" of a body's affectual doings and undoings' and with the humour with which they write, 'So, there it is: now, we know all that a body can do! Let's call it a day' (Gregg and Seigworth, 2010: 3).

This plateau, the plateau that will appear at the end of this book can, therefore, be given life through the presencing of Spinoza's 'not yet'. I sense a beautiful madness in, what I have referred to elsewhere in this book as the presencing of this madness of methodology of event that revels in its becoming, in its not-yet-ness.

REFERENCES

Althusser, L. (2014) *On the reproduction of capitalism: Ideology and ideological state apparatuses*, trans. and ed. G. Goshgarian. London: Verso.

Artaud, A. (1976) To have done with the judgment of God. In S. Sontag (ed.) *Selected writings*. Berkeley, CA: University of California Press.

Atkinson, P. (1990) *The ethnographic imagination: textual constructions of reality*. London: Routledge.

Austin, J. (1962) *How to do things with words: The William James Lectures delivered at Harvard University in 1955*. Oxford: Clarendon Press.

Ayer, A. J. (1936) *Language, truth and logic*. London: Gollancz.

Bachelard, G. (1969) *The poetics of space*, trans. M. Jolas. Boston, MA: Beacon Press.

Bachelard, G. (2014) *On poetic imagination and reverie,* trans. Colette Gaudin. Putnam, Conn: Spring Publications.

Bakhtin, M. (1981) *The dialogic imagination: Four essays*, ed. M. Holquist. Austin: University of Texas Press.

Barad, K. (2007) *Meeting the universe halfway: Quantum physics and the entanglement of matter and meaning*. London: Duke University Press.

Barnes, M. and Berke, J. (1982) *Mary Barnes: Two accounts of a journey through madness*. Harmondsworth: Penguin.

Bennett, J. (2010) *Vibrant matter: The political ecology of things*. London: Duke University Press.

Berg, L. (1968) *Risinghill: Death of a comprehensive school*. Harmondsworth: Penguin.

Bergson, H. (1911) *Creative evolution*, trans. Arthur Mitchell. New York: Henry Holt.

Berlant, L. (2011) *Cruel optimism*. Durham and London: Duke University Press.

Boal, A. (1993). *Theatre of the oppressed*. New York: Theatre Communications Group.

Bogue, R. (2003) *Deleuze on music, painting, and the arts*. London: Routledge.

Bonta, M. and Protevi, J. (2004) *Deleuze and geophilosophy: A guide and glossary*. Edinburgh: Edinburgh University Press.

Borges, J.-L. (1970) *Labyrinths: Selected stories and other writings*. Harmondsworth: Penguin.

Bourdieu, P. and Passeron, J.-C. (1990) *Reproduction in education, society and culture*. London: Sage.

Braidotti, R. (2013) Posthuman humanities, *European Educational Research Journal* 12(1). www.wwwords.eu/EERJ, http://dx.doi.org/10.2304/eerj.2013.12.1.1

Butler, J. (2006) *Gender trouble.* London: Routledge.

Carr, W. and Kemmis, S. (1989) Becoming critical: Education, knowledge and action research, *The Journal of Educational Thought* 23(3): 209–216.

Causley, C. (2017) *A certain man: Charles Causley in his own words,* compiled and ed. S. Parker. scryfa.co.uk.

Chadwick, W. and De Courtivron, I. (eds) (1993) *Significant others: Creativity and intimate partnership.* London: Thames and Hudson.

Cixous, H. (1991) *Coming to writing and other essays,* ed. D. Jenson, trans. S. Cornell, D. Jenson, A. Liddle and S. Sellers. Cambridge, MA: Harvard University Press.

Clough, P. (2010) The affective turn: Political economy, biomedia, and bodies. In M. Gregg, and G. Seigworth (eds) *The affect theory reader.* Durham and London: Duke University Press, pp. 206–229.

Cohen, L., Mannion, L. and Morrison, K. (2000) *Research methods in education,* 5th edn. London and New York: RoutledgeFalmer.

Colebrook, C. (2002) *Gilles Deleuze.* London: Routledge.

Davies, B. and Gannon, S. (2006) *Doing collective biography.* Buckingham: Open University Press.

Davies, B. and Gannon, S. (eds) (2009) *Pedagogical encounters.* New York: Peter Lang.

De Freitas, E. (2012) The classroom as rhizome: New strategies for diagramming knotted interactions, *Qualitative Inquiry* 18(7): 557–570.

Deleuze, G. (1988) *Spinoza: Practical philosophy,* trans. R. Hurley. San Francisco: City Lights Books.

Deleuze, G. (1989) *Cinema 2: The time-image,* trans. H. Tomlinson and R. Galeta. Minneapolis: University of Minnesota Press.

Deleuze, G. (1991) *Empiricism and subjectivity: An essay on Hume's theory of human nature,* trans. C. Boundas. New York: Columbia University Press.

Deleuze, G. (1993) *The fold: Leibniz and the baroque,* trans. T. Conley. London: Athlone Press.

Deleuze, G. (1994) He stuttered. In C. Boundas and D. Olkowski (eds) *Gilles Deleuze and the theatre of philosophy.* London: Routledge.

Deleuze, G. (1995) *Negotiations 1972–1990,* trans. M. Joughin. New York: Columbia University Press.

Deleuze, G. (1997) *Essays critical and clinical,* trans. D. W. Smith and M. A. Greco. Minneapolis: University of Minnesota Press.

Deleuze, G. (2001) *Pure immanence: Essays on a life,* trans. A. Boyman. New York: Zone Books.

Deleuze, G. (2003) *The fold: Leibniz and the Baroque,* Foreword and trans. T. Conley. London: Continuum.

Deleuze, G. (2004a) *The logic of sense,* trans. M. Lester with C. Stivale. London: Continuum.

Deleuze, G. (2004b) *Francis Bacon: The logic of sensation,* trans. D. Smith. London: Continuum.

Deleuze, G. (2004c) *Difference and repetition,* trans. Paul Patton, London: Continuum.

Deleuze, G. (2005) *Cinema 1: The movement-image,* trans. Hugh Tomlinson and Barbara Habberjam, London: Continuum.

Deleuze, G. (2007) *Desert Islands: And other texts 1953–1974,* ed. D. Lapoujade, trans. M. Taormina. New York: Semiotext(e).

Deleuze, G. and Guattari, F. (1986) *Kafka: Toward a minor literature,* trans. Dana Polan. Minneapolis: University of Minnesota Press.

Deleuze, G. and Guattari, F. (1987) *A thousand plateaus: Capitalism and schizophrenia,* trans. B. Massumi. London: Athlone.

Deleuze, G. and Guattari, F. (1994) *What is philosophy?*, trans. G. Burchell and H. Tomlinson. London: Verso.

Deleuze, G. and Guattari, F. (2004) *Anti-Oedipus: Capitalism and schizophrenia*, trans. R. Hurley, M. Seem and H. Lane. London: Continuum.

Deleuze, G. and Parnet, C. (2002) *Dialogues II*. London: Athlone.

Done, E. (2013) *The supervisory assemblage: A singular doctoral experience*. Newcastle upon Tyne: Cambridge Scholars Publishing.

Dosse, F. (2010) *Gilles Deleuze and Felix Guattari: Intersecting lives*, trans. D. Glassman. New York: Columbia University Press.

Dylan, B. (1965) Gates of Eden, *Bringing It All Back Home*, released 22 March 1965 on Columbia Records, Columbia Recording Studios, New York City, produced by Tom Wilson.

Ellis, C. (2004) *The Ethnographic I: A methodological novel about autoethnography*. Walnut Creek, CA: Altamira Press.

Ellis, C. (2013) Preface: Carrying the torch for autoethnography. In S. Holman Jones, T. Adams and C. Ellis (eds) *Handbook of autoethnography*. Walnut Creek, CA: Left Coast Press.

Ellis, C. and Bochner, A. (2000). Autoethnography, personal narrative, reflexivity: Researcher as subject. In N. Denzin and Y. Lincoln (eds) *Handbook of qualitative research*, 2nd edn.,Thousand Oaks, CA: Sage, pp. 733–768.

Foucault, M. (1980) *Power/Knowledge*. New York: Pantheon.

Foucault, M. (1991) Question of method. In G. Burchell, C. Gordon and P. Miller (eds) *The Foucault effect: Studies in governmentality*. Brighton: Harvester/Wheatsheaf.

Foucault, M. (1992) *The use of pleasure: The history of sexuality, Volume 2*, trans. R. Hurley. Harmondsworth: Penguin.

Foucault, M. (2000) Interview with Michel Foucault. In J. Faubion (ed.), trans. R.Hurley *Power: The essential works of Michel Foucault 1954–1984, Volume Three*. New York: New Press.

Gale, K. (2003) Creative pedagogies of resistance in post compulsory (teacher) education. In J. Satterthwaite, E. Atkinson and K. Gale (eds) *Discourse, power and resistance: Challenging the rhetoric of contemporary education*. Stoke on Trent: Trentham Books.

Gale, K. (2007) Teacher education in the university: Working with policy, practice and Deleuze, *Teaching in Higher Education* 12(4): 471–583.

Gale, K. (2010) An inquiry into the ethical nature of a Deleuzian creative educational practice, *Qualitative Inquiry* 16(5): 303–309.

Gale, K. (2014) Moods, tones, flavours: Living with intensities as inquiry, *Qualitative Inquiry* 20(8): 998–1005.

Gale, K. (2016a) Writing minor literature: Working with flows, intensities and the welcome of the unknown, *Qualitative Inquiry* 22(5): 301–308.

Gale, K. (2016b) Theorising *as* practice: Engaging the posthuman as method of inquiry and pedagogic practice within contemporary higher education. In C. Taylor and C. Hughes (eds) *Posthuman research practices in education*. London: Palgrave MacMillan, pp. 242–258.

Gale, K. and Wyatt, J. (2016) Working at the Wonder: Collaborative Writing as Method of Inquiry, *Qualitative Inquiry* 23(5): 335–364.

Gale, K. (2017) Not all who wander are lost and all who wonder are found, *International Review of Qualitative Research* 10(1): 4–9.

Gale, K. and Pineau, E. (2011) Flows, tides, and transatlantic drifts: An emergent methodology of collaborative performative writing, *International Review of Qualitative Research* 4(4): 317–334.

Gale, K. and Wyatt, J. (2008a) Two men talking: A nomadic inquiry into collaborative writing, *International Review of Qualitative Research* 1(3): 361–380.

Gale, K. and Wyatt, J. (2008b) Becoming men, becoming-men? A collective biography, *International Review of Qualitative Research* 1(2): 235–255.

Gale, K. and Wyatt, J. (2008c) *Between the two: A nomadic inquiry into collaborative writing and subjectivity*. Doctoral dissertation, University of Bristol.

Gale, K. and Wyatt J. (2009) *Between the two: A nomadic inquiry into collaborative writing and subjectivity*. Newcastle: Cambridge Scholars Press.

Gale, K. and Wyatt, J. (eds) (2014) Collaborative writing as a method of inquiry. Special Edition of *Cultural Studies ó Critical Methodologies* 14(4).

Gale, K., Speedy, J. and Wyatt, J. (2010) Gatecrashing the oasis? A joint doctoral dissertation play, *Qualitative Inquiry* 16(1): 21–28.

Gale, K. Turner, R. and McKenzie, L. (2013) Action research, becoming and the assemblage: A Deleuzian reconceptualisation of professional practice, *Educational Action Research* 21(4): 549–564.

Gale, K., Martin, V., Sakellariadis, A., Speedy, J. and Spry, T. (2012a) Collaborative writing in real time, *Cultural Studiesó Critical Methodologies* 12(5): 401–407.

Gale, K., Pelias, R., Russell, L., Spry, T. and Wyatt, J. (2012b) *How writing touches: An intimate scholarly collaboration*. Newcastle: Cambridge Scholars Publishing.

Gingras, Y. (2002). Les formes specifique de l'internationalité du champ scientifique, *Actes de la recherché en sciences sociales* 141–145: 31–45.

Gregg, M. and Seigworth, G. (eds) (2010) *The affect theory reader*. Durham and London: Duke University Press.

Grosz, E. (1994) A thousand tiny sexes: Feminism and rhizomatics. In C. Boundas and D. Olkowski (eds) *Gilles Deleuze and the theatre of philosophy*. London: Routledge.

Guattari, F. (1992) *Chaosmosis: An ethico-aesthetic paradigm*, trans. P. Bains and J. Pefanis. Bloomington and Indianapolis: Indiana University Press.

Halsey, A., Heath, A. and Ridge, J. (1980) *Origins and destinations*. Oxford: Clarendon Press.

Halverson, K. (ed.) (2016) *Shakespeare and Company, Paris: History of a rag and bone shop of the heart*. Paris: Shakespeare and Company.

Haraway, D. (2000) *How like a leaf*, an interview with Thyrza Nichols Goodeve. New York: Routledge.

Haraway, D. (2008) *When species meet*. Minneapolis: University of Minnesota Press.

Heidegger, M. (1962) *Being and time*, trans. J. McQuarrie and E. Robinson. Oxford: Blackwell.

Heron, J. (1989) *The Facilitators Handbook*. London: Kogan Page.

Holman Jones, S. (2005). Autoethnography: Making the personal political. In N. Denzin and Y. Lincoln (eds), *Handbook of qualitative research*. Thousand Oaks, CA: Sage, pp. 763–791.

Honan, E. and Bright, D. (2016) Writing a thesis differently, *International Journal of Qualitative Studies in Education* 29(5): 731–743.

I-D (2017) No. 348, The creativity issue, Summer.

Irigaray, L. (1974) *Speculum of the other woman*. Ithaca, NY: Cornell University Press.

Jackson, A. and Mazzei, L. (2012) *Thinking with theory in qualitative research: Viewing data across multiple perspectives*. London: Routledge.

Joyce, J. (2000) *Finnegans Wake*, Introduction by Seamus Deane. London: Penguin.

Kent, A. (2010) *The hope of place: Selected poems in English 1990–2010*. London: Francis Boutle.

Kerouac, J. (1972) *On the road*. Harmondsworth: Penguin.

Koro-Ljundberg, M. (2016) *Reconceptualising qualitative research: Methodologies without methodology*. Thousand Oaks CA: Sage.

Lather, P. (2007) *Getting lost: Feminist efforts toward a double(d) science.* New York: SUNY.

Lecercle, J.-J. (1985) *Philosophy through the Looking-Glass: Language, nonsense, desire.* La Salle, IL: Open Court.

Leys, R. (2011) The turn to affect: A critique, *Critical Inquiry* 37: 434–472.

Liptrot, A. (2016) *The Outrun.* Edinburgh: Canongate.

Macfarlane, R. (2007) *The wild places.* London: Granta.

MacLure, M. (2013a) The wonder of data, *Cultural Studies ó Critical Methodologies* 13(4): 228–232.

MacLure, M. (2013b). Researching with out representation? Language and materiality in post-qualitative methodology, *International Journal of Qualitative Studies in Education* 26(6), 658–667,

MacLure, M. (2017) Qualitative methodology and the new materialisms: 'A little of Dionysus's blood'. In N. Denzin and M. Giardina (eds) *Qualitative inquiry in neoliberal times.* New York: Routledge, pp. 48–58.

Madison. D. S. (2010) *Acts of activism: Human rights as radical performance.* Cambridge: Cambridge University Press.

Mallett, F. and Penwill, M. A. (1997) *R.O. Lenkiewicz.* Plymouth: White Lane Press.

Malone, K. (2016) Reconsidering children's encounters with nature and place using posthumanism, *Australian Journal of Environmental Education* 32(1): 42–56.

Manning, E. (2007) *Politics of touch: Sense, movement, sovereignty.* Minneapolis: University of Minnesota Press.

Manning, E. (2009) What if it all didn't begin with containment? Toward a leaky sense of self *Body and Society* 15(3): 33–45.

Manning, E. (2010) Always more than one: The collectivity of *a life, Body and Society* 16(1): 117–127.

Manning, E. (2013) *Always more than one: Individuation's dance.* Durham, NC: Duke University Press.

Manning, E. (2014) Wondering the world directly – or, how movement outruns the subject *Body and Society* 20(3 and 4): 162–188.

Martin, R. (1988) Truth, power, self: An interview with Michel Foucault. In L. H. Martin, H. Gutman and P. H. Hutton (eds) *Technologies of the self: A seminar with Michel Foucault.* Amherst, MA: University of Massachusetts Press, pp. 9–15.

Maslow, A. H. (1943). A theory of human motivation, *Psychological Review* 50(4): 370–396.

Masny, D. (2013) Multiple literacies theory: Exploring spaces. In I. Semetsky and D. Masny (eds) *Deleuze and education.* Edinburgh: Edinburgh University Press.

Massumi, B. (1987) Translator's introduction to G. Deleuze and F. Guattari (1987) *A thousand plateaus: Capitalism and schizophrenia,* trans. Brian Massumi. London: Athlone.

Massumi, B. (1998) Sensing the virtual, building the insensible, *Hypersurface Architecture* (special issue of *Architectural Design,* profile no. 133) 68(5/6): 16–24.

Massumi, B. (2002) *Parables for the virtual: Movement, affect, sensation.* Durham and London: Duke University Press.

Massumi, B. (2013) Prelude to Manning, E. (2013) *Always more than one: Individuation's dance* Durham, NC: Duke University Press.

Massumi, B (2015) *Politics of affect.* Cambridge: Polity Press.

McIntyre, A. (1981) *After Virtue.* London: Duckworth Press.

Meillassoux, Q. (2008) *After finitude: An essay on the necessity of contingency,* trans. Ray Brasier. London: Continuum.

Nagel, T. (1986) *The view from nowhere.* Oxford: Oxford University Press.

Newman, S. (2016) *Postanarchism.* Cambridge: Polity Press.

Nietzsche, F. (1968) *The will to power,* trans. W. Kaufmann and R. Hollingdale. New York: Vintage Books.

Ondaatje, M. (1992) *The English patient.* Toronto: McClelland and Stewart.

Parr, A. (ed.) (2010) *The Deleuze dictionary,* revised edn. Edinburgh: Edinburgh University Press.

Pedersen, H. (2010) Is 'the posthuman' educable? On the convergence of educational philosophy, animal studies, and posthumanist theory, *Discourse: Studies in the Cultural Politics of Education* 31(2): 237–250.

Pelias, R. (1999) *Writing performance: Poeticizing the researcher's body.* Carbondale: Southern Illinois University Press.

Pelias, R. (2005) Performative writing as scholarship: An apology, an argument, an anecdote, *Cultural Studies—Critical Methodologies* 5: 415–424.

Pessoa, F. (2002) *The book of disquiet.* London: Penguin Classics.

Pineau, E. (2011) *Performance as radical educational praxis,* invited research presentation for School of Education, Plymouth University, UK, October.

Postman, N. and Weingartner, C. (1971) *Teaching as a subversive activity.* London: Pitman Publishing.

Probyn, E. (2010) Writing shame. In M. Gregg and G. Seigworth (eds) *The affect theory reader.* Durham and London: Duke University Press, pp. 71–90.

Proulx, A. (1995) *The shipping news.* London: Fourth Estate.

Rabinow, P. (ed.) (1991) *The Foucault reader: An introduction to Foucault's thought.* Harmondsworth: Penguin Social Sciences.

Reynolds, S. (1998) *Energy flash: A journey through rave music and dance culture.* London: Pan Macmillan.

Rhinehart, L. (1972) *The dice man.* London: Panther.

Rich, A. (1975) *The burning of paper instead of children. Poems: Selected and new, 1950–1974.* New York: W. W. Norton.

Richardson, L. (2000) Writing: A method of inquiry. In N. Denzin and Y. Lincoln (eds) *The Sage handbook of qualitative research,* 2nd edn. Thousand Oaks, CA: Sage, pp. 923–948.

Richardson, L. and St Pierre, E. A. (2005) Writing: A method of inquiry. In N. Denzin and Y. Lincoln (eds) *The Sage handbook of qualitative research,* 3rd edn. Thousand Oaks, CA: Sage, pp. 959–979.

Rogers, C. (1961) *On becoming a person: A therapist's view of psychotherapy.* London: Constable.

Royal Society for the Protection of Birds (RSPB) www.rspb.org.uk/discoverandenjoynature/discoverandlearn/birdguide/name/s/starling/roosting.aspx

Schon, D. A. (1983) *The reflective practitioner.* San Francisco: Jossey Bass.

Schon, D. A. (1987) *Educating the reflective practitioner.* San Francisco: Jossey Bass.

Sellers, W. and Gough, N. (2010) Sharing outsider thinking: Thinking (differently) with Deleuze in educational philosophy and curriculum inquiry, *International Journal of Qualitative Studies in Education* 23(5): 589–614.

Serres, M. (2008) *The five senses: A philosophy of mingled bodies,* trans. Margaret Sankey and Peter Crowley. London: Continuum.

Shouse, E. (2005) Feeling, emotion, affect. *M/C Journal* 8(6). http://journal.media-culture.org.au/0512/03-shouse.php (accessed 24 August 2016).

Smith, P. (2015) *M train.* London: Bloomsbury.

Soja, E. (2010) *Seeking spatial justice.* Minneapolis: University of Minnesota Press.

Somekh, B. and Zeichner, K. (2009) Action research for educational reform: Remodelling action research theories and practices in local contexts, *Educational Action Research* 17(1): 5–21.

Sorell, T. (1994) *Scientism: Philosophy and the infatuation with science.* London: Routledge.

Speedy, J. and Wyatt, J. (eds) (2014) *Collaborative writing as inquiry.* Newcastle: Cambridge Scholars Publishing.

Stengers, I. (2011). Wondering about materialism. In L. Bryant, N. Srnicek and G. Harman (eds) *The speculative turn: Continental materialism and realism*. Melbourne: re. press, pp. 368–380.

Stewart, K. (2007) *Ordinary affects*. London: Duke University Press.

St Pierre, E. (1997) Methodology in the fold and the irruption of transgressive data, *Qualitative Studies in Education* 10(20): 175–189.

St Pierre, E. (2004) Deleuzian concepts for education: The subject undone, *Educational Philosophy and Theory* 36(3): 283–296.

St Pierre, E. (2011) Post qualitative research: The critique and the coming after. In N. Denzin and Y. Lincoln (eds), *The Sage handbook of qualitative research*, 4th edn. Thousand Oaks, CA: Sage.

St Pierre, E. (2015) Practices for the 'new' in the new empiricisms, the new materialisms and post qualitative inquiry. In N. Denzin and M. Giardina (eds) *Qualitative inquiry and the politics of research*. Walnut Creek, CA: Left Coast Press, pp. 75–93.

St Pierre, E. (2017) Post qualitative inquiry: The next generation. In N. Denzin and M. Giardina (eds) *Qualitative inquiry in neoliberal times*. New York: Routledge, pp. 37–47.

Thrift, N. (2006) Space, *Theory, Culture and Society* 23(2–3): 139–146.

Tufnell, B. (2006) *On the very edge of he ocean: The Porthmeor studios and painting in St. Ives*. St Ives: Tate St Ives.

Usher, R., Bryant, I. and Johnston, R. (1997) *Adult education and the postmodern challenge*. London: Routledge.

Whitehead, A. N. (1929) Process and reality: An essay in cosmology. Gifford lectures delivered in the University of Edinburgh during the session 1927–1928. New York: Macmillan; Cambridge: Cambridge University Press.

Wittgenstein, L. (1922) *Tractatus Logico-Philosophicus*, trans. F P. Ramsey and C. K. Ogden. London: Kegan Paul.

Woolf, V. (1985) *Moments of being*, 2nd edn, ed. Jeanne Schulkind. London: Harcourt Brace.

Wyatt, J. and Gale, K. (2013a) Assemblage/ethnography: Troubling constructions of the self in the play of materiality and representation. In P. Short, L. Turner and A. Grant (eds) *Contemporary British autoethnography*. Rotterdam: Sense, pp. 139–157.

Wyatt, J. and Gale, K. (2013b) Getting out of selves: An assemblage/ethnography? In T. Adams, C. Ellis and S. Holman-Jones (eds) *The autoethnography handbook*. Thousand Oaks, CA: Sage, pp. 300–313.

Wyatt, J. and Gale, K. (2013c) (eds) Collaborative writing, special edition of *International Review of Qualitative Research* 5(4).

Wyatt, J. and Gale, K. (2017) Writing to it: Creative engagements with writing practice in and with the not yet known in today's academy, *International Journal of Qualitative Studies in Education*.

Wyatt, J., Gale, K., Gannon, S. and Davies, B. (2011) *Deleuze and collaborative writing: An immanent plane of composition*. New York: Peter Lang.

Wyatt, J., Gale, K., Gannon, S. and Davies, B. (2017) Creating a space in between: Collaborative inquiries. In N. Denzin and Y. Lincoln (eds) *The Sage handbook of qualitative research*, 5th edn. Thousand Oaks, CA: Sage.

INDEX

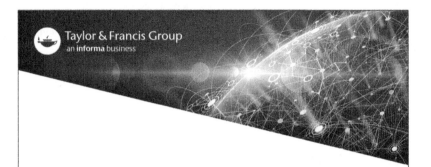

Taylor & Francis eBooks

www.taylorfrancis.com

A single destination for eBooks from Taylor & Francis
with increased functionality and an improved user
experience to meet the needs of our customers.

90,000+ eBooks of award-winning academic content in
Humanities, Social Science, Science, Technology, Engineering,
and Medical written by a global network of editors and authors.

TAYLOR & FRANCIS EBOOKS OFFERS:

A streamlined
experience for
our library
customers

A single point
of discovery
for all of our
eBook content

Improved
search and
discovery of
content at both
book and
chapter level

REQUEST A FREE TRIAL
support@taylorfrancis.com